AI-Powered Robotics:
From Concept to Application

By

SHARATH CHANDRA MACHA

Contents

Chapter 3

Chapter 6

Chapter 1

Introduction to Artificial Intelligence and Robotics

Overview of Artificial Intelligence

Artificial Intelligence (AI) is a multidisciplinary field of study focused on the development of intelligent systems that can perform tasks typically requiring human intelligence. The concept of AI dates back to ancient times, with myths and stories featuring artificial beings endowed with human-like intelligence. However, it wasn't until the mid-20th century that AI emerged as a distinct academic discipline, spurred by advances in mathematics, computer science, and cognitive psychology.

Historical Background

The roots of AI can be traced back to the seminal work of mathematician and logician Alan Turing, who proposed the concept of a "universal machine" capable of simulating any computable function. Turing's theoretical framework laid the groundwork for the development of digital computers and the exploration of machine intelligence. In 1950, Turing published his famous paper "Computing Machinery and Intelligence," in which he introduced the Turing Test as a criterion for determining whether a machine exhibits human-like intelligence.

The 1950s and 1960s saw the birth of AI as a formal academic discipline, marked by the establishment of research institutions such as the Dartmouth Conference in 1956, where the term "artificial intelligence" was coined. During this period, early AI pioneers such as John McCarthy, Marvin Minsky, Herbert Simon, and Allen Newell made significant contributions to the field, laying the groundwork for the development of AI techniques and methodologies.

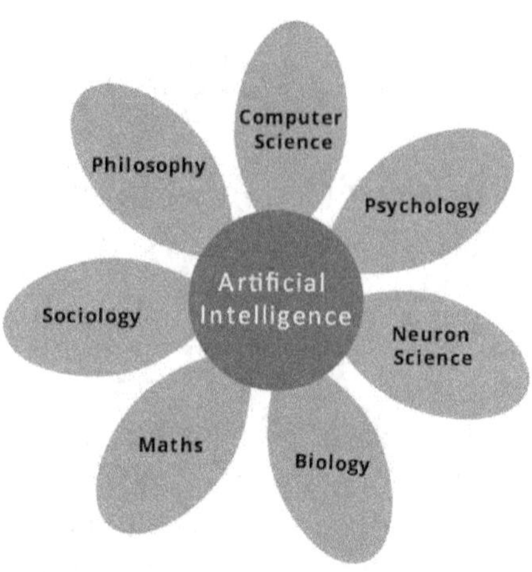

Figure 1. Artificial Intelligence (AI)

Key Concepts in AI

AI encompasses a wide range of techniques and methodologies aimed at creating intelligent systems capable of reasoning, learning, problem-solving, perception, and language understanding. Some key concepts in AI include:

Machine Learning: A subfield of AI concerned with the development of algorithms and models that enable computers to learn from data and improve their performance over time. Machine learning techniques include supervised learning, unsupervised learning, reinforcement learning, and deep learning.

Neural Networks: Inspired by the structure and function of the human brain, neural networks are computational models composed of interconnected nodes (neurons) that process information and learn complex patterns from data. Deep neural networks, in particular, have revolutionized many AI applications, achieving remarkable performance in tasks such as image recognition, natural language processing, and game playing.

Natural Language Processing (NLP): NLP is the branch of AI concerned with the interaction between computers and human languages. NLP techniques enable computers to understand, interpret, and generate human language, facilitating applications such as machine translation, sentiment analysis, and chatbots.

Computer Vision: Computer vision is the field of AI focused on enabling computers to interpret and understand visual information from the real world. Computer vision techniques enable applications such as object detection, image classification, and facial recognition, with widespread applications in robotics, autonomous vehicles, and healthcare.

Applications of AI

AI has found applications in a wide range of domains, revolutionizing industries and transforming the way we live and work. Some notable applications of AI include:

Healthcare: AI-powered systems are being used to diagnose diseases, analyze medical images, and personalize treatment plans. Machine learning algorithms can analyze large datasets of patient records to identify patterns and trends, assisting healthcare providers in making more accurate diagnoses and treatment decisions.

Finance: In the finance industry, AI is used for algorithmic trading, fraud detection, credit scoring, and risk management. Machine learning models analyze market data and financial transactions to identify trading opportunities and mitigate risks, while natural language processing techniques extract insights from news articles and social media for sentiment analysis and market prediction.

Autonomous Vehicles: AI plays a crucial role in the development of autonomous vehicles, enabling cars, drones, and other vehicles to perceive their environment, make decisions, and navigate safely without human intervention. Computer vision, sensor fusion, and machine learning algorithms enable autonomous vehicles to recognize objects, predict their movements, and plan optimal trajectories in real-time.

Manufacturing and Robotics: In manufacturing and industrial automation, AI-powered robots are transforming production processes, increasing efficiency, and reducing costs.

Robots equipped with machine learning algorithms can adapt to changing environments, optimize production schedules, and perform complex tasks with precision and accuracy, leading to improvements in quality and productivity.

Ethical and Societal Implications

While AI holds immense potential to benefit society, it also raises important ethical and societal considerations that must be addressed. Concerns related to privacy, bias, accountability, and job displacement have prompted calls for ethical guidelines, regulations, and responsible AI development practices. It is essential for AI researchers, practitioners, and policymakers to consider the ethical implications of AI technologies and ensure that they are deployed in a manner that promotes fairness, transparency, and human welfare.

In Artificial Intelligence is a rapidly evolving field that holds the promise of revolutionizing industries, enhancing human capabilities, and addressing some of the most pressing challenges facing society. By understanding the historical roots, key concepts, applications, and ethical implications of AI, we can harness its potential to create a better future for all.

History and Evolution of Robotics

Origins of Robotics

The history of robotics traces back to ancient civilizations where the concept of automatons and mechanical devices captivated the human imagination. In ancient Greece, for instance, mythological tales featured beings like Talos, a giant automaton created by Hephaestus to protect Crete. Similarly, ancient Chinese and Egyptian civilizations depicted mechanisms resembling robots in their folklore and religious texts. These early manifestations, though mythical in nature, laid the conceptual groundwork for the eventual development of robotics.

Early Mechanical Automata

The Renaissance period witnessed significant advancements in mechanical engineering, setting the stage for the birth of modern robotics. Inventors and scholars such as Leonardo da Vinci conceptualized and designed various mechanical devices resembling human and animal movements. Da Vinci's intricate designs, including the famous humanoid robot known as Leonardo's robot, demonstrated an early fascination with creating lifelike machines.

Industrial Revolution and Automata

The Industrial Revolution of the 18th and 19th centuries marked a pivotal moment in the evolution of robotics. The mechanization of labor and the invention of steam-powered machinery revolutionized manufacturing processes. During this period, inventors like Jacques de Vaucanson and his famous automata, such as "The Digesting Duck" and "The Flute Player," showcased the potential of mechanical devices to mimic human actions with remarkable precision.

Emergence of Modern Robotics

The 20th century witnessed significant advancements in technology, leading to the birth of modern robotics. The term "robot" was coined by the Czech playwright Karel Čapek in his play "R.U.R. (Rossum's Universal Robots)" in 1920, where he introduced the concept of artificial beings called "robots" derived from the Czech word "robota," meaning forced labor or servitude.

World War II and Technological Innovations

The outbreak of World War II spurred rapid technological advancements, including developments in robotics. Both Allied and Axis powers explored the use of unmanned vehicles and remotely controlled devices for military purposes. Notable examples include the German V-1 flying bomb, and the American Goliath tracked mine, which laid the groundwork for future robotic innovations.

Post-War Developments and Industrial Robotics

The post-war era witnessed the rise of industrial robotics, driven by the need to improve efficiency and productivity in manufacturing processes. In 1954, George Devol and Joseph Engelberger introduced the first programmable robot, the Unimate, which revolutionized automotive assembly lines. This marked the beginning of the widespread adoption of robotic automation in various industries worldwide.

Advancements in Robotics Research

The latter half of the 20th century saw rapid progress in robotics research and development. Academic institutions, research laboratories, and technology companies dedicated resources to advancing robotics technology. Breakthroughs in artificial intelligence, sensor technology, and materials science paved the way for the development of more sophisticated and capable robots.

Robotics in the 21st Century

The 21st century has witnessed an unprecedented surge in robotics innovation across diverse fields, including healthcare, entertainment, agriculture, and space exploration. Robotics technology has become increasingly integrated with artificial intelligence, enabling robots to perceive and interact with their environments autonomously.

Future Prospects and Challenges

Looking ahead, robotics holds immense promise for addressing societal challenges and transforming various industries. However, significant challenges remain, including ethical considerations, safety concerns, and the impact of automation on employment. As robotics continues to evolve, navigating these challenges will be crucial in realizing the full potential of robotic technology.

The history and evolution of robotics reflect humanity's enduring fascination with creating intelligent machines. From ancient myths to modern-day innovations, robotics has undergone a remarkable journey driven by human ingenuity and technological progress. As we stand on the cusp of a new era of robotics, the possibilities for innovation and discovery are limitless.

Basic Concepts in Robotics

In the realm of robotics, understanding the foundational concepts is crucial for grasping the intricacies of this interdisciplinary field. In this section, we delve into the fundamental principles that underpin robotics, from the anatomy of robots to the mathematical frameworks that govern their behavior.

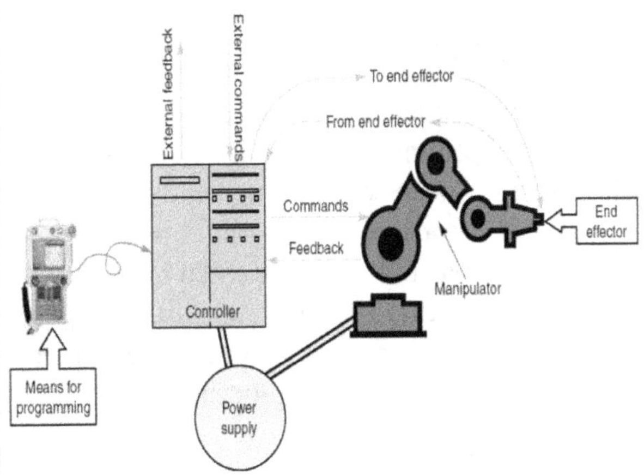

Figure 2. Basic Concepts in Robotics

Anatomy of a Robot

Robots, in their most basic form, consist of a multitude of components working in concert to execute tasks autonomously or under human supervision. At the heart of every robot lies its structure, comprising mechanical, electrical, and computational elements.

Mechanical Components

The mechanical structure of a robot encompasses its physical body, joints, and limbs. Depending on its intended application, a robot may possess a rigid or flexible body, with joints facilitating movement along various axes. These joints enable robots to mimic human or animal motion, allowing for a wide range of actions and interactions with the environment.

Electrical Components

Electrical systems within a robot encompass the circuits, sensors, and actuators responsible for converting electrical signals into physical actions. Sensors serve as the robot's sensory organs, detecting external stimuli such as light, sound, touch, and proximity. Actuators, on the other hand, act as the muscles of the robot, translating electrical impulses into mechanical motion. Common types of actuators include motors, solenoids, and pneumatic or hydraulic systems.

Computational Components

Central to the operation of a robot is its computational infrastructure, comprising processors, memory units, and software algorithms. These components enable robots to perceive their surroundings, process information, and make decisions based on predefined instructions or learned behaviors. Advanced robotics systems often incorporate artificial intelligence techniques, such as machine learning and neural networks, to adapt to changing environments and optimize performance.

Kinematics and Dynamics

Kinematics and dynamics form the mathematical framework that governs the motion and behavior of robots. Kinematics deals with the study of motion without considering the forces involved, focusing instead on parameters such as position, velocity, and acceleration. Dynamics, on the other hand, examines the forces and torques acting on a robot and their effects on its motion.

Forward Kinematics

Forward kinematics involves determining the position and orientation of a robot's end-effector, such as its gripper or tool, given the joint angles or actuator positions. This process enables robots to plan and execute precise movements in three-dimensional space, essential for tasks ranging from pick-and-place operations to complex manipulation.

Inverse Kinematics

Inverse kinematics, conversely, entails calculating the joint angles or actuator positions required to achieve a desired end-effector pose. This computational task is particularly important in robotics applications where precise control over the end-effector position is necessary, such as robotic arm manipulation or trajectory planning.

Robot Dynamics

Robot dynamics consider the forces, torques, and accelerations involved in the motion of a robot's mechanical components. By modeling the dynamic behavior of a robot, engineers can optimize its performance, stability, and energy efficiency. Dynamic analysis also plays a crucial role in the design of control algorithms for tasks such as trajectory tracking, force control, and collision avoidance.

Robot Control Systems

Robot control systems dictate how robots perceive, interpret, and respond to their environment, enabling them to execute tasks with precision and reliability. These systems encompass both hardware components, such as sensors and actuators, and software algorithms responsible for decision-making and feedback control.

Open-loop vs. Closed-loop Control

Open-loop control involves executing predefined sequences of actions without feedback from the environment, relying solely on internal commands. While suitable for simple tasks with predictable outcomes, open-loop control lacks adaptability and robustness in dynamic environments. Closed-loop control, in contrast, incorporates feedback from sensors to adjust the robot's behavior in real time, enhancing accuracy and resilience to disturbances.

Feedback Control

Feedback control systems utilize sensory information to continuously monitor and adjust the robot's state or trajectory. Proportional-Integral-Derivative (PID) control is a widely used feedback control technique that maintains desired performance criteria by adjusting control signals based on the error between the desired and actual states. Advanced control strategies, such as model predictive control and adaptive control, further enhance the agility and responsiveness of robotic systems.

Robot Programming

Programming lies at the heart of empowering robots to perform a diverse range of tasks, from simple pick-and-place operations to complex assembly sequences. Robot programming languages and frameworks provide engineers with the tools to design, simulate, and deploy robotic applications efficiently.

Programming Paradigms

Robot programming paradigms vary depending on the level of abstraction and the intended application. Low-level programming involves directly controlling individual actuators and sensors, often using languages such as C or assembly language. High-level programming, on the other hand, abstracts the underlying hardware, enabling developers to specify tasks in terms of higher-level concepts such as motion planning, perception, and decision-making.

Simulation and Visualization

Simulation environments play a vital role in the development and testing of robotic systems, allowing engineers to validate algorithms, optimize parameters, and assess performance in virtual environments before deployment in the real world. Visualization tools provide intuitive interfaces for designing robot behaviors, simulating sensor data, and analyzing results, fostering rapid iteration and refinement of robotic applications.

In this, we have explored the basic concepts that form the foundation of robotics, from the anatomy of robots to the mathematical principles governing their motion and behavior. By understanding these fundamental principles, engineers and enthusiasts alike can embark on a journey to unlock the full potential of robotics in addressing real-world challenges and advancing human-robot interaction.

Types of Robots and Applications

In this, we delve into the diverse landscape of robots, exploring the various types of robots and their wide-ranging applications. From industrial robots revolutionizing manufacturing processes to autonomous drones mapping out disaster zones, the realm of robotics is expanding rapidly, driven by advancements in artificial intelligence (AI) and robotic technologies. By understanding the different types of robots and their applications, we gain insight into the ever-evolving role of robotics in our society.

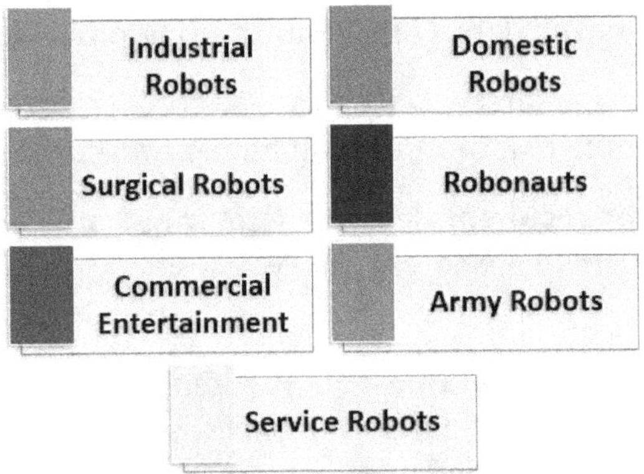

Figure 3. Types of Robots

Industrial Robots

Industrial robots are perhaps the most well-known and widely used type of robot, playing a pivotal role in modern manufacturing industries. These robots are designed to perform repetitive tasks with high precision and efficiency, thus enhancing productivity and reducing production costs. From automotive assembly lines to electronics manufacturing, industrial robots handle a diverse range of tasks, including welding, painting, material handling, and assembly.

Applications of Industrial Robots

Automotive industry: Robotic arms are used for welding, painting, and assembling vehicles on production lines.

Electronics manufacturing: Robots handle delicate components with precision, improving efficiency and quality control.

Food and beverage industry: Automated packaging and palletizing systems streamline food production processes.

Advantages of Industrial Robots

Increased productivity: Robots can work continuously without fatigue, leading to higher output.

Improved quality: Consistent performance and precision reduce errors and defects in manufacturing processes.

Enhanced safety: Robots perform hazardous tasks, minimizing the risk of injuries to human workers.

Initial investment costs: Acquiring and implementing robotic systems can be expensive for small and medium-sized enterprises.

Programming complexity: Programming industrial robots requires specialized skills and expertise, posing a barrier to adoption for some companies.

Human-robot collaboration: Ensuring safe interaction between robots and human workers remains a challenge in collaborative manufacturing environments.

Service Robots

Service robots are designed to assist humans in various tasks, ranging from household chores to healthcare and hospitality services. Unlike industrial robots, which operate in controlled environments, service robots interact directly with humans in dynamic and unstructured environments. These robots often incorporate AI algorithms and sensors to perceive and respond to their surroundings, enabling them to adapt to changing conditions and interact intelligently with users.

Types of Service Robots

Domestic robots: Vacuum cleaning robots, lawn mowing robots, and other home automation devices simplify household chores.

Healthcare robots: Robotic assistants help patients with mobility issues, rehabilitation exercises, and medication management in hospitals and rehabilitation centers.

Hospitality robots: Robots greet guests, deliver room service, and provide concierge services in hotels and resorts, enhancing the guest experience.

Applications of Service Robots

Elderly care: Companion robots provide companionship and assistance to elderly individuals, monitoring their health and well-being.

Education: Educational robots engage students in interactive learning activities, teaching programming, STEM concepts, and foreign languages.

Public safety: Autonomous security robots patrol public spaces, monitoring for suspicious activities and providing real-time surveillance.

Advantages of Service Robots

Increased efficiency: Service robots automate repetitive tasks, allowing humans to focus on more complex and value-added activities.

Improved accessibility: Robots assist individuals with disabilities or limited mobility, enabling them to live independently and participate fully in society.

Enhanced customer experience: Service robots provide personalized and responsive services, enhancing customer satisfaction in various industries.

Challenges in Service Robotics

Social acceptance: Overcoming societal skepticism and fear of robots is essential for the widespread adoption of service robots in diverse settings.

Ethical considerations: Ensuring ethical use of service robots and addressing concerns about privacy, surveillance, and job displacement are critical issues.

Technical limitations: Developing robots that can navigate complex environments, interact naturally with humans, and perform tasks with dexterity remains a significant challenge in service robotics.

Autonomous Robots

Autonomous robots are equipped with sensors, actuators, and onboard intelligence to operate independently in uncontrolled environments without direct human intervention. These robots rely on AI algorithms, machine learning, and sensor fusion techniques to perceive their surroundings, make decisions, and navigate complex terrains. From self-driving cars navigating city streets to drones conducting search and rescue missions, autonomous robots are revolutionizing transportation, exploration, and disaster response efforts.

Types of Autonomous Robots

Autonomous vehicles: Self-driving cars, trucks, and drones navigate roads, highways, and airspace autonomously, relying on sensors and AI algorithms to detect obstacles and plan safe routes.

Mobile robots: Autonomous mobile robots patrol warehouses, logistics centers, and industrial facilities, performing tasks such as inventory management, picking, and delivery.

Unmanned aerial vehicles (UAVs): Drones equipped with cameras and sensors are used for aerial photography, mapping, surveillance, and environmental monitoring.

Applications of Autonomous Robots

Transportation: Autonomous vehicles promise to revolutionize transportation systems, reducing traffic congestion, accidents, and carbon emissions.

Exploration: Autonomous robots explore remote and hazardous environments, such as deep-sea habitats, polar regions, and outer space, gathering scientific data and conducting research.

Disaster response: Drones and other autonomous robots assist emergency responders in disaster scenarios, assessing damage, delivering supplies, and conducting search and rescue operations.

Advantages of Autonomous Robots

Safety: Autonomous robots reduce the risk of accidents and injuries by eliminating human error and fatigue in critical tasks such as driving and surveillance.

Efficiency: Autonomous systems operate continuously and adaptively, optimizing resource allocation and response strategies in dynamic environments.

Scalability: Autonomous robots can be deployed in large-scale operations, such as disaster relief efforts and logistics management, to cover vast areas and handle complex tasks efficiently.

Challenges in Autonomous Robotics

Regulatory hurdles: Addressing legal and regulatory challenges related to liability, safety standards, and privacy concerns is essential for the widespread adoption of autonomous robots.

Technological limitations: Improving sensor technologies, AI algorithms, and communication systems is necessary to enhance the reliability and performance of autonomous robots in real-world environments.

Ethical dilemmas: Ethical issues surrounding autonomous decision-making, accountability, and the impact on employment and society must be carefully considered in the development and deployment of autonomous robots.

In this we have explored the diverse landscape of robots, including industrial robots, service robots, and autonomous robots, and examined their wide-ranging applications in various industries and domains. From enhancing productivity and efficiency in manufacturing to providing personalized services and enabling scientific exploration, robots are transforming our world in profound ways. As advancements in AI and robotic technologies continue to accelerate, the possibilities for innovation and impact are endless, shaping the future of robotics and redefining the relationship between humans and machines.

Robot Components: Sensors, Actuators, and Controllers

In the realm of robotics, understanding the fundamental components that enable a machine to perceive, act, and make decisions is crucial. At the heart of any robotic system lie three key elements: sensors, actuators, and controllers. These components form the foundation upon which robots interact with their environment, execute tasks, and adapt to changing circumstances. In this chapter, we delve into the intricate workings of sensors, actuators, and controllers, exploring their functionalities, types, and significance in the realm of robotics.

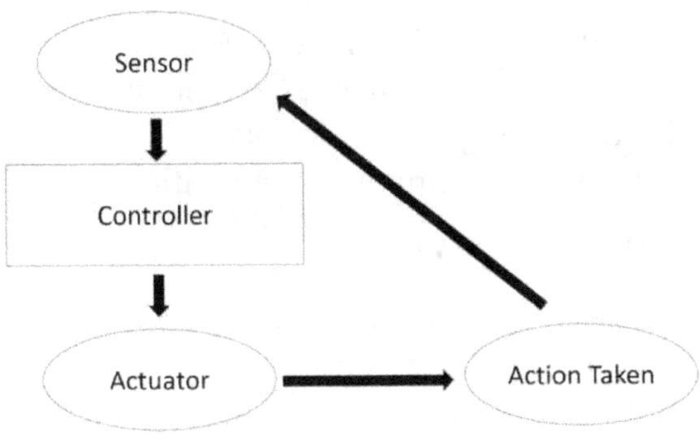

Figure 4. Robot Components

Sensors: Perception of the Environment

Sensors serve as the sensory organs of a robot, providing vital information about its surroundings. These devices detect various physical stimuli such as light, sound, temperature, pressure, proximity, and motion, enabling robots to perceive and interact with the world around them.

Types of Sensors

1. Vision Sensors: Cameras and other vision sensors capture visual data, allowing robots to recognize objects, navigate environments, and perform tasks requiring visual perception.

2. Tactile Sensors: Tactile sensors detect touch and pressure, enabling robots to interact with objects safely and efficiently. These sensors are crucial in tasks requiring delicate manipulation and object recognition through touch.

3. Proximity Sensors: Proximity sensors detect the presence or absence of nearby objects without physical contact. They are commonly used in obstacle detection, object avoidance, and proximity-based control systems.

4. Inertial Sensors: Inertial sensors, including accelerometers and gyroscopes, measure motion, orientation, and changes in velocity. They play a vital role in robotics applications such as navigation, stabilization, and motion control.

5. Environmental Sensors: Sensors for measuring environmental parameters such as temperature, humidity, and atmospheric pressure provide robots with essential data for adapting to different environmental conditions.

Actuators: Executing Actions

Actuators are the muscle of a robot, responsible for converting electrical signals into physical motion or manipulation. These devices enable robots to perform a wide range of actions, from simple movements to complex tasks requiring precision and dexterity.

Types of Actuators

1. Electric Motors: Electric motors, including DC motors, stepper motors, and servo motors, convert electrical energy into rotational motion. They are commonly used in robotic joints, wheels, and manipulators for precise control of movement.

2. Pneumatic Actuators: Pneumatic actuators utilize compressed air to generate linear or rotary motion. They are lightweight, fast-acting, and suitable for applications requiring high force-to-weight ratios, such as industrial automation and robotics.

3. Hydraulic Actuators: Hydraulic actuators use pressurized hydraulic fluid to produce linear or rotary motion. They are capable of exerting high forces and are commonly employed in heavy-duty industrial robots and construction machinery.

4. Piezoelectric Actuators: Piezoelectric actuators rely on the piezoelectric effect to generate precise and rapid movements. They are used in micro-robotics, precision positioning systems, and applications requiring nanoscale actuation.

5. Shape Memory Alloys (SMAs): SMAs undergo reversible changes in shape in response to temperature variations. They are utilized in robotics for shape-changing structures, adaptive mechanisms, and minimally invasive medical devices.

Controllers: Brain of the Robot

Controllers serve as the central nervous system of a robot, orchestrating its actions based on sensory inputs, predefined algorithms, and programmed instructions. These devices regulate the operation of sensors and actuators, enabling robots to perceive their environment, make decisions, and execute tasks autonomously or under human supervision.

Types of Controllers

1. Microcontrollers: Microcontrollers are small, embedded computing devices equipped with processing units, memory, and input/output interfaces. They are commonly used in low-cost robotic systems for basic control tasks and interfacing with sensors and actuators.

2. Programmable Logic Controllers (PLCs): PLCs are industrial-grade controllers designed for robustness, reliability, and real-time control of industrial automation systems. They are widely used in manufacturing, assembly lines, and process automation in various industries.

3. Single-Board Computers (SBCs): SBCs such as Raspberry Pi and Arduino provide versatile computing platforms for robotics prototyping, development, and experimentation. They offer a wide range of connectivity options, software libraries, and development tools for creating custom robotic solutions.

4. Embedded Systems: Embedded systems are specialized computing devices integrated into robotic hardware for dedicated control and processing tasks. They are tailored to the specific requirements of robotic applications, offering optimized performance, power efficiency, and real-time capabilities.

5. Robot Operating Systems (ROS): ROS is a flexible, open-source framework for robot software development, providing libraries, tools, and middleware for building complex robotic systems. It facilitates communication between sensors, actuators, and higher-level software components, enabling modular and distributed control architectures.

Sensors, actuators, and controllers are the essential building blocks of robotic systems, enabling robots to perceive their environment, execute tasks, and adapt to changing conditions. Understanding the functionalities and characteristics of these components is vital for designing, developing, and deploying effective robotic solutions across various domains and applications.

Robot Kinematics: Forward and Inverse Kinematics

In the realm of robotics, understanding the movement of robotic systems is paramount. Robot kinematics is the branch of robotics concerned with the study of motion, specifically the motion of robotic manipulators. In this chapter, we delve into the fundamental concepts of robot kinematics, focusing on forward and inverse kinematics.

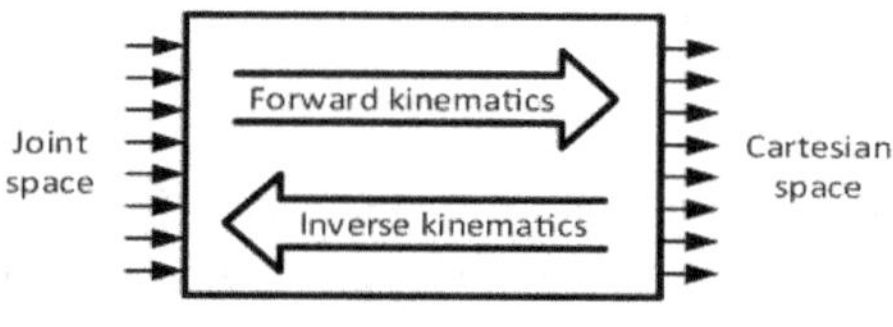

Figure 5. Robot Kinematics

Understanding Robot Kinematics

Robot kinematics deals with the geometric and spatial properties of robot motion. It encompasses the study of how robotic manipulators move through space and how their various components interact to achieve desired end-effector positions. At its core, robot kinematics enables us to analyze and predict the movement of robotic systems, laying the groundwork for precise control and manipulation.

Forward Kinematics

Forward kinematics is the process of determining the position and orientation of the end-effector of a robot, given the joint angles or parameters of the robot's manipulator. In simpler terms, it answers the question: "Where is the end-effector located in space?" This calculation involves traversing the kinematic chain from the robot's base to its end-effector, taking into account the lengths and orientations of each link and the angles of each joint.

Forward kinematics is typically represented using homogeneous transformation matrices or Denavit-Hartenberg (DH) parameters. These mathematical representations allow us to efficiently compute the end-effector pose based on the robot's joint configurations. Through forward kinematics, engineers can design robotic systems capable of precise positioning and trajectory planning.

Inverse Kinematics

Inverse kinematics, on the other hand, involves the opposite calculation: determining the joint configurations required to place the end-effector at a specified position and orientation in space. In essence, it addresses the question: "What joint angles are needed to reach a desired end-effector pose?" Inverse kinematics is particularly crucial in robotics applications where precise control over the end-effector position is necessary, such as robot manipulators used in manufacturing or surgical robotics.

Unlike forward kinematics, which follows a straightforward chain of transformations from the base to the end-effector, inverse kinematics often requires solving complex mathematical equations or optimization problems. This is because there may be multiple solutions or constraints involved, such as joint limits or singularities, which must be accounted for to ensure the robot's movements are physically feasible and within its operational limits.

Practical Considerations and Applications

In real-world robotics applications, both forward and inverse kinematics play vital roles in enabling robots to perform tasks accurately and efficiently. For example, in industrial automation, forward kinematics is used to plan robotic trajectories for tasks such as pick-and-place operations on assembly lines. In contrast, inverse kinematics enables robots to adapt to changes in the environment or interact with objects in a controlled manner, such as manipulating objects with a robotic arm in a cluttered workspace.

Furthermore, advancements in robotics research have led to the development of sophisticated algorithms and techniques for solving kinematic problems in real time, allowing robots to operate in dynamic and unpredictable environments with greater autonomy and precision. These advancements have fueled the growth of various robotics applications, from autonomous vehicles and drones to humanoid robots and exoskeletons for rehabilitation.

In robot kinematics, encompassing forward and inverse kinematics forms the foundation of robotic motion control and manipulation. By understanding the geometric relationships between a robot's components and applying mathematical principles to calculate the robot's motion, engineers and researchers can design robots capable of performing a wide range of tasks with accuracy and efficiency. As robotics technology continues to evolve, advancements in kinematic analysis and control will undoubtedly play a central role in shaping the future of robotics and its applications across diverse industries.

Robot Dynamics: Newton-Euler and Lagrange Methods

Robotic dynamics, a crucial aspect of robotics, entails understanding the motion and forces acting on robots as they interact with their environment. In this chapter, we delve into two fundamental methods used for analyzing robot dynamics: the Newton-Euler method and the Lagrange method. Through comprehensive exploration, we aim to provide readers with a deep understanding of these methods and their applications in the field of robotics.

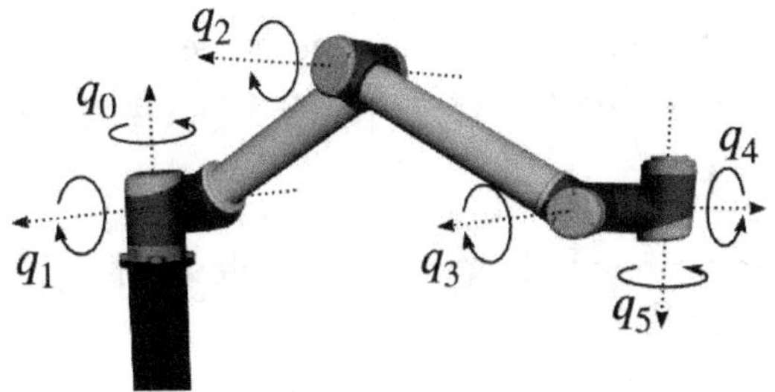

Figure 6. Robot Dynamics

Before delving into the specific methods of robot dynamics analysis, it's essential to grasp the foundational concepts. At its core, robot dynamics deals with the study of motion, forces, and torques acting on a robot system. Understanding these dynamics is vital for various applications, including robot control, motion planning, and stability analysis.

Newton-Euler Method

The Newton-Euler method, also known as the recursive Newton-Euler algorithm, is a widely used approach for calculating the forward and inverse dynamics of robotic systems. This method employs a recursive formulation to compute the velocities, accelerations, forces, and torques experienced by each link of the robot.

Basic Principles

At the heart of the Newton-Euler method lies the principle of applying Newton's laws of motion and Euler's equations of motion to derive dynamic equations for each link in the robot. By recursively propagating these equations from the base to the end-effector, we can compute the dynamic behavior of the entire robot system.

Recursive Formulation

The recursive nature of the Newton-Euler method enables efficient computation of robot dynamics by propagating motion and force information along the robot's kinematic chain. Through a step-by-step process, we can calculate the velocity, acceleration, force, and torque experienced by each link, taking into account the effects of gravity, inertia, and external forces.

Application Examples

To illustrate the application of the Newton-Euler method, we provide examples of its use in robotic manipulators, mobile robots, and humanoid robots. By understanding how to apply this method in practical scenarios, readers can gain insights into its utility for real-world robotics applications.

Lagrange Method

In contrast to the recursive nature of the Newton-Euler method, the Lagrange method offers a systematic and elegant approach to deriving the dynamic equations of motion for robotic systems. Named after the mathematician Joseph-Louis Lagrange, this method leverages the principle of least action to formulate the robot's dynamics.

Principle of Least Action

The Lagrangian formulation of mechanics rests on the principle of least action, which states that the actual motion of a mechanical system follows a path that minimizes the action integral. By expressing the Lagrangian as the kinetic energy minus the potential energy of the system, we can derive the equations of motion using Euler-Lagrange equations.

Derivation of Dynamic Equations

Using the Lagrangian formulation, we derive the dynamic equations of motion for robotic systems by applying the Euler-Lagrange equations to the Lagrangian function. This results in a set of coupled differential equations that describe the robot's dynamics in terms of its generalized coordinates, velocities, and accelerations.

Advantages and Limitations

While the Lagrange method offers a systematic approach to deriving robot dynamics equations, it may involve more complex mathematical formalism compared to the Newton-Euler method.

However, its elegance and generality make it well-suited for theoretical analysis and control design in robotics.

Applications and Case Studies

To demonstrate the practical relevance of robot dynamics analysis, we present case studies and applications where the Newton-Euler and Lagrange methods are employed. These include scenarios such as robot manipulator control, trajectory planning, and dynamic simulation, showcasing the importance of understanding robot dynamics in real-world settings.

The Newton-Euler and Lagrange methods provide powerful tools for analyzing the dynamics of robotic systems. By mastering these methods, roboticists can gain insights into the motion, forces, and torques experienced by robots, enabling them to design more efficient, stable, and capable robotic systems. Through continued research and application, the field of robot dynamics continues to evolve, driving innovation and advancements in robotics.

Robot Control Systems: Open Loop and Closed Loop

In the realm of robotics, control systems serve as the backbone, dictating the behavior and functionality of robots. Understanding the nuances between open-loop and closed-loop control systems is paramount for engineers and enthusiasts alike, as it underpins the very essence of how robots interact with their environment. In this chapter, we delve into the intricate workings of these control systems, elucidating their principles, applications, and implications in the field of robotics.

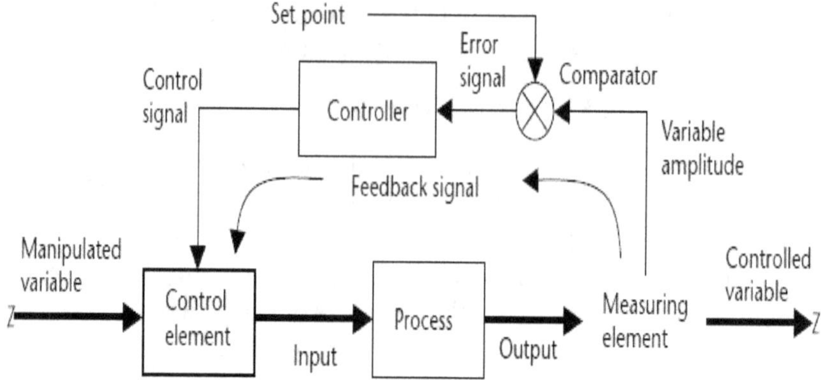

Figure 7. Robot Control Systems

Understanding Control Systems

Control systems, in their essence, are mechanisms that govern the behavior of a system or device. In the context of robotics, control systems are instrumental in regulating the motion, navigation, and interaction capabilities of robots. At its core, a control system comprises sensors, actuators, and a controller, working in tandem to achieve desired outcomes.

Open-Loop Control Systems

Open-loop control systems, also known as non-feedback control systems, operate based on predefined inputs without considering the system's output. In simpler terms, these systems execute actions without monitoring or adjusting based on the system's performance. While open-loop control systems exhibit simplicity and efficiency in certain applications, they lack adaptability and robustness, making them susceptible to disturbances and uncertainties in the environment.

Components of Open-Loop Control Systems

Input: The desired command or setpoint provided to the system.

Controller: Translates the input into control signals for the actuators.

Actuators: Execute the specified actions based on the control signals.

Output: Represents the system's response to the input without feedback or correction.

Applications of Open-Loop Control Systems

Simple Operations: Open-loop control systems are suitable for tasks with predictable environments and well-defined objectives, such as conveyor belt systems in manufacturing.

High-Speed Operations: In scenarios where real-time feedback is unnecessary, open-loop control systems offer rapid and efficient execution, such as in CNC machining.

Closed-Loop Control Systems

Closed-loop control systems, also referred to as feedback control systems, incorporate feedback mechanisms to continuously monitor and adjust the system's behavior based on its output. By comparing the actual output with the desired setpoint, these systems can dynamically adapt to changes in the environment, enhancing accuracy, stability, and robustness.

Components of Closed-Loop Control Systems

Feedback Sensor: Monitors the system's output or performance.

Controller: Analyzes the feedback signal and computes corrective actions.

Actuators: Receive commands from the controller to adjust the system's behavior.

Output: Represents the system's response to the feedback, enabling refinement and optimization.

Advantages of Closed-Loop Control Systems

Adaptability: Closed-loop systems can adjust their behavior in real time, compensating for disturbances or variations in the environment.

Accuracy: By continuously comparing the desired setpoint with the actual output, closed-loop control systems maintain precise control over the system's performance.

Robustness: Feedback mechanisms enable closed-loop systems to withstand uncertainties and external influences, ensuring reliable operation in diverse conditions.

Applications of Closed-Loop Control Systems

Autonomous Vehicles: Closed-loop control systems play a pivotal role in navigation, collision avoidance, and trajectory planning for self-driving cars and drones.

Robot Manipulation: In tasks requiring precise manipulation, such as robotic arms in manufacturing or surgical robotics, closed-loop control systems ensure accurate positioning and force control.

Environmental Monitoring: Closed-loop systems are employed in environmental monitoring platforms, such as weather stations and oceanographic buoys, to gather data and adjust operations based on feedback.

Comparative Analysis

In comparing open-loop and closed-loop control systems, it becomes evident that each approach has distinct advantages and limitations. While open-loop systems offer simplicity and efficiency for certain applications, closed-loop systems excel in adaptability, accuracy, and robustness, making them indispensable for dynamic and complex environments.

In the realm of robotics, control systems serve as the linchpin, orchestrating the intricate dance between input, output, and feedback. Through the exploration of open-loop and closed-loop control systems, we gain profound insights into the mechanisms that govern robotic behavior. By embracing the principles of feedback and adaptation, we pave the way for the evolution of intelligent and responsive robots capable of navigating the complexities of the world with grace and precision.

Robot Programming: Languages and Environments

Robot programming is a fundamental aspect of robotics that enables robots to perform various tasks autonomously or under human supervision. In this chapter, we delve into the diverse landscape of robot programming languages and environments, exploring their characteristics, functionalities, and applications. From traditional programming languages to domain-specific languages tailored for robotics, we examine how each language contributes to the development and operation of robotic systems.

Robot programming encompasses the techniques and methodologies used to instruct robots to perform specific tasks. It involves defining sequences of actions, controlling robot movements, processing sensor data, and making decisions based on environmental inputs.

Types of Robot Programming Languages

Traditional Programming Languages: Common programming languages such as C/C++, Python, and Java are widely used in robotics for their versatility and extensive libraries. These languages enable developers to create complex algorithms and control systems for robots.

Domain-Specific Languages (DSLs): DSLs are specialized languages designed specifically for robotics applications. Examples include Robotic Operating System (ROS) with its own language, RobotFlow for visual programming, and Blockly for educational purposes. DSLs often provide higher-level abstractions tailored to robotic tasks, simplifying the development process.

Behavior-Based Languages: Behavior-based languages focus on defining robot behaviors as a collection of simple reactive rules. Examples include Behavior-Based Robotics Language (B4GL) and Subsumption Architecture. These languages emphasize modularity and reactivity, making them suitable for real-time control systems.

Simulation and Modeling Languages: Simulation environments such as Gazebo and Webots use modeling languages like Unified Robot Description Format (URDF) and RobotML to describe robot geometries, dynamics, and sensor properties. These languages facilitate the simulation and testing of robotic algorithms before deployment on physical robots.

Key Features and Characteristics

Syntax and Semantics: Each programming language has its syntax and semantics, defining how instructions are structured and interpreted by the robot.

Concurrency and Parallelism: Robotics often requires handling multiple tasks concurrently, making support for concurrency and parallelism crucial in programming languages.

Real-Time Capabilities: Real-time systems demand precise timing and responsiveness, necessitating programming languages with deterministic execution and low-latency communication.

Interoperability: Integration with external libraries, frameworks, and hardware components enhances the versatility and interoperability of robot programming languages.

Support for Perception and Control: Effective robot programming languages should provide mechanisms for sensor data processing, perception, and feedback control to enable robust interaction with the environment.

Programming Environments and Tools

Integrated Development Environments (IDEs): IDEs such as Visual Studio Code, Eclipse, and JetBrains' PyCharm offer comprehensive development environments with features like code highlighting, debugging, and version control integration.

Simulation Platforms: Simulation platforms like ROS (Robot Operating System), V-REP, and Webots provide environments for testing and validating robotic algorithms in virtual environments before deployment on physical robots.

Online Resources and Communities: Online resources such as GitHub repositories, ROS wikis, and robotics forums foster collaboration, knowledge sharing, and access to open-source robotics projects.

Applications and Case Studies

Industrial Robotics: Programming languages like C/C++ and Python are widely used in industrial robotics for tasks such as assembly, welding, and material handling.

Autonomous Vehicles: Autonomous vehicles rely on programming languages such as C++ and Python for perception, decision-making, and control algorithms.

Service Robotics: DSLs like ROS facilitate the development of service robots for applications in healthcare, logistics, and domestic assistance.

Educational Robotics: Blockly and Scratch offer intuitive visual programming environments for teaching robotics concepts to students of all ages, fostering creativity and problem-solving skills.

Challenges and Future Directions

Complexity and Scalability: As robotic systems become more complex and interconnected, programming languages and environments must evolve to handle increasing complexity and scale.

Safety and Reliability: Ensuring the safety and reliability of robot programs is paramount, requiring robust programming paradigms and verification techniques.

Human-Robot Interaction: Programming languages and environments need to support natural and intuitive human-robot interaction paradigms to enable seamless collaboration between humans and robots.

Continued Innovation: The field of robot programming will continue to evolve with advancements in AI, machine learning, and hardware technologies, driving innovation in programming languages, tools, and methodologies.

In this we have explored the diverse landscape of robot programming languages and environments, from traditional languages like C/C++ to domain-specific languages like ROS and behavior-based languages. By understanding the characteristics, features, and applications of these languages, roboticists can effectively develop and deploy robotic systems for a wide range of applications.

Robot Vision Systems

Robot vision systems play a crucial role in enabling robots to perceive and interpret the world around them. Vision, as a sensory modality, allows robots to gather information from their environment, recognize objects, navigate obstacles, and perform various tasks autonomously. In this chapter, we will delve deep into the principles, technologies, and applications of robot vision systems.

Fundamentals of Robot Vision

Robot vision systems are inspired by human vision but implemented through sensors and algorithms. These systems typically consist of:

Cameras: Capturing visual data from the environment.

Image Processing Algorithms: Analyzing and interpreting the captured images.

Machine Learning Techniques: Training models for object recognition, scene understanding, etc.

Types of Robot Vision Systems

Robot vision systems can be categorized based on their functionality and application:

2D Vision Systems: Processing images in two dimensions, suitable for tasks like object detection and tracking.

3D Vision Systems: Providing depth information in addition to 2D data, enabling tasks like depth perception and spatial mapping.

Stereo Vision Systems: Using multiple cameras to create a 3D representation of the environment.

Time-of-Flight (ToF) Cameras: Measuring the time taken for light to travel to objects and back, enabling depth sensing.

Lidar Systems: Emitting laser beams and measuring the time taken for reflection, suitable for mapping and navigation.

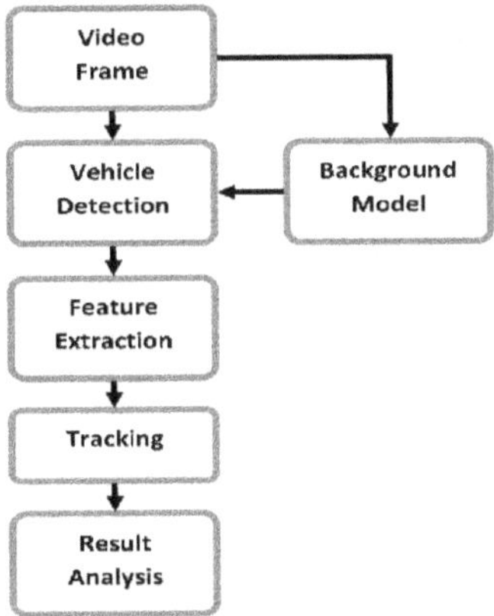

Figure 8. Robot Vision Systems

Principles of Robot Vision

Robot vision systems rely on various principles to interpret visual data effectively:

Feature Extraction: Identifying key features such as edges, corners, and textures in images.

Object Recognition: Classifying objects based on their visual appearance or characteristics.

Scene Understanding: Interpreting the context of a scene and extracting relevant information.

Depth Estimation: Inferring the distance of objects from the camera using depth sensing techniques.

Motion Detection: Detecting and tracking moving objects in real-time.

Technologies Empowering Robot Vision

Several technologies have advanced the capabilities of robot vision systems:

Deep Learning: Leveraging neural networks to learn complex patterns and features from visual data.

Convolutional Neural Networks (CNNs): Specialized neural networks for image processing tasks like object detection and classification.

Reinforcement Learning: Training robots to improve their vision-based decision-making through interaction with the environment.

Simultaneous Localization and Mapping (SLAM): Integrating vision with mapping techniques for navigation and localization.

Augmented Reality (AR): Overlaying digital information onto the robot's visual perception, enhancing its understanding of the environment.

Applications of Robot Vision Systems

Robot vision systems find applications across various domains:

Manufacturing: Quality inspection, object manipulation, and assembly line automation.

Logistics and Warehousing: Inventory management, package sorting, and robotic picking systems.

Healthcare: Surgical robots, patient monitoring, and medical imaging analysis.

Autonomous Vehicles: Visual perception for navigation, object detection, and pedestrian recognition.

Agriculture: Crop monitoring, pest detection, and robotic harvesting.

Surveillance and Security: Intrusion detection, facial recognition, and activity monitoring.

Challenges and Future Directions

Despite the advancements, robot vision systems still face several challenges:

Robustness: Ensuring reliable performance under varying lighting conditions, occlusions, and cluttered environments.

Real-time Processing: Meeting the computational requirements for processing large amounts of visual data in real-time.

Interpretability: Making AI-driven vision systems more interpretable and transparent in their decision-making process.

Ethical Considerations: Addressing concerns related to privacy, bias, and misuse of visual data.

Looking ahead, future research directions include:

Continued Advances in Deep Learning: Developing more efficient and versatile neural network architectures for vision tasks.

Integration with Other Sensors: Combining vision with other sensory modalities like lidar, radar, and ultrasound for multimodal perception.

Human-Robot Interaction: Enhancing robots' ability to understand and respond to human gestures, expressions, and intentions through vision.

Explainable AI: Developing techniques to provide insights into how vision-based decisions are made, fostering trust and transparency.

Robot vision systems have transformed the capabilities of robots, enabling them to perceive and interact with the world in increasingly sophisticated ways. By leveraging advances in imaging technology, artificial intelligence, and robotics, these systems hold immense potential to revolutionize industries, enhance human-robot collaboration, and shape the future of automation.

Mobile Robotics: Navigation and Mapping

Mobile robotics encompasses a vast array of applications, from autonomous vehicles to delivery drones, exploring environments that are dynamic and constantly changing. Key to the functionality of these robots is their ability to navigate through space effectively and map their surroundings accurately. In this chapter, we delve into the intricacies of mobile robotics navigation and mapping, exploring the underlying principles, techniques, and challenges involved in creating robots that can autonomously move and operate in diverse environments.

Mobile robotics involves the design and development of robots capable of locomotion in various environments. Unlike stationary robots, mobile robots possess the ability to move and navigate autonomously, making them well-suited for applications such as exploration, surveillance, and logistics.

Fundamentals of Navigation

Navigation is the process by which a robot determines its position and moves from one location to another. It involves several fundamental concepts, including localization, path planning, and obstacle avoidance.

Localization Techniques

Localization refers to the ability of a robot to determine its position within its environment. There are several techniques for achieving localization, including landmark-based methods, odometry, and simultaneous localization and mapping (SLAM).

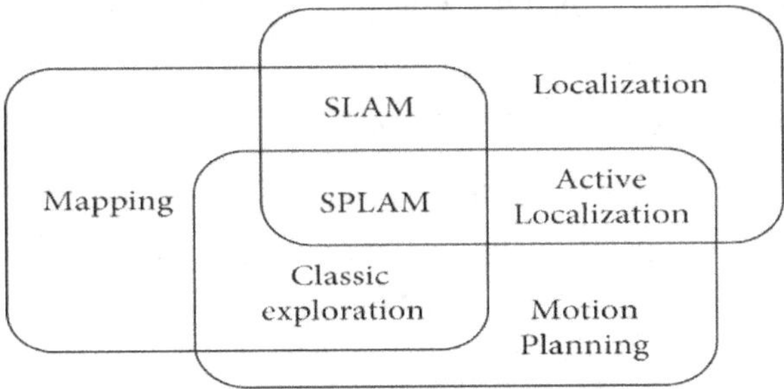

Figure 9. Mobile Robotics

Path Planning Algorithms

Path planning is the process of determining the optimal path for a robot to reach its destination while avoiding obstacles. Various algorithms, such as A search, Dijkstra's algorithm, and Rapidly-exploring Random Trees (RRT), are used to generate efficient paths in different environments.

Obstacle Avoidance

Obstacle avoidance is essential for ensuring the safety and efficiency of mobile robots. Robots must be able to detect obstacles in their path and navigate around them without colliding. Techniques for obstacle detection and avoidance include sensors such as LiDAR, cameras, and ultrasonic sensors.

Mapping Strategies

Mapping involves creating a representation of the robot's environment, including obstacles, landmarks, and other features. Mapping techniques range from simple grid-based maps to more complex probabilistic methods like occupancy grid mapping and feature-based mapping.

Simultaneous Localization and Mapping (SLAM)

SLAM is a fundamental problem in mobile robotics that involves building a map of an unknown environment while simultaneously localizing the robot within that map. SLAM algorithms utilize sensor data, such as odometry and range measurements, to estimate both the robot's pose and the map of the environment.

Challenges and Considerations

Mobile robotics navigation and mapping present numerous challenges, including sensor noise, environmental variability, and computational complexity. Additionally, ethical considerations, such as privacy concerns and the impact on society, must be taken into account when deploying autonomous robots in real-world scenarios.

Applications of Mobile Robotics

Mobile robotics has a wide range of applications across various industries, including logistics, agriculture, search and rescue, and space exploration. Autonomous drones, self-driving cars, and warehouse robots are just a few examples of how mobile robots are revolutionizing different sectors.

Future Directions

The field of mobile robotics continues to advance rapidly, driven by innovations in AI, sensor technology, and robotics. Future developments may include more robust navigation and mapping algorithms, enhanced sensor capabilities, and the integration of mobile robots into smart cities and infrastructure systems.

In mobile robotics, navigation and mapping are critical components of autonomous systems that enable robots to operate effectively in dynamic and unpredictable environments. By understanding the principles and techniques discussed in this chapter, researchers and engineers can develop mobile robots capable of navigating and mapping their surroundings with precision and reliability.

Robot Localization and SLAM

Robot localization is a fundamental problem in robotics that involves determining a robot's position and orientation within its environment. It is akin to a robot's sense of self-awareness in the physical world. Without accurate localization, a robot would be unable to navigate effectively or interact meaningfully with its surroundings.

Importance of Localization

Accurate robot localization is crucial for a wide range of applications, including autonomous navigation, mapping, and object manipulation. In scenarios such as search and rescue missions or warehouse automation, the ability of a robot to know its precise location can mean the difference between success and failure.

Challenges in Localization

Several challenges must be addressed to achieve reliable robot localization:

Sensor Noise: Sensors used for localization, such as GPS, lidar, and cameras, are prone to noise and inaccuracies. This noise can lead to erroneous position estimates if not properly handled.

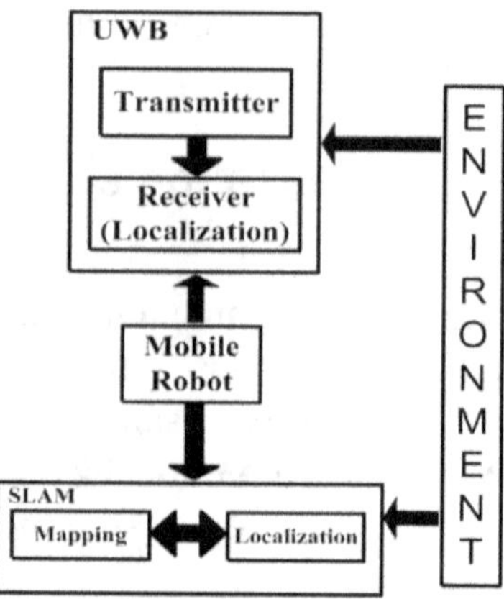

Figure 10. Robot Localization and SLAM

Ambiguity: In environments with symmetrical or repetitive features, it can be challenging for a robot to distinguish its current location from similar-looking positions.

Dynamic Environments: Changes in the environment, such as moving objects or varying lighting conditions, can further complicate localization efforts.

Techniques for Robot Localization

Several techniques and algorithms have been developed to tackle the problem of robot localization. These methods leverage different sensor modalities and mathematical models to estimate the robot's pose accurately.

Odometry

Odometry is a localization technique that relies on measuring the motion of a robot's wheels or other actuators. By tracking the distance traveled and the changes in orientation, odometry estimates the robot's position relative to a starting point. However, odometry is prone to cumulative errors, especially in environments with uneven terrain or wheel slippage.

Sensor Fusion

Sensor fusion involves integrating data from multiple sensors to improve localization accuracy. Common sensor modalities used in sensor fusion include:

GPS: Global Positioning System provides absolute position information but may suffer from signal loss or multipath interference in urban or indoor environments.

Lidar: Light Detection and Ranging sensors use laser beams to measure distances to surrounding objects. Lidar scans can provide detailed maps of the environment, aiding in localization.

IMU: Inertial Measurement Units combine accelerometers and gyroscopes to measure a robot's linear and angular velocity. IMUs are particularly useful for short-term localization but suffer from drift over time.

Visual Sensors: Cameras and depth sensors capture visual information about the environment, allowing robots to recognize landmarks and infer their position relative to known features.

Kalman Filters

Kalman filters are a class of recursive Bayesian filters used to estimate the state of a dynamic system based on noisy sensor measurements. Kalman filters are widely employed in robot localization due to their effectiveness in handling sensor noise and uncertainty. Extended Kalman filters (EKF) and Unscented Kalman filters (UKF) are variants commonly used in localization applications.

Particle Filters

Particle filters, also known as Monte Carlo localization, are another popular approach to robot localization. Particle filters maintain a set of probabilistic hypotheses about the robot's pose and update these hypotheses based on sensor measurements. By sampling from the posterior distribution of possible poses, particle filters can accommodate nonlinearities and multimodal distributions in the localization problem.

Simultaneous Localization and Mapping (SLAM)

Simultaneous Localization and Mapping (SLAM) is an advanced robotics technique that addresses the challenge of robot localization in unknown environments while simultaneously building a map of the surroundings. SLAM algorithms enable robots to navigate autonomously in unexplored or dynamically changing environments, making them indispensable for applications such as robotic exploration, autonomous driving, and mobile robotics.

Key Components of SLAM

SLAM algorithms typically consist of the following key components:

Mapping: The mapping component of SLAM involves building a representation of the environment using sensor measurements. This can be done using techniques such as occupancy grid mapping, feature-based mapping, or 3D reconstruction.

Localization: The localization component estimates the robot's pose within the map generated by the mapping module. This is often achieved by integrating sensor measurements with motion models to track the robot's position over time.

Loop Closure Detection: Loop closure detection is a critical aspect of SLAM that involves identifying previously visited locations based on current sensor measurements. Detecting loop closures allows SLAM algorithms to correct drift errors and improve map consistency.

SLAM Algorithms

Several SLAM algorithms have been developed, each with its own strengths and weaknesses:

Extended Kalman Filter SLAM (EKF-SLAM): EKF-SLAM applies the extended Kalman filter to estimate both the robot's pose and the map of the environment. However, EKF-SLAM is limited by its linearization assumptions and can struggle in environments with nonlinearities or sparse features.

Graph-Based SLAM: Graph-based SLAM formulates the SLAM problem as a graph optimization task, where nodes represent robot poses and edges encode constraints between poses. Graph-based SLAM algorithms, such as pose graph optimization and bundle adjustment, can handle loop closures and non-Gaussian uncertainty more effectively than EKF-SLAM.

Particle Filter SLAM: Particle filter-based SLAM methods, such as FastSLAM and Monte Carlo Localization (MCL), use particle filters to maintain a posterior distribution over the robot's trajectory and the map. Particle filter SLAM algorithms are well-suited for handling nonlinearities and multimodal distributions in the SLAM problem.

Challenges and Future Directions

While SLAM has made significant strides in recent years, several challenges remain to be addressed:

Real-Time Performance: Many SLAM algorithms struggle to achieve real-time performance, especially in large-scale environments or with high-resolution sensor data. Improving computational efficiency is a key area of research in SLAM.

Robustness to Dynamic Environments: SLAM algorithms often assume static environments and can struggle to cope with dynamic obstacles or changes in lighting conditions. Developing robust SLAM algorithms that can adapt to dynamic environments is an active area of research.

Semantic Mapping: Beyond geometric maps, there is growing interest in semantic mapping, where robots not only localize themselves but also understand the semantic meaning of the environment. Integrating semantic information into SLAM algorithms could enable robots to perform more intelligent navigation and interaction tasks.

Robot localization and SLAM are essential capabilities for autonomous robots operating in real-world environments. By leveraging sensor data and advanced algorithms, robots can accurately determine their position, navigate complex surroundings, and interact effectively with the world around them.

Human-Robot Interaction (HRI)

Human-Robot Interaction (HRI) is a multidisciplinary field that focuses on understanding, designing, and evaluating interactions between humans and robots. In recent years, HRI has garnered significant attention due to the increasing presence of robots in various domains, ranging from manufacturing and healthcare to entertainment and domestic settings. This chapter explores the intricacies of HRI, including its importance, challenges, key concepts, and future directions.

Importance of HRI

In today's rapidly evolving technological landscape, the integration of robots into human-centric environments necessitates seamless and intuitive interactions between humans and machines. HRI plays a pivotal role in ensuring effective communication, collaboration, and cooperation between humans and robots. By understanding human behaviors, preferences, and social cues, robots can better adapt to their environments and fulfill their intended tasks. Moreover, fostering positive interactions between humans and robots is crucial for enhancing user acceptance, trust, and satisfaction, ultimately leading to the successful deployment and adoption of robotic systems.

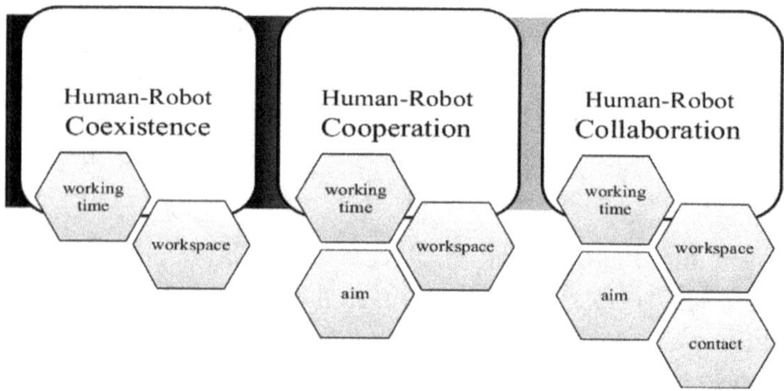

Figure 11. Human-Robot Interaction (HRI)

Challenges in HRI

Despite its potential benefits, HRI poses several challenges that stem from the complex nature of human behavior and social interaction. One of the primary challenges is designing robots that can perceive, interpret, and respond to human gestures, facial expressions, and verbal cues accurately. Achieving natural and intuitive communication between humans and robots requires advanced sensor technologies, robust perception algorithms, and sophisticated natural language processing capabilities. Additionally, cultural differences, individual preferences, and societal norms influence human-robot interactions, necessitating cross-cultural studies and adaptive interaction strategies. Moreover, ensuring the safety and ethical implications of HRI is paramount, particularly in applications involving vulnerable populations such as children, the elderly, and individuals with disabilities.

Key Concepts in HRI

a. Social Robots: Social robots are designed to engage with humans in social interactions, such as conversation, emotional support, and companionship. These robots often possess anthropomorphic features, such as human-like faces and gestures, to facilitate empathetic communication and establish rapport with users.

b. Collaborative Robots (Cobots): Collaborative robots, or cobots, work alongside humans in shared workspaces, performing tasks that require close coordination and cooperation. Ensuring safe and effective collaboration between humans and cobots involves implementing intuitive interfaces, adaptive control strategies, and robust safety mechanisms.

c. User-Centered Design: User-centered design (UCD) emphasizes the importance of incorporating user feedback and preferences into the design process to create products and systems that are intuitive, usable, and enjoyable for the intended users. In the context of HRI, UCD involves conducting user studies, usability testing, and iterative design iterations to refine the interaction experience and enhance user satisfaction.

d. Ethical Considerations: Ethical considerations in HRI encompass a wide range of issues, including privacy, autonomy, transparency, and accountability. As robots become increasingly integrated into various aspects of human life, addressing ethical concerns surrounding data privacy, algorithmic bias, and human-robot power dynamics is essential to ensure equitable and responsible interactions between humans and robots.

Future Directions in HRI

Looking ahead, the field of HRI is poised for continued growth and innovation, driven by advancements in robotics, artificial intelligence, and human-computer interaction. Future research directions in HRI include:

Personalized Interaction: Tailoring robot behaviors and responses to individual user preferences and characteristics.

Multi-modal Interaction: Integrating multiple modalities, such as speech, gesture, and touch, to enable richer and more natural communication between humans and robots.

Long-term Interaction: Investigating the dynamics of long-term human-robot relationships and the factors that contribute to user engagement, trust, and attachment.

Ethical Robotics: Developing ethical frameworks and guidelines for the responsible design, deployment, and use of robots in society.

Human-Robot Interaction is a dynamic and interdisciplinary field that bridges the gap between humans and machines, enabling seamless collaboration and communication in diverse domains. By addressing the challenges and harnessing the opportunities of HRI, we can unlock the full potential of robots as valuable partners in our daily lives.

Robotics Projects and Case Studies

In this we delve into real-world applications of robotics through a series of projects and case studies. These examples illustrate how artificial intelligence is integrated into robotic systems to solve complex problems and accomplish various tasks across different industries.

Autonomous Delivery Drones in Logistics

Autonomous delivery drones have gained significant attention in recent years due to their potential to revolutionize the logistics industry. Case studies of companies like Amazon Prime Air and Google's Wing showcase how AI-powered drones are used for efficient and timely delivery of packages to customers. These drones utilize advanced algorithms for route planning, obstacle avoidance, and navigation, demonstrating the capabilities of AI in autonomous aerial vehicles.

Robotic Surgeons in Healthcare

Robotic surgeons, such as the da Vinci Surgical System, have transformed minimally invasive surgery by providing surgeons with enhanced precision and control. Through case studies of hospitals and medical centers worldwide, we explore how AI algorithms enable robotic surgeons to perform delicate procedures with greater accuracy and safety. These case studies highlight the integration of computer vision, machine learning, and haptic feedback in robotic surgical systems, leading to improved patient outcomes and reduced recovery times.

AI-Powered Agricultural Robots

The agriculture industry is embracing robotics to address labor shortages and improve crop yield. Case studies of companies like Blue River Technology (acquired by John Deere) and FarmWise demonstrate how AI-powered robots are deployed for tasks such as weed control, crop monitoring, and harvesting. These robots leverage computer vision and machine learning algorithms to identify and classify plants, enabling targeted application of herbicides and fertilizers while minimizing environmental impact.

Autonomous Vehicles for Urban Mobility

Autonomous vehicles are poised to revolutionize urban transportation, offering the promise of safer and more efficient mobility. Case studies of companies like Waymo and Tesla provide insights into the development and deployment of self-driving cars equipped with AI-driven perception, decision-making, and control systems. These case studies examine the technological challenges of autonomous driving, such as real-time object detection, localization, and path planning, as well as regulatory and ethical considerations.

Humanoid Robots in Service Industries

Humanoid robots are increasingly being deployed in service industries such as hospitality, retail, and entertainment to enhance customer experience and streamline operations. Case studies of robots like Pepper and SoftBank Robotics' Whiz showcase their roles in greeting customers, providing information, and performing tasks such as cleaning and inventory management. These case studies explore the design principles and AI algorithms behind humanoid robots, as well as their integration with existing systems and workflows.

Robotic Exploration of Extreme Environments

Robots equipped with AI capabilities are utilized for exploring extreme environments such as deep-sea environments, outer space, and disaster zones. Case studies of projects like NASA's Mars rovers and underwater exploration vehicles highlight the challenges and opportunities of robotic exploration in harsh and remote environments. These case studies discuss the autonomy and adaptability of robotic systems in navigating unpredictable terrain, collecting scientific data, and executing complex missions with limited human intervention.

In each case study, we analyze the technical aspects, challenges, and outcomes of the robotics projects, providing readers with valuable insights into the real-world applications of AI in robotics across diverse domains.

Ethical and Social Implications of Robotics

As we delve deeper into the realm of robotics, it becomes imperative to critically examine the ethical and social implications of these technologies. While robotics holds immense potential to revolutionize various aspects of our lives, it also raises significant ethical concerns that warrant careful consideration.

Impact on Employment

One of the foremost concerns surrounding the integration of robotics into various industries is its potential impact on employment. The automation of tasks traditionally performed by humans has the potential to displace workers, leading to unemployment and economic upheaval. While proponents argue that automation can lead to increased efficiency and productivity, critics raise concerns about the widening gap between the skilled and unskilled workforce. Addressing this issue requires proactive measures, such as retraining programs and policies aimed at ensuring a fair transition for workers affected by automation.

Privacy and Surveillance

The proliferation of robotic technologies equipped with sensors and cameras raises significant concerns regarding privacy and surveillance. Autonomous robots deployed in public spaces, workplaces, and even private residences have the capability to collect vast amounts of data about individuals without their consent. This raises questions about the ethical implications of surveillance and the potential for abuse of power by governments and corporations. Striking a balance between the benefits of surveillance for security and the protection of individual privacy rights is essential to ensuring the ethical use of robotic technologies.

Autonomous Decision-Making

Advancements in artificial intelligence have led to the development of robots capable of autonomous decision-making, raising ethical questions about accountability and liability. In situations where robots are entrusted with critical tasks, such as autonomous vehicles making split-second decisions on the road, it becomes crucial to establish clear guidelines for ethical behavior and accountability. Who bears responsibility in the event of accidents or harm caused by autonomous robots? Addressing these ethical dilemmas requires interdisciplinary collaboration between ethicists, policymakers, and technologists to develop robust frameworks for responsible AI and robotics.

Impact on Human Relationships

The increasing integration of robots into various aspects of society, including healthcare, education, and companionship, raises complex questions about the nature of human relationships. Can robots truly emulate human empathy and emotional intelligence? What are the ethical implications of forming emotional attachments to robots? While proponents argue that robots can provide valuable support and companionship, critics caution against the erosion of genuine human connections and the potential for exploitation. Navigating these ethical complexities requires careful reflection on the ethical boundaries of human-robot interactions and the promotion of empathy and compassion in the design and deployment of robotic technologies.

Bias and Fairness

AI algorithms powering robotic systems are not immune to bias, reflecting the biases present in the data used to train them. This raises concerns about algorithmic fairness and the perpetuation of societal biases, such as gender, race, and socioeconomic status, in robotic decision-making. Addressing algorithmic bias requires transparency and accountability in the design and implementation of AI systems, as well as efforts to diversify the datasets used for training to mitigate bias. Additionally, ongoing monitoring and evaluation of AI systems are necessary to identify and rectify biases that may emerge over time.

Moral Agency and Rights

The concept of moral agency, traditionally associated with human beings, raises profound questions about the ethical status of robots and their entitlement to rights and protections. As robots become increasingly autonomous and capable of exhibiting complex behaviors, questions arise about their moral standing and the ethical implications of treating them as mere tools or possessions. Some argue for the recognition of robot rights, such as the right to autonomy and freedom from harm, while others caution against anthropomorphizing robots and blurring the distinction between humans and machines. Exploring these ethical questions requires interdisciplinary dialogue and a nuanced understanding of the relationship between technology, ethics, and human values.

The ethical and social implications of robotics are multifaceted and complex, touching upon fundamental questions about the nature of humanity, morality, and society. As we continue to advance the field of robotics, it is essential to approach these ethical challenges with humility, empathy, and a commitment to fostering responsible innovation that prioritizes the well-being of individuals and communities.

Chapter 2

Robot Perception and Sensing

Sensor Technologies for Robotics

Sensors serve as the eyes and ears of robotic systems, enabling them to perceive and interact with their environment. From detecting objects and obstacles to measuring temperature and humidity, sensors play a crucial role in equipping robots with the ability to sense and respond to the world around them. In this section, we will explore various sensor technologies commonly used in robotics, ranging from visual and auditory sensors to tactile and environmental sensors.

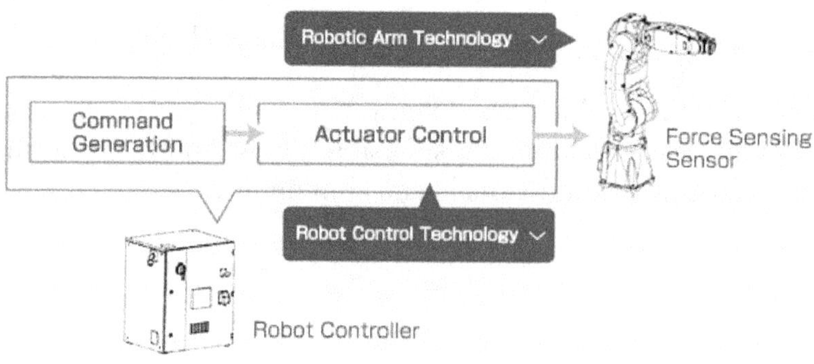

Figure 1. Sensor Technologies for Robotics

Visual Sensors

Visual sensors, such as cameras and depth sensors, provide robots with the ability to perceive the visual aspects of their environment. Cameras capture images or videos, allowing robots to extract visual information about objects, shapes, and colors. Depth sensors, such as LiDAR (Light Detection and Ranging) and time-of-flight cameras, measure the distance to objects in the robot's surroundings, enabling depth perception and 3D mapping. Visual sensors are essential for tasks such as object recognition, navigation, and scene understanding.

Auditory Sensors

Auditory sensors, including microphones and sound detectors, enable robots to perceive and interpret auditory signals in their environment. Microphones capture sound waves, allowing robots to detect speech, environmental sounds, and other acoustic cues. Speech recognition algorithms process audio input, enabling robots to understand and respond to verbal commands. Auditory sensors are particularly useful in applications such as human-robot interaction, voice-controlled interfaces, and acoustic monitoring.

Tactile Sensors

Tactile sensors provide robots with the ability to sense physical contact and pressure, enabling them to interact with objects and surfaces in a tactile manner. Tactile sensors can take various forms, including pressure-sensitive materials, force-sensitive resistors, and tactile arrays. By detecting changes in pressure or deformation, tactile sensors enable robots to grasp objects with precision, manipulate delicate materials, and perceive tactile feedback during interaction. Tactile sensing is essential for tasks such as grasping, manipulation, and haptic exploration.

Inertial Sensors

Inertial sensors, such as accelerometers and gyroscopes, measure the acceleration and angular velocity of the robot's body, enabling it to perceive changes in its orientation and motion. Accelerometers detect linear acceleration along the three axes, while gyroscopes measure rotational motion around these axes. Inertial sensors provide robots with information about their posture, velocity, and changes in direction, enabling precise motion control, stabilization, and navigation. Inertial sensors are particularly useful in mobile robots, drones, and wearable devices.

Environmental Sensors

Environmental sensors measure various physical parameters of the robot's surroundings, including temperature, humidity, pressure, and gas concentrations. Temperature sensors detect changes in temperature, enabling robots to monitor thermal conditions and detect heat sources. Humidity sensors measure the moisture content of the air, important for applications such as climate control and environmental monitoring. Pressure sensors measure atmospheric pressure, useful for altitude sensing and weather forecasting. Gas sensors detect the presence of gases in the environment, enabling robots to detect pollutants, toxic gases, and other hazardous substances.

Proximity Sensors

Proximity sensors detect the presence or absence of objects in the robot's vicinity, enabling it to perceive obstacles and avoid collisions. Proximity sensors can take various forms, including ultrasonic sensors, infrared sensors, and capacitive sensors. Ultrasonic sensors emit high-frequency sound waves and measure the time it takes for the sound waves to bounce back from objects, enabling distance measurement and object detection. Infrared sensors detect infrared radiation emitted or reflected by objects, useful for proximity sensing and object detection in low-light conditions. Capacitive sensors detect changes in capacitance caused by the presence of objects, enabling touchless sensing and proximity detection.

Fusion of Sensor Technologies

In many robotic applications, multiple sensor modalities are combined to provide a more comprehensive perception of the environment. Sensor fusion techniques integrate data from different sensors to enhance the accuracy, reliability, and robustness of robotic perception. The fusion of visual, auditory, tactile, and inertial sensors enables robots to perceive and interpret complex environmental cues, enabling tasks such as object recognition, navigation, and human-robot interaction. Sensor fusion plays a crucial role in enabling robots to operate effectively in diverse and dynamic environments.

Sensor technologies form the foundation of robotic perception, enabling robots to sense and interact with their environment. From visual and auditory sensors to tactile and environmental sensors, a diverse range of sensor modalities equip robots with the ability to perceive the world around them. By harnessing the capabilities of sensor technologies, robots can perform a wide range of tasks, from autonomous navigation and manipulation to human-robot interaction and environmental monitoring.

Vision Systems and Image Processing

Vision systems play a crucial role in enabling robots to perceive and interact with their environment. By emulating the human sense of sight, robots equipped with vision systems can recognize objects, navigate through complex environments, and perform tasks with precision. In this section, we will explore the principles of vision systems and the role of image processing in robotics.

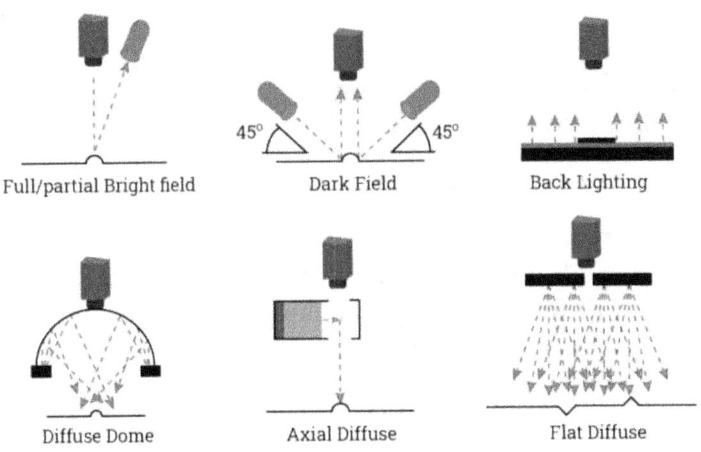

Figure 2. Vision Systems

Vision systems in robotics refer to the integration of cameras and image-processing algorithms to enable robots to interpret visual information from their surroundings. These systems are essential for tasks such as object detection, localization, navigation, and manipulation. By capturing images of the environment and analyzing them using computer vision techniques, robots can make informed decisions and perform tasks autonomously.

Types of Vision Systems

There are various types of vision systems used in robotics, each tailored to specific applications and environments:

2D Vision Systems: Utilize traditional cameras to capture two-dimensional images of the environment. These systems are widely used for tasks such as object recognition, tracking, and navigation.

3D Vision Systems: Employ depth-sensing technologies, such as stereo cameras, time-of-flight cameras, or structured light sensors, to capture three-dimensional information about the environment. This enables robots to perceive depth and accurately estimate the size and shape of objects.

Multi-camera Systems: Combine multiple cameras to provide a wider field of view and better coverage of the environment. Multi-camera systems are commonly used in applications requiring panoramic vision or simultaneous monitoring of multiple areas.

Image Processing Techniques

Image processing plays a crucial role in extracting meaningful information from visual data captured by vision systems. A variety of image processing techniques are employed to enhance image quality, extract features, and analyze visual patterns:

Image Filtering: Involves the application of filters to remove noise, blur, or enhance specific features in an image. Common filtering techniques include Gaussian blur, median filtering, and edge enhancement.

Feature Extraction: Focuses on identifying key features or patterns in an image, such as edges, corners, or keypoints. Feature extraction techniques, such as edge detection, corner detection, and blob detection, are essential for tasks like object recognition and tracking.

Object Detection and Recognition: Involves detecting and identifying objects of interest within an image. Object detection algorithms, such as Haar cascades, HOG (Histogram of Oriented Gradients), and deep learning-based approaches like CNNs (Convolutional Neural Networks), are widely used for this purpose.

Image Segmentation: Divides an image into meaningful regions or segments based on similarities in color, texture, or intensity. Image segmentation techniques, such as thresholding, region growing, and clustering, are useful for tasks like image analysis and scene understanding.

Applications of Vision Systems in Robotics

Vision systems find applications across a wide range of robotic domains, including:

Autonomous Navigation: Vision-based navigation systems enable robots to perceive obstacles, detect landmarks, and plan collision-free paths in dynamic environments.

Object Manipulation: Vision-guided robots can identify and grasp objects with precision, facilitating tasks such as pick-and-place operations in manufacturing and logistics.

Quality Inspection: Vision systems are used for inspecting product quality, identifying defects, and ensuring compliance with quality standards in manufacturing processes.

Surveillance and Security: Vision-based surveillance systems enable robots to monitor and analyze activity in various environments, enhancing security and situational awareness.

Assistive Robotics: Vision systems are employed in assistive robots to aid individuals with disabilities or impairments in tasks such as navigation, object recognition, and daily living activities.

Challenges and Future Directions

Despite the advancements in vision systems, several challenges remain in the field of robotics:

Robustness to Environmental Variability: Vision systems must be robust to variations in lighting conditions, occlusions, and cluttered environments to perform reliably in real-world scenarios.

Real-Time Processing: Many robotics applications require real-time image processing to make timely decisions and responses. Ensuring efficient algorithms and hardware acceleration are essential to meet these requirements.

Integration with Other Sensors: Vision systems often complement other sensor modalities, such as lidar, radar, and inertial sensors. Integrating data from multiple sensors and fusing information to enhance perception remains a challenging task.

Looking ahead, the future of vision systems in robotics holds exciting prospects:

Advancements in Deep Learning: Deep learning techniques, particularly convolutional neural networks (CNNs), continue to revolutionize image processing and object recognition tasks, enabling robots to achieve higher levels of accuracy and robustness.

Emerging Technologies: Technologies such as neuromorphic sensors, event-based vision, and bio-inspired algorithms hold promise for enhancing the capabilities of vision systems and overcoming current limitations.

Ethical Considerations: As vision systems become more pervasive in robotics, ethical considerations regarding privacy, surveillance, and bias in image processing algorithms must be carefully addressed to ensure responsible development and deployment.

Vision systems and image processing are integral components of robotics, enabling robots to perceive and interpret visual information from their environment. By leveraging advances in computer vision and image processing techniques, robots can navigate, interact, and collaborate with humans in diverse real-world scenarios, paving the way for the advancement of robotics in the years to come.

Object Detection and Recognition

Object detection and recognition are fundamental tasks in robotics that enable robots to perceive and interact with their environment. By identifying and understanding objects in their surroundings, robots can navigate safely, manipulate objects, and perform various tasks autonomously. In this section, we will explore the principles, techniques, and applications of object detection and recognition in robotics.

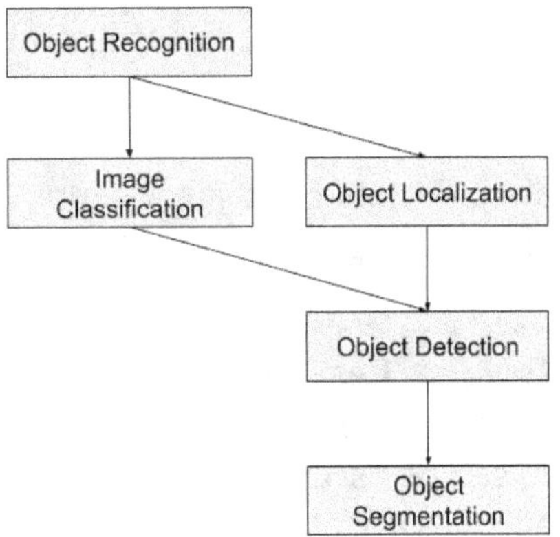

Figure 3. Object Detection

Object detection and recognition involve identifying and categorizing objects in images or sensor data captured by robots. These tasks are essential for robots to understand and interact with the world around them. Object detection refers to the process of locating objects within an image or scene, while object recognition involves identifying the type or class of each detected object.

Techniques for Object Detection

There are several techniques for object detection in robotics, each with its strengths and limitations:

Traditional Computer Vision Methods: Traditional computer vision methods rely on handcrafted features and algorithms to detect objects. Techniques such as edge detection, corner detection, and template matching are commonly used.

Machine Learning Approaches: Machine learning techniques, particularly deep learning, have revolutionized object detection in recent years. Convolutional Neural Networks (CNNs), such as the YOLO (You Only Look Once) and SSD (Single Shot MultiBox Detector) architectures, have achieved remarkable performance in real-time object detection tasks.

Feature-Based Methods: Feature-based methods extract distinctive features from images, such as keypoints or descriptors, to detect objects. Techniques like SIFT (Scale-Invariant Feature Transform) and SURF (Speeded-Up Robust Features) are examples of feature-based approaches.

Object Recognition Techniques

Once objects are detected, the next step is to recognize them and assign labels or categories. Object recognition techniques include:

Classical Machine Learning: Classical machine learning algorithms, such as Support Vector Machines (SVMs) and Random Forests, can be used for object recognition tasks. These algorithms learn to classify objects based on handcrafted features extracted from images.

Deep Learning Approaches: Deep learning has revolutionized object recognition by enabling end-to-end learning from raw sensor data. Convolutional Neural Networks (CNNs) are widely used for image classification tasks, achieving state-of-the-art performance on benchmark datasets.

Transfer Learning: Transfer learning techniques leverage pre-trained deep learning models to perform object recognition tasks with limited labeled data. By fine-tuning pre-trained models on specific datasets, robots can recognize a wide range of objects with high accuracy.

Applications of Object Detection and Recognition in Robotics

Object detection and recognition have numerous applications in robotics across various domains:

Autonomous Navigation: Robots use object detection to identify obstacles and navigate safely in their environment. By detecting and avoiding obstacles in real-time, robots can autonomously navigate complex environments.

Object Manipulation: In tasks such as pick-and-place operations in manufacturing or household chores, robots must detect and recognize objects to manipulate them effectively. Object detection and recognition enable robots to grasp and manipulate objects with precision.

Scene Understanding: Object detection and recognition contribute to scene understanding by providing robots with contextual information about their surroundings. By identifying objects and their spatial relationships, robots can make informed decisions and adapt to changing environments.

Human-Robot Interaction: In social robotics and assistive technology, object detection and recognition facilitate human-robot interaction. Robots can recognize objects used by humans and assist with tasks such as fetching objects or providing information.

Challenges and Future Directions

Despite significant advancements, object detection and recognition in robotics still face several challenges:

Robustness to Variability: Object detection algorithms must be robust to variations in lighting conditions, occlusions, and object poses. Robustness to environmental variability is essential for real-world deployment.

Real-Time Processing: Many robotics applications require real-time object detection and recognition to operate efficiently. Achieving real-time performance while maintaining high accuracy is a challenge, particularly for deep learning-based approaches.

Generalization: Object detection and recognition algorithms should generalize well to unseen objects and environments. Ensuring that robots can recognize a diverse range of objects in various contexts remains a significant challenge.

Object detection and recognition are foundational tasks in robotics that enable robots to perceive and interact with their environment autonomously. By leveraging techniques from computer vision and machine learning, robots can detect and recognize objects with high accuracy, enabling a wide range of applications across different domains. Despite remaining challenges, ongoing research and innovation continue to advance the field of object detection and recognition, paving the way for more intelligent and capable robotic systems.

Environment Modeling and Mapping

In the realm of robotics, the ability to perceive and understand the surrounding environment is fundamental to the autonomy and intelligence of robotic systems. Environment modeling and mapping play a crucial role in enabling robots to navigate and interact with their surroundings effectively. This section delves into the intricacies of environment modeling and mapping, exploring the techniques, challenges, and applications of these foundational concepts in robotics.

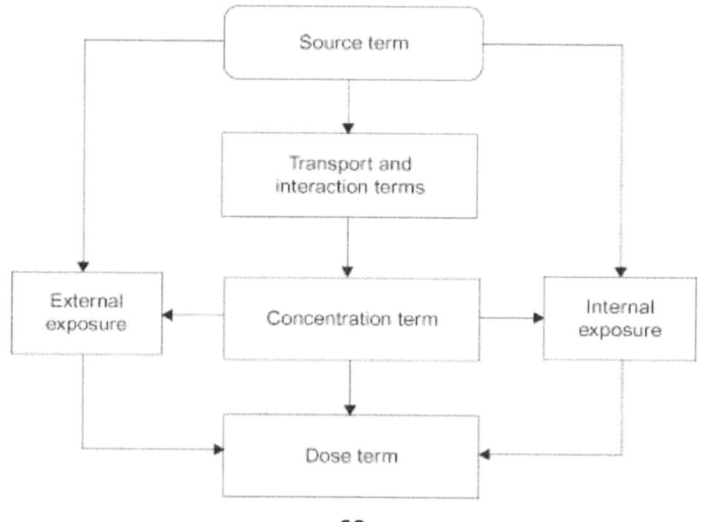

Environment modeling and mapping encompass the processes of creating representations of the physical world and capturing spatial information about the robot's surroundings. These representations serve as the basis for decision-making, navigation, and interaction in robotic systems. By constructing accurate models of the environment, robots can navigate complex terrains, avoid obstacles, and accomplish tasks autonomously.

Sensor Technologies for Environment Perception

Central to environment modeling and mapping are the sensors employed by robots to perceive their surroundings. Various sensor modalities, including cameras, LiDAR (Light Detection and Ranging), sonar, and depth sensors, provide rich data about the environment. Each sensor type has its strengths and limitations, and the choice of sensors depends on the specific requirements of the robotic application.

Localization Techniques

Localization, the process of determining the robot's position and orientation within the environment, is a critical component of environment modeling and mapping. Techniques such as Global Positioning System (GPS), odometry, and inertial navigation systems (INS) are commonly used for robot localization. Simultaneous Localization and Mapping (SLAM) algorithms enable robots to build maps of unknown environments while simultaneously estimating their own pose relative to these maps.

Mapping Approaches

Mapping involves the creation of spatial representations of the environment based on sensor data. There are various mapping approaches, including occupancy grid mapping, feature-based mapping, and semantic mapping. Occupancy grid mapping divides the environment into grid cells and represents each cell as either occupied or free based on sensor observations. Feature-based mapping focuses on identifying distinctive features in the environment, such as corners or edges, to create a sparse representation. Semantic mapping incorporates higher-level semantic information, such as object categories or room labels, into the map representation.

Challenges in Environment Modeling and Mapping

Despite advancements in sensor technologies and mapping algorithms, several challenges persist in environment modeling and mapping. These challenges include sensor noise and uncertainty, dynamic environments with moving obstacles, perceptual aliasing, and the need for real-time processing and memory-efficient representations. Addressing these challenges requires interdisciplinary research efforts spanning robotics, computer vision, and machine learning.

Applications of Environment Modeling and Mapping

Environment modeling and mapping have diverse applications across various domains, including robotics, autonomous vehicles, virtual reality, and augmented reality. In robotics, accurate environment models enable robots to perform tasks such as navigation in indoor environments, exploration of unknown terrains, and interaction with objects in cluttered spaces. Autonomous vehicles rely on environment mapping for localization and obstacle avoidance, contributing to safer and more efficient transportation systems.

Future Directions and Emerging Technologies

The field of environment modeling and mapping continues to evolve with advancements in sensor technologies, algorithms, and computational resources. Emerging technologies such as neuromorphic sensors, event-based vision, and 3D reconstruction techniques hold promise for improving the accuracy and efficiency of environment modeling and mapping. Furthermore, the integration of machine learning and artificial intelligence into mapping algorithms enables robots to learn from experience and adapt to changing environments autonomously.

Ethical Considerations

As robots become increasingly integrated into human environments, ethical considerations surrounding privacy, surveillance, and data security in environment modeling and mapping become paramount. It is essential to develop transparent and accountable practices for data collection, processing, and storage to mitigate potential risks and ensure the ethical use of robotic technologies.

Environment modeling and mapping are foundational pillars of robotic autonomy, enabling robots to perceive, understand, and interact with their surroundings effectively. By leveraging advances in sensor technologies, localization algorithms, and mapping techniques, researchers and engineers continue to push the boundaries of what robots can accomplish in diverse real-world scenarios.

Localization and Positioning Systems

Localization and positioning systems play a crucial role in enabling robots to navigate and interact with their environment autonomously. These systems provide robots with the ability to determine their position and orientation relative to their surroundings, allowing them to perform tasks such as mapping, exploration, and navigation with precision and accuracy. In this section, we will explore the various techniques and technologies used in robot localization and positioning, along with their applications and challenges.

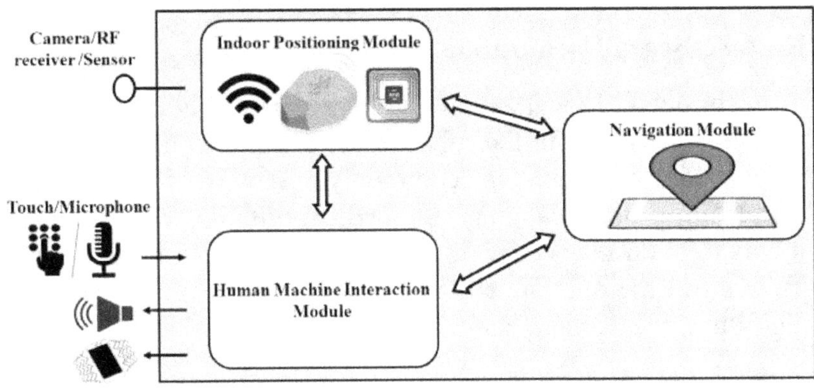

71

Localization refers to the process of determining a robot's position and orientation within a known environment. This information is essential for enabling robots to navigate effectively and perform tasks autonomously. Localization is often achieved using a combination of sensor data and mathematical algorithms, which allow the robot to estimate its position relative to a map of its surroundings.

Sensor-Based Localization

Sensor-based localization relies on data collected from onboard sensors to estimate the robot's position. Common sensors used for localization include:

Odometry: Odometry sensors measure the robot's movement by tracking wheel rotations or other motion parameters.

Inertial Measurement Units (IMUs): IMUs measure accelerations and angular velocities to determine changes in the robot's orientation.

Global Navigation Satellite Systems (GNSS): GNSS receivers use signals from satellites to determine the robot's position on Earth's surface.

Visual Sensors: Cameras and other visual sensors can be used for landmark detection and feature-based localization.

Feature-Based Localization

Feature-based localization involves identifying and matching distinctive features in the robot's environment to a pre-existing map. This approach is commonly used in Simultaneous Localization and Mapping (SLAM) algorithms, which enable robots to build maps of their surroundings while simultaneously estimating their own position within these maps. SLAM algorithms use techniques such as:

Scan Matching: Matching sensor readings to features in the map to estimate the robot's position.

Loop Closure: Detecting previously visited locations to correct errors in the estimated trajectory.

Bundle Adjustment: Optimizing the estimated trajectory based on observed features and sensor measurements.

Probabilistic Localization

Probabilistic localization techniques model the uncertainty associated with the robot's position using probability distributions. Bayesian filtering algorithms, such as the Extended Kalman Filter (EKF) and the Particle Filter, are commonly used for probabilistic localization. These algorithms integrate sensor measurements with prior knowledge about the robot's motion and the environment to compute the most likely pose of the robot.

Challenges in Localization

Despite advances in localization technology, several challenges remain:

Sensor Noise and Drift: Sensor noise and errors can lead to inaccuracies in localization estimates, particularly over long periods of operation.

Environmental Variability: Changes in lighting conditions, obstacles, and other environmental factors can affect sensor readings and complicate localization.

Computational Complexity: Real-time localization algorithms must process large amounts of sensor data quickly, which can pose computational challenges for resource-constrained robotic systems.

Applications of Localization Systems

Localization systems have diverse applications across various domains, including:

Autonomous Vehicles: Self-driving cars rely on precise localization to navigate safely in urban environments.

Robotics: Industrial robots use localization systems to navigate factory floors and perform manufacturing tasks.

Agriculture: Agricultural robots use localization to optimize planting, watering, and harvesting operations in fields.

Search and Rescue: Search and rescue robots use localization to navigate hazardous environments and locate survivors.

Future Directions in Localization

Future research in localization is focused on addressing existing challenges and improving the accuracy, robustness, and efficiency of localization systems. Key areas of research include:

Multi-Sensor Fusion: Integrating data from multiple sensors to improve localization accuracy and reliability.

Machine Learning: Using machine learning techniques to learn models of sensor behavior and environment dynamics for better localization performance.

Distributed Localization: Developing algorithms for collaborative localization among multiple robots or sensor nodes in dynamic environments.

Localization and positioning systems are fundamental to the operation of autonomous robots in a wide range of applications. By accurately determining their position and orientation, robots can navigate complex environments and perform tasks with precision and efficiency. Despite the challenges posed by sensor noise, environmental variability, and computational complexity, ongoing research and development efforts continue to advance the state-of-the-art in localization technology, paving the way for increasingly capable and intelligent robotic systems.

Sensor Fusion Techniques

Sensor fusion, also known as data fusion, is the process of integrating data from multiple sensors to obtain a more accurate and reliable representation of the environment. In the context of robotics, sensor fusion plays a crucial role in enhancing perception, navigation, and decision-making capabilities. By combining information from different sensory modalities, such as vision, auditory, and tactile sensors, sensor fusion enables robots to robustly perceive and interact with their surroundings. In this section, we will explore various sensor fusion techniques employed in robotics, their advantages, and their applications.

Sensor fusion addresses the inherent limitations and uncertainties associated with individual sensors by leveraging the complementary nature of different sensory modalities. By combining data from multiple sensors, sensor fusion enhances the accuracy, reliability, and robustness of perception systems in robotics applications. The goal of sensor fusion is to create a coherent and comprehensive representation of the environment that enables robots to make informed decisions and adapt to dynamic changes in their surroundings.

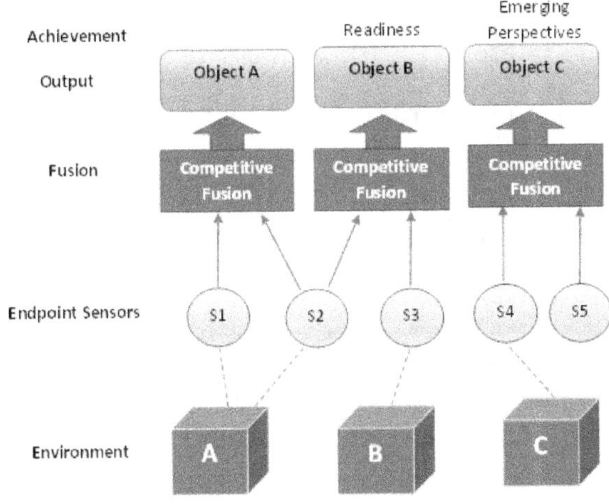

Figure 6. sensor fusion

Types of Sensor Fusion

Sensor fusion techniques can be broadly categorized into two main types: centralized fusion and distributed fusion.

Centralized Fusion:

In centralized fusion, data from multiple sensors are collected and processed in a central unit, often referred to as a fusion center. The fusion center integrates the sensor data using various fusion algorithms to generate a unified perception of the environment. Centralized fusion offers the advantage of global optimization and consistency but may suffer from scalability and computational complexity issues, particularly in large-scale robotic systems.

Distributed Fusion:

In distributed fusion, sensor data are processed locally by individual sensors or sensor nodes, and the fused information is shared and combined collaboratively among neighboring nodes. Distributed fusion is well-suited for decentralized robotic systems where communication bandwidth and computational resources are limited. It offers the advantage of scalability, fault tolerance, and real-time responsiveness but may require sophisticated coordination and synchronization mechanisms.

Fusion Algorithms

Several fusion algorithms are commonly used in robotics to combine sensor data effectively. These algorithms can be categorized based on their mathematical principles and computational techniques:

Probabilistic Methods:

Probabilistic fusion methods, such as Bayesian inference and Kalman filtering, model the uncertainty associated with sensor measurements and fuse them probabilistically to estimate the state of the environment. Bayesian inference combines prior knowledge with sensor observations to update the belief about the environment, while Kalman filtering recursively estimates the state of a dynamic system based on noisy sensor measurements.

Feature-based Fusion:

Feature-based fusion techniques extract salient features from sensor data, such as keypoints in visual images or landmarks in sensor readings, and fuse them to generate a consistent representation of the environment. Feature-based fusion is commonly used in simultaneous localization and mapping (SLAM) algorithms, where landmarks are detected and matched across multiple sensor modalities to estimate the robot's pose and map of the environment.

Machine Learning Approaches:

Machine learning techniques, such as neural networks and deep learning, have gained popularity in sensor fusion for their ability to learn complex relationships and patterns from high-dimensional sensor data. Deep learning models, such as convolutional neural networks (CNNs) and recurrent neural networks (RNNs), can be trained to directly fuse raw sensor data and extract meaningful features for perception tasks, such as object detection and scene understanding.

Advantages of Sensor Fusion

Sensor fusion offers several advantages for robotics applications:

Improved Accuracy: By combining information from multiple sensors, sensor fusion reduces the effects of noise, outliers, and uncertainties, resulting in more accurate perception and localization.

Enhanced Robustness: Sensor fusion increases the reliability and robustness of perception systems by mitigating sensor failures or discrepancies through redundancy and cross-validation.

Increased Sensitivity: Sensor fusion enables robots to detect and perceive environmental cues that may be imperceptible or ambiguous to individual sensors, leading to enhanced situational awareness and adaptability.

Dynamic Adaptation: Sensor fusion allows robots to dynamically adapt to changes in the environment, such as variations in lighting conditions, terrain characteristics, or sensor characteristics, by adjusting the fusion parameters or sensor weighting factors.

Applications of Sensor Fusion

Sensor fusion techniques find wide-ranging applications in robotics across various domains:

Autonomous Vehicles: Sensor fusion is essential for autonomous vehicles to perceive and navigate complex traffic environments, combining data from cameras, lidar, radar, and inertial sensors to detect obstacles, localize the vehicle, and plan safe trajectories.

Mobile Robotics: Mobile robots, such as drones and ground robots, use sensor fusion for localization and mapping in unknown or GPS-denied environments, integrating data from odometry, visual odometry, lidar, and IMU sensors to estimate their pose and construct maps of the surroundings.

Human-Robot Interaction: Sensor fusion enables robots to perceive and interpret human gestures, expressions, and speech, facilitating natural and intuitive interaction with users in social robotics, healthcare, and assistive technology applications.

Industrial Automation: Sensor fusion is employed in industrial robots for quality inspection, object manipulation, and assembly tasks, combining data from vision, force, and tactile sensors to ensure precise and reliable operation in manufacturing environments.

Challenges and Future Directions

While sensor fusion offers numerous benefits for robotics applications, it also poses several challenges:

Integration Complexity: Integrating data from heterogeneous sensors with different characteristics, resolutions, and coordinate frames requires careful calibration, synchronization, and alignment to ensure accurate fusion.

Computational Overhead: Sensor fusion algorithms often involve complex mathematical computations and data processing, which can be computationally intensive and resource-demanding, particularly for real-time applications on embedded platforms.

Uncertainty Management: Managing uncertainty and modeling sensor noise, biases, and correlations accurately is essential for robust and reliable fusion results, requiring sophisticated probabilistic models and estimation techniques.

Scalability and Flexibility: Scaling sensor fusion techniques to large-scale robotic systems and diverse operating environments while maintaining efficiency, adaptability, and scalability remains a significant challenge for future research.

Future research directions in sensor fusion for robotics include:

Multi-modal Fusion: Exploring new fusion paradigms and algorithms for integrating data from emerging sensor modalities, such as 3D cameras, thermal sensors, and chemical sensors, to enrich perception capabilities and enable new applications.

Context-aware Fusion: Incorporating contextual information, such as scene semantics, temporal dynamics, and task requirements, into sensor fusion algorithms to enhance perception and decision-making in complex and dynamic environments.

Distributed Fusion Architectures: Developing decentralized and distributed fusion architectures that leverage edge computing, networked sensors, and collaborative sensing to enable scalable and resilient fusion in large-scale robotic systems.

Adaptive Fusion Strategies: Designing adaptive fusion strategies that dynamically adjust sensor weighting, fusion parameters, and fusion algorithms based on the confidence, reliability, and relevance of sensor measurements to improve adaptability and robustness.

In sensor fusion is a fundamental technology for robotics that enables robots to perceive, understand, and interact with their environment effectively. By integrating data from multiple sensors, sensor fusion enhances the accuracy, reliability, and robustness of perception systems, enabling robots to navigate complex environments, interact with humans, and perform diverse tasks autonomously. While sensor fusion presents numerous opportunities for advancing robotics capabilities, addressing challenges such as integration complexity, computational overhead, uncertainty management, and scalability remains critical for realizing the full potential of sensor fusion in future robotic systems.

Infrared and Ultrasonic Sensors

In the realm of robotics, sensors play a pivotal role in enabling machines to perceive and interact with their environment. Among the diverse array of sensors available, infrared (IR) and ultrasonic sensors stand out for their ability to detect objects and obstacles using non-visible forms of energy. In this section, we delve into the principles of operation, applications, and considerations of IR and ultrasonic sensors in robotics.

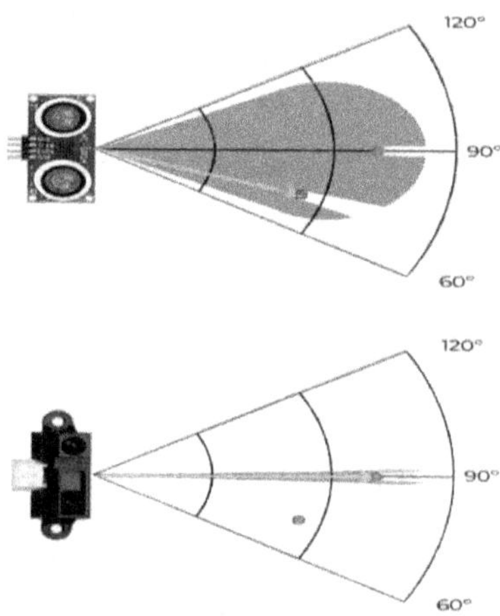

Figure 7. Infrared and Ultrasonic Sensors

Principles of Operation

Infrared Sensors:

Infrared sensors operate by detecting infrared radiation emitted or reflected by objects in their vicinity. These sensors typically consist of an emitter that emits infrared radiation and a receiver that detects the reflected or emitted radiation. The intensity of the received signal is then used to determine the proximity of objects.

There are two main types of infrared sensors:

1. Passive Infrared (PIR) Sensors: These sensors detect changes in infrared radiation caused by the movement of objects. They are commonly used in motion detection applications, such as security systems and automatic lighting.

2. Active Infrared (AIR) Sensors: In AIR sensors, an infrared emitter emits a beam of infrared radiation, and the receiver detects the reflected signal. The time it takes for the signal to return is used to calculate the distance to the object.

Ultrasonic Sensors:

Ultrasonic sensors utilize sound waves with frequencies higher than the audible range of humans (typically above 20 kHz) to detect objects. These sensors emit ultrasonic pulses and measure the time it takes for the pulses to reflect off objects and return to the sensor. By calculating the time of flight of the ultrasonic waves, the distance to the object can be determined using the speed of sound in the air.

Ultrasonic sensors can be categorized into two types based on their operating mode:

Transmitter-Receiver Sensors: These sensors consist of separate transmitters and receivers. The transmitter emits ultrasonic pulses, and the receiver detects the reflected waves.

Transceiver Sensors: Transceiver sensors integrate both the transmitter and receiver functions into a single device. This simplifies the sensor design and reduces complexity in robotic systems.

Applications

Infrared Sensors:

Infrared sensors find widespread applications in robotics, including:

Obstacle Detection: IR sensors are commonly used in robot navigation systems to detect obstacles and avoid collisions.

Line Following: IR sensors can be used to detect lines or tracks on the ground, enabling robots to follow predefined paths.

Gesture Recognition: IR sensors are utilized in human-robot interaction systems for detecting hand gestures and commands.

Object Counting: IR sensors are employed in industrial automation for counting objects on conveyor belts or in manufacturing processes.

Ultrasonic Sensors:

Ultrasonic sensors are versatile and find applications in various robotic tasks, such as:

Distance Measurement: Ultrasonic sensors are used to measure distances to objects in robotics applications, such as object detection and navigation.

Obstacle Avoidance: Robots equipped with ultrasonic sensors can navigate through environments by detecting obstacles and adjusting their trajectory accordingly.

Liquid Level Sensing: Ultrasonic sensors are employed in liquid-level sensing applications, such as monitoring fluid levels in tanks or reservoirs.

Parking Assistance: Ultrasonic sensors are integrated into automotive systems for parking assistance, providing drivers with proximity warnings to avoid collisions.

Considerations and Challenges

While IR and ultrasonic sensors offer numerous benefits in robotics applications, they also pose certain considerations and challenges:

Environmental Factors: Both IR and ultrasonic sensors can be affected by environmental conditions such as ambient light, humidity, and temperature. Careful calibration and sensor fusion techniques may be required to mitigate these effects.

Range and Accuracy: The range and accuracy of IR and ultrasonic sensors may vary depending on factors such as sensor design, operating conditions, and the properties of the objects being detected.

Interference: In environments with multiple robots or electronic devices emitting similar signals, interference may occur, affecting the performance of IR and ultrasonic sensors. Shielding and frequency management techniques can help mitigate interference.

Future Directions

Despite their widespread use, IR and ultrasonic sensors continue to evolve with advancements in technology. Future developments may focus on:

Miniaturization: Shrinking the size of IR and ultrasonic sensors to enable integration into smaller and more agile robotic platforms.

Enhanced Sensing Capabilities: Improving the sensitivity and resolution of sensors to detect smaller objects and finer details in the environment.

Integration with Other Sensors: Combining IR and ultrasonic sensors with complementary sensing modalities, such as cameras and LIDAR, to enhance perception and enable more robust robotic systems.

IR and ultrasonic sensors are invaluable tools in the robotics toolkit, enabling robots to perceive their surroundings and interact with the world in diverse ways. By understanding the principles of operation, applications, considerations, and future directions of these sensors, roboticists can leverage their capabilities to create more capable and intelligent machines.

Tactile and Force Sensors

Tactile and force sensors play a crucial role in enabling robots to interact with and understand the physical world. By providing feedback about the forces exerted on their surfaces and the properties of objects they come into contact with, these sensors allow robots to perform a wide range of tasks, from delicate manipulation to robust grasping. In this chapter, we will delve into the principles behind tactile and force sensing technologies, their applications in robotics, and the challenges and advancements shaping their development.

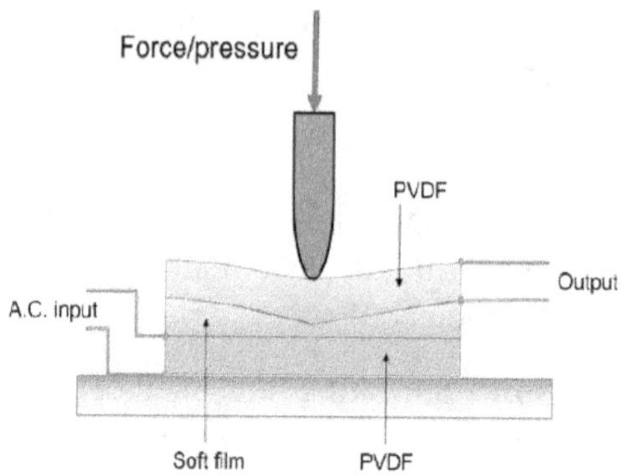

Figure 8. Tactile and force sensor

Tactile sensing refers to the ability of robots to perceive and interpret physical contact with objects through the sense of touch. Force sensing, on the other hand, involves the measurement of forces exerted on a robot's body or end effector during interactions with the environment. Together, tactile and force sensors enable robots to gather rich tactile information about their surroundings, facilitating tasks such as object recognition, grasping, and manipulation.

Principles of Tactile Sensing

Tactile sensors detect mechanical stimuli, such as pressure, shear, and vibration, using various transduction mechanisms. Capacitive sensors, for example, measure changes in capacitance resulting from the deformation of flexible materials, while piezoresistive sensors detect changes in resistance caused by mechanical stress. Other tactile sensing technologies include piezoelectric sensors, optical sensors, and elastomer-based sensors, each offering unique advantages and trade-offs in terms of sensitivity, resolution, and robustness.

Types of Tactile Sensors

Capacitive Tactile Sensors: These sensors utilize changes in capacitance to detect contact and pressure, offering high sensitivity and spatial resolution.

Piezoresistive Tactile Sensors: By measuring changes in resistance in response to mechanical deformation, piezoresistive sensors provide precise force measurements and are suitable for applications requiring high dynamic range.

Optical Tactile Sensors: Optical sensors use light-based techniques, such as reflection or diffraction, to detect tactile stimuli, offering advantages such as immunity to electromagnetic interference and compatibility with transparent materials.

Piezoelectric Tactile Sensors: Piezoelectric materials generate electrical charges in response to mechanical stress, allowing for the detection of dynamic tactile events such as vibrations and impacts.

Elastomer-Based Tactile Sensors: These sensors utilize deformable elastomers embedded with conductive materials to detect changes in shape and pressure, offering flexibility and conformability to curved surfaces.

Applications of Tactile Sensing in Robotics

Tactile sensors find diverse applications in robotics across various domains:

Object Recognition and Manipulation: Tactile feedback enables robots to identify objects based on their tactile properties, such as texture, shape, and compliance, and to manipulate them with precision.

Grasping and Dexterous Manipulation: By providing feedback about the forces exerted during grasping, tactile sensors enable robots to adjust their grip and apply appropriate force to objects of varying shapes and sizes.

Human-Robot Interaction: Tactile sensing facilitates natural and intuitive interactions between humans and robots, allowing robots to respond to tactile cues and gestures in real-time.

Medical Robotics: In surgical robotics, tactile sensors provide surgeons with haptic feedback during minimally invasive procedures, enhancing dexterity and precision.

Principles of Force Sensing

Force sensors measure the forces and torques exerted on a robot's body or end effector during interactions with the environment. These sensors typically rely on strain gauges, piezoelectric materials, or capacitive elements to transduce mechanical forces into measurable electrical signals, providing feedback about contact forces, object weight, and torque.

Types of Force Sensors

Strain Gauge Force Sensors: These sensors measure changes in electrical resistance resulting from mechanical deformation, offering high sensitivity and accuracy for force measurements.

Piezoelectric Force Sensors: Piezoelectric materials generate electrical charges in response to mechanical stress, allowing for the detection of dynamic force events such as impacts and vibrations.

Capacitive Force Sensors: Capacitive sensors measure changes in capacitance resulting from the displacement of conductive plates under applied force, offering high linearity and stability.

Applications of Force Sensing in Robotics

Force sensing technologies find widespread applications in robotics, including:

Industrial Automation: Force sensors enable robots to perform tasks such as assembly, welding, and polishing with precision, ensuring consistent quality and reducing the risk of damage to workpieces.

Collaborative Robotics: Force sensing enables robots to safely interact with human operators and adapt their behavior based on tactile feedback, facilitating collaborative tasks in shared workspaces.

Haptic Feedback Systems: Force feedback devices use force sensors to provide users with tactile feedback in virtual reality simulations and teleoperation systems, enhancing immersion and realism.

Mobile Robotics: In mobile platforms such as unmanned aerial vehicles (UAVs) and autonomous vehicles, force sensors provide feedback about ground contact forces and terrain properties, enabling adaptive locomotion and navigation.

Challenges and Advancements

Despite their widespread use, tactile and force sensing technologies still face several challenges:

Sensor Integration and Robustness: Integrating tactile and force sensors into robotic systems while ensuring reliability and robustness in diverse operating conditions remains a challenge.

Calibration and Accuracy: Achieving accurate and consistent measurements across different tactile and force sensing modalities requires precise calibration and compensation for environmental factors.

Multimodal Integration: Integrating tactile and force sensing with other sensory modalities, such as vision and proprioception, to enable robust perception and manipulation is an ongoing research area.

Future Directions

Soft Robotics: Advances in soft robotics are driving the development of new tactile sensing technologies based on flexible and compliant materials, enabling robots to interact with delicate objects and navigate unstructured environments.

Bioinspired Sensing: Drawing inspiration from biological systems, researchers are exploring novel tactile sensing approaches based on principles such as hierarchical sensing, distributed sensing, and adaptive compliance.

Machine Learning and AI: Machine learning techniques are being applied to improve the interpretation of tactile and force sensor data, enabling robots to learn from experience and adapt their behavior in response to tactile feedback.

In tactile and force sensors are indispensable components of robotic systems, enabling robots to perceive and interact with the physical world in a manner analogous to human touch. As robotics continues to advance, the development of robust and versatile tactile and force sensing technologies will play a pivotal role in unlocking new capabilities and applications for robots across diverse domains.

Lidar and Radar Sensing

In the realm of robotics, the ability to perceive and interpret the surrounding environment is paramount for autonomous navigation and interaction. While vision-based sensors, such as cameras, provide valuable information about the visual appearance of objects, they are limited in their ability to operate effectively in adverse weather conditions or low-light environments. In such scenarios, lidar and radar sensing technologies offer complementary capabilities, enabling robots to perceive their surroundings using active sensing methods that do not rely on visible light. In this section, we explore the principles, applications, and advancements in lidar and radar sensing for robotics.

Principles of Lidar Sensing

Lidar, which stands for Light Detection and Ranging, is a remote sensing technology that measures the distance to objects by emitting laser pulses and measuring the time it takes for the pulses to reflect off surfaces and return to the sensor. The basic principle of lidar sensing involves the emission of short pulses of laser light in various directions, typically using a rotating laser scanner or a phased array of lasers. The reflected light is then detected by the sensor, allowing for the calculation of the distance to objects based on the time-of-flight of the laser pulses.

One of the key advantages of lidar sensing is its ability to provide accurate three-dimensional representations of the environment, often referred to as point clouds. By scanning the surroundings from multiple vantage points and combining the resulting point clouds, lidar systems can create detailed maps of the terrain, obstacles, and other objects in the robot's vicinity. This spatial awareness is essential for autonomous navigation, obstacle avoidance, and environmental mapping in diverse robotic applications.

Applications of Lidar Sensing

Lidar sensing finds wide-ranging applications in robotics, spanning industries such as autonomous vehicles, agriculture, environmental monitoring, and infrastructure inspection. In the field of autonomous vehicles, lidar sensors play a crucial role in perceiving the surrounding traffic environment, detecting obstacles, and enabling safe navigation in complex urban environments. High-resolution lidar systems can capture detailed information about the shape, size, and position of objects, facilitating precise localization and path planning for autonomous vehicles.

Beyond transportation, lidar sensing is also utilized in agricultural robotics for tasks such as crop monitoring, yield estimation, and precision farming. By scanning agricultural fields with lidar sensors mounted on drones or ground-based robots, farmers can gather valuable data about crop health, soil moisture levels, and vegetation density, enabling targeted interventions to optimize crop yields and resource usage.

In environmental monitoring and conservation efforts, lidar sensing provides valuable insights into terrain topography, forest structure, and habitat characteristics. By generating detailed elevation maps and vegetation profiles, lidar data can aid in biodiversity assessments, forest management, and land-use planning initiatives. Furthermore, lidar sensors mounted on airborne platforms, such as aircraft and drones, enable large-scale mapping of natural landscapes and ecosystems with high spatial resolution.

Advancements in Lidar Technology

In recent years, significant advancements have been made in lidar technology, leading to improvements in sensor performance, cost-effectiveness, and miniaturization. Traditional mechanical lidar systems, which rely on rotating components to scan the environment, have been complemented by solid-state lidar sensors that offer higher reliability and faster scanning speeds. Additionally, the development of MEMS (Micro-Electro-Mechanical Systems) lidar technology has enabled the production of compact and lightweight lidar sensors suitable for integration into small robotic platforms and wearable devices.

Furthermore, innovations in lidar hardware and signal processing algorithms have led to enhanced capabilities such as longer-range sensing, higher spatial resolution, and improved noise filtering. For example, frequency-modulated continuous-wave (FMCW) lidar systems leverage the Doppler effect to measure both distance and velocity, enabling the detection of moving objects and the estimation of their trajectories. Similarly, multi-beam lidar architectures utilize multiple laser beams and advanced beamforming techniques to achieve faster scanning rates and increased coverage of the surrounding environment.

Principles of Radar Sensing

Radar, short for Radio Detection and Ranging, is a sensing technology that utilizes radio waves to detect the presence, location, and motion of objects in the surrounding environment. Unlike lidar, which relies on the reflection of laser light, radar operates at longer wavelengths and can penetrate various atmospheric conditions, making it suitable for use in adverse weather conditions such as fog, rain, and snow. The basic principle of radar sensing involves the transmission of radio frequency (RF) signals from a transmitter antenna, which are then reflected off objects in the environment and detected by a receiver antenna.

Radar sensors emit electromagnetic waves in the microwave or millimeter-wave frequency bands, which interact with objects in their path, causing them to scatter and reflect the incident waves. By measuring the time delay, amplitude, and phase shift of the reflected signals, radar systems can infer the distance, velocity, and angular position of objects relative to the sensor. Furthermore, the Doppler effect enables radar sensors to detect the relative motion of objects, making them particularly suited for applications such as automotive collision avoidance and traffic monitoring.

Applications of Radar Sensing

Radar sensing is widely used in robotics and autonomous systems for a variety of applications, including automotive safety, maritime navigation, aerospace surveillance, and industrial automation. In the automotive industry, radar sensors play a critical role in advanced driver assistance systems (ADAS), such as adaptive cruise control, collision warning, and blind spot detection. By continuously monitoring the surrounding traffic environment and detecting potential hazards, radar-equipped vehicles can enhance safety and reduce the risk of accidents.

In maritime applications, radar sensors are employed for navigation, collision avoidance, and search and rescue operations. Marine radar systems use radio waves to detect other vessels, obstacles, and landmasses in the vicinity, providing crucial information to ship captains and maritime authorities for safe navigation and situational awareness. Furthermore, radar sensors mounted on unmanned aerial vehicles (UAVs) and satellites enable remote sensing and surveillance of the Earth's surface for applications such as environmental monitoring, disaster response, and border security.

In industrial automation and robotics, radar sensing offers advantages such as robustness to adverse environmental conditions, long-range detection capabilities, and the ability to penetrate non-metallic materials. Radar sensors are used for applications such as object detection and tracking in warehouses, collision avoidance in mobile robots, and level sensing in industrial processes. Additionally, ground-penetrating radar (GPR) systems are utilized for subsurface imaging and geological surveys in construction, archaeology, and geophysics.

Advancements in Radar Technology

In recent years, radar technology has undergone significant advancements, driven by innovations in antenna design, signal processing algorithms, and semiconductor technology. Modern radar sensors feature compact and lightweight designs, improved sensitivity, and enhanced range resolution, making them suitable for integration into a wide range of robotic platforms and IoT devices. Furthermore, the development of phased arrays and electronically scanned antennas enables radar systems to achieve beamforming and beam steering capabilities, enabling adaptive sensing and tracking of multiple targets simultaneously.

The integration of radar sensors with other sensing modalities, such as lidar, cameras, and inertial sensors, enables multimodal perception and robust environmental awareness for robotic systems. By fusing data from multiple sensors, robots can compensate for the limitations and uncertainties inherent in individual sensing modalities, enhancing their ability to navigate complex and dynamic environments. Furthermore, advancements in radar signal processing techniques, such as synthetic aperture radar (SAR) imaging and inverse synthetic aperture radar (ISAR) imaging, enable high-resolution imaging of stationary and moving objects for applications such as remote sensing and surveillance.

In lidar and radar, sensing technologies play crucial roles in enabling autonomous perception and navigation for robotic systems across a wide range of applications. While lidar sensors excel in providing high-resolution 3D maps of the environment, radar sensors offer robustness to adverse weather conditions and long-range detection capabilities. By leveraging the complementary strengths of lidar and radar sensing, robots can achieve robust and reliable perception in diverse operating environments, enabling safe and efficient interaction with the world around them.

Neural Networks for Sensor Data Processing

In the realm of robotics, sensor data processing plays a pivotal role in enabling machines to perceive and interact with their environment autonomously. Traditional methods of sensor data processing often rely on handcrafted algorithms and heuristics, which may struggle to generalize across diverse environments and tasks. In recent years, however, neural networks have emerged as powerful tools for processing sensor data, offering the potential to learn complex patterns and representations directly from raw sensor inputs. In this chapter, we delve into the principles of neural networks for sensor data processing, exploring their architectures, training methods, and applications across various domains of robotics.

Neural networks, inspired by the structure and function of the human brain, are computational models composed of interconnected nodes, or neurons, organized into layers. These networks are capable of learning from data through a process known as training, wherein they adjust their internal parameters to minimize the difference between their predicted outputs and the ground truth labels. The flexibility and scalability of neural networks make them well-suited for a wide range of tasks, including classification, regression, and pattern recognition.

Neural Network Architectures for Sensor Data Processing

Convolutional Neural Networks (CNNs):

CNNs are specialized neural network architectures designed for processing structured grid-like data, such as images.

They consist of convolutional layers, which apply filters to input data to extract spatial features, followed by pooling layers for downsampling and reducing dimensionality.

CNNs have been successfully applied to various tasks in robotics, including object detection, image classification, and visual odometry.

Recurrent Neural Networks (RNNs):

RNNs are neural network architectures equipped with recurrent connections, allowing them to process sequences of data.

They are well-suited for tasks involving temporal dependencies, such as time series prediction, natural language processing, and sensor data processing.

RNN variants, such as Long Short-Term Memory (LSTM) and Gated Recurrent Unit (GRU), address the vanishing gradient problem and enable more effective learning of long-term dependencies.

Graph Neural Networks (GNNs):

GNNs are a class of neural network architectures designed for processing data structured as graphs, such as social networks, molecular structures, and sensor networks.

They operate directly on graph-structured data, enabling tasks such as node classification, graph classification, and graph generation.

GNNs hold promise for applications in robotics, particularly in scenarios involving spatial reasoning, sensor fusion, and semantic mapping.

Training Neural Networks for Sensor Data Processing

Supervised Learning:

In supervised learning, neural networks are trained on labeled datasets, where each input is associated with a corresponding target output.

Training proceeds by minimizing a loss function, which quantifies the discrepancy between the predicted outputs and the ground truth labels.

Common optimization algorithms, such as stochastic gradient descent (SGD) and its variants, are used to update the network parameters iteratively.

Unsupervised Learning:

Unsupervised learning techniques, such as autoencoders and generative adversarial networks (GANs), enable neural networks to learn patterns and structures from unlabeled data.

Autoencoders learn to reconstruct input data from compressed representations, while GANs learn to generate realistic samples from a given distribution.

Unsupervised learning holds promise for tasks such as anomaly detection, data clustering, and data denoising in sensor data processing.

Reinforcement Learning:

Reinforcement learning (RL) enables neural networks to learn decision-making policies through interaction with an environment.

Agents receive feedback in the form of rewards or penalties based on their actions, allowing them to learn optimal strategies for achieving specified goals.

RL has been applied to robotics tasks such as robot navigation, manipulation, and control, where learning from trial and error is essential.

Applications of Neural Networks in Robotics

Neural networks have found widespread applications in robotics, revolutionizing the way machines perceive, interpret, and act upon sensor data. Some notable applications include:

Object Detection and Recognition: CNNs are used to detect and recognize objects in images or point clouds obtained from sensors such as cameras and LiDAR.

Gesture Recognition: RNNs and CNNs are employed to recognize and interpret human gestures captured by depth sensors or vision systems.

Speech Recognition: Recurrent neural networks, particularly LSTMs, are utilized for speech recognition tasks, enabling robots to understand and respond to spoken commands.

Navigation and Mapping: Neural networks, including CNNs and RNNs, are employed for tasks such as simultaneous localization and mapping (SLAM), enabling robots to navigate and build maps of their environments autonomously.

Human-Robot Interaction: Neural networks play a crucial role in enabling natural and intuitive interactions between humans and robots, facilitating tasks such as emotion recognition, facial expression analysis, and gesture-based control.

Challenges and Future Directions

While neural networks have shown remarkable success in processing sensor data for robotics applications, several challenges remain:

Data Efficiency: Neural networks often require large amounts of labeled data for training, which may be expensive or impractical to acquire in real-world robotic scenarios.

Robustness and Generalization: Neural networks trained on specific datasets may struggle to generalize to unseen environments or variations in sensor inputs, leading to performance degradation or unexpected behavior.

Interpretability and Explainability: The inherently black-box nature of neural networks poses challenges in understanding and interpreting their decisions, raising concerns about safety, reliability, and accountability in critical robotic systems.

Continual Learning and Adaptation: Robotic systems operate in dynamic and uncertain environments, necessitating the ability to adapt and learn from experience over time. Continual learning techniques for neural networks aim to address this challenge by enabling incremental learning and adaptation to changing conditions.

Future research directions in neural networks for sensor data processing include:

Learning from Limited Data: Developing techniques for efficient learning from limited labeled data, such as transfer learning, few-shot learning, and active learning, to alleviate the data scarcity problem in robotics.

Robustness and Safety: Investigating methods for improving the robustness and safety of neural network-based systems through techniques such as adversarial training, uncertainty estimation, and formal verification.

Interpretability and Explainability: Advancing methods for interpreting and explaining the decisions of neural networks, such as attention mechanisms, saliency maps, and model-agnostic approaches, to enhance trust and transparency in robotic systems.

Continual Learning and Lifelong Adaptation: Exploring strategies for continual learning and lifelong adaptation in neural networks, including online learning, memory-augmented architectures, and meta-learning approaches, to enable robots to acquire and refine their capabilities over time.

Neural networks hold immense promise for processing sensor data in robotics, offering unprecedented capabilities for perception, cognition, and action. By harnessing the power of neural networks, we can pave the way for more intelligent, adaptive, and autonomous robotic systems that can thrive in a diverse range of environments and applications.

Applications of Perception in Robotics

Robot perception, encompassing the ability to sense and interpret information from the environment, plays a fundamental role in enabling robots to interact intelligently with their surroundings and perform a wide range of tasks. In this section, we explore various applications of perception in robotics across different domains, highlighting the transformative impact of perception technologies on automation, efficiency, and safety.

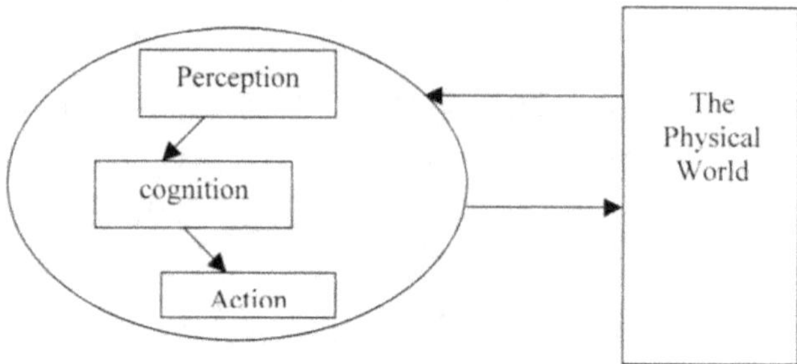

Figure 9. Perception in Robotics

Autonomous Vehicles

One of the most prominent applications of perception in robotics is in the field of autonomous vehicles. Self-driving cars rely on a suite of sensors, including cameras, lidar, radar, and ultrasonic sensors, to perceive the surrounding environment and make real-time decisions to navigate safely and efficiently. Perception algorithms process sensor data to detect lane markings, traffic signs, pedestrians, cyclists, and other vehicles, enabling autonomous vehicles to perceive and react to dynamic traffic conditions. The integration of perception technologies in autonomous vehicles holds the promise of reducing accidents, alleviating traffic congestion, and revolutionizing transportation systems.

Industrial Automation

In industrial settings, robot perception plays a crucial role in automating manufacturing processes and enhancing productivity. Robots equipped with vision systems can accurately perceive and manipulate objects on assembly lines, perform quality inspection tasks, and adapt to changes in production environments. Perception technologies enable robots to recognize parts, detect defects, and precisely position components, leading to improved efficiency, consistency, and cost-effectiveness in manufacturing operations. From automotive assembly plants to electronics manufacturing facilities, robot perception is driving innovation and transforming traditional manufacturing practices.

Service Robotics

Service robots designed to assist humans in various tasks benefit greatly from advanced perception capabilities. In environments such as homes, hospitals, and retail spaces, robots equipped with sensors and vision systems can perceive and navigate through cluttered environments, interact safely with humans, and perform tasks such as cleaning, delivery, and caregiving. Perception technologies enable service robots to recognize objects, understand natural language commands, and adapt their behavior to the preferences and needs of users. As the demand for automation in service industries continues to grow, perception-enabled robots have the potential to enhance convenience, efficiency, and quality of life for individuals and communities.

Agricultural Robotics

In agriculture, robots equipped with perception technologies are revolutionizing traditional farming practices and addressing challenges such as labor shortages and resource inefficiency. Agricultural robots equipped with cameras, multispectral imaging systems, and other sensors can monitor crop health, identify weeds, and optimize irrigation and fertilization practices. Perception algorithms process sensor data to generate actionable insights for farmers, enabling precision agriculture techniques that improve crop yields, reduce chemical usage, and conserve water and energy resources. From autonomous drones surveying fields to robotic harvesters picking crops, perception-driven robotics is reshaping the future of agriculture.

Healthcare Robotics

In healthcare settings, robots with perception capabilities are being deployed to assist healthcare professionals, support patients, and enhance medical procedures. Surgical robots equipped with vision systems can provide surgeons with enhanced visualization and dexterity during minimally invasive procedures, improving surgical outcomes and patient recovery times. Service robots in hospitals and care facilities can assist with tasks such as patient monitoring, medication delivery, and eldercare, enhancing the efficiency and quality of healthcare services. Perception technologies enable healthcare robots to navigate complex environments, interact safely with patients, and adapt their behavior to changing circumstances, contributing to improved patient care and healthcare delivery.

Search and Rescue Robotics

In emergency situations such as natural disasters or urban accidents, robots equipped with perception capabilities play a crucial role in search and rescue operations. Unmanned aerial vehicles (UAVs) equipped with cameras and thermal imaging sensors can survey disaster areas from above, identifying survivors and assessing the extent of damage. Ground robots equipped with cameras, lidar, and other sensors can navigate through rubble and hazardous environments, searching for survivors and relaying critical information to rescue teams. Perception technologies enable search and rescue robots to operate autonomously in challenging conditions, augmenting human efforts and saving lives in emergency situations.

Environmental Monitoring

Robotic systems equipped with sensors for environmental monitoring play a vital role in studying and preserving natural ecosystems, monitoring air and water quality, and detecting environmental hazards. Autonomous underwater vehicles (AUVs) equipped with sonar and other sensors can survey marine environments, map underwater habitats, and monitor marine life. Unmanned aerial vehicles (UAVs) equipped with cameras and sensors can survey terrestrial environments, monitoring deforestation, wildlife populations, and pollution levels. Perception technologies enable environmental monitoring robots to collect data in remote or hazardous locations, providing valuable insights for scientific research, conservation efforts, and environmental management.

The applications of perception in robotics are diverse and far-reaching, spanning domains such as autonomous vehicles, industrial automation, service robotics, agriculture, healthcare, search and rescue, and environmental monitoring. Perception technologies enable robots to perceive and interpret information from the environment, enabling them to perform tasks autonomously, interact safely with humans, and adapt to changing circumstances. As robotics continues to advance, the integration of perception technologies holds the promise of revolutionizing industries, improving quality of life, and addressing pressing societal challenges.

Challenges in Perception and Sensing

The field of robotics has made significant strides in advancing the capabilities of robots to perceive and sense their environment. However, despite these advancements, numerous challenges persist, hindering the development of robust and reliable perception systems. In this section, we will explore some of the key challenges facing researchers and engineers in the domain of robot perception and sensing.

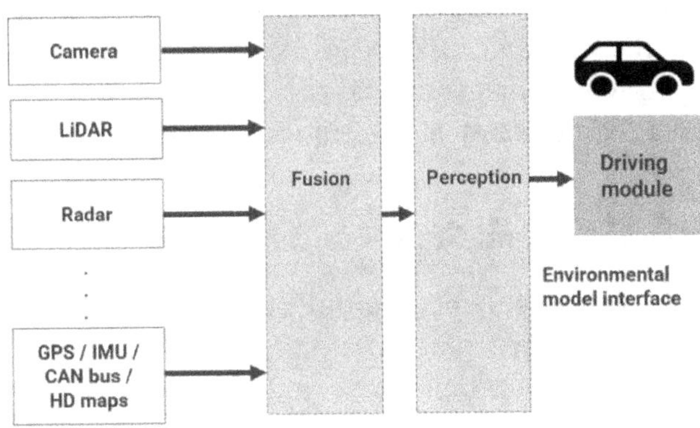

Figure 10. Perception and Sensing

Environmental Variability

One of the primary challenges in robot perception is the inherent variability of real-world environments. Robots are required to operate in diverse settings with varying lighting conditions, weather conditions, and cluttered surroundings. This variability can pose significant challenges for perception systems, affecting the reliability and accuracy of sensor data. Developing perception algorithms that are robust to environmental variability remains a major research challenge in the field of robotics.

Sensor Noise and Uncertainty

Another major challenge in perception and sensing is the presence of sensor noise and uncertainty in the data collected by robotic sensors. Sensors such as cameras, lidars, and IMUs are prone to noise, errors, and inaccuracies, which can affect the performance of perception algorithms. Dealing with sensor noise and uncertainty requires sophisticated signal processing techniques, sensor calibration, and error modeling to ensure accurate perception in real-world scenarios.

Perception in Dynamic Environments

Robots often operate in dynamic environments where objects and obstacles are in motion. Tracking moving objects and predicting their future trajectories pose significant challenges for perception systems, particularly in crowded and dynamic scenes. Robust perception algorithms capable of accurately detecting and tracking moving objects in real-time are essential for enabling safe and reliable robot navigation and interaction in dynamic environments.

Data Association and Multi-Object Tracking

In scenarios involving multiple objects or agents, such as crowded urban environments or busy factory floors, data association, and multi-object tracking become critical challenges for perception systems. Associating sensor measurements with individual objects and maintaining track of their identities over time is a non-trivial task, particularly in cluttered and occluded environments. Developing efficient and accurate algorithms for data association and multi-object tracking remains an active area of research in robotics.

Semantic Understanding of Scenes

While traditional perception systems focus on low-level tasks such as object detection and localization, achieving a semantic understanding of scenes remains a challenging problem in robotics. Semantic understanding involves not only recognizing objects but also understanding their relationships, attributes, and contextual information. For example, understanding that a person is holding a cup and drinking from it requires not only object recognition but also a semantic understanding of human actions and interactions. Developing perception systems capable of semantic scene understanding is essential for enabling more intelligent and context-aware robots.

Real-Time Processing Constraints

Many robotics applications require perception systems to operate in real-time, processing sensor data and making decisions within strict time constraints. Real-time processing is particularly challenging for perception algorithms that involve computationally intensive tasks such as image processing and deep learning inference. Balancing the trade-off between accuracy and speed while meeting real-time processing constraints remains a significant challenge in the design and implementation of perception systems for robotics applications.

Adaptability and Generalization

Robotic perception systems are often trained and tested on specific datasets or environments, which may not fully capture the diversity and complexity of real-world scenarios. Achieving adaptability and generalization, i.e., the ability of perception systems to perform reliably across different environments and conditions, is a critical challenge in robotics. Developing perception algorithms that can adapt to novel environments, learn from limited data, and generalize to unseen scenarios is essential for enabling the deployment of robots in real-world applications.

Ethical and Privacy Considerations

As robots become increasingly capable of perceiving and sensing their surroundings, ethical and privacy considerations come to the forefront. Privacy concerns arise from the potential for invasive surveillance and the collection of sensitive personal data by robotic sensors. Ensuring the ethical use of perception technologies and protecting individuals' privacy rights are essential considerations for the responsible development and deployment of robotic systems.

While significant progress has been made in advancing the capabilities of robot perception and sensing, numerous challenges remain to be addressed. From environmental variability and sensor noise to real-time processing constraints and ethical considerations, overcoming these challenges requires interdisciplinary collaboration and innovative solutions. By addressing these challenges, we can pave the way for the development of more robust, reliable, and ethically responsible robotic perception systems that can effectively navigate and interact with the complex and dynamic world around us.

Perception Algorithms and Techniques

In the realm of robotics, perception serves as the foundation upon which intelligent behavior is built. Perception algorithms and techniques enable robots to interpret and understand their environment through sensory input, allowing them to make informed decisions and interact with their surroundings effectively. In this section, we will explore a variety of perception algorithms and techniques employed by robots to sense and interpret the world around them.

Visual Perception

Visual perception plays a crucial role in enabling robots to perceive and understand their environment through visual sensory input. Several algorithms and techniques are utilized in visual perception, including:

Image Processing: Image processing techniques are employed to preprocess raw image data captured by cameras and vision sensors. These techniques may include image filtering, edge detection, and feature extraction, which help enhance the quality of visual information and facilitate subsequent analysis.

Object Detection and Recognition: Object detection algorithms enable robots to identify and locate objects of interest within their visual field. Techniques such as Haar cascades, Histogram of Oriented Gradients (HOG), and Convolutional Neural Networks (CNNs) are commonly used for object detection tasks. Once objects are detected, recognition algorithms classify them into predefined categories, allowing robots to understand the identity and significance of observed objects.

Semantic Segmentation: Semantic segmentation algorithms partition images into meaningful regions and assign semantic labels to individual pixels. This enables robots to understand the spatial layout of their environment and distinguish between different objects and surfaces. Deep learning approaches, such as Fully Convolutional Networks (FCNs) and U-Net, have demonstrated remarkable performance in semantic segmentation tasks.

Auditory Perception

Auditory perception enables robots to sense and interpret sound signals from their environment, facilitating tasks such as speech recognition, audio localization, and environmental sound analysis. Key algorithms and techniques in auditory perception include:

Speech Recognition: Speech recognition algorithms convert audio input into textual representations, allowing robots to understand and respond to spoken commands and queries. Techniques such as Hidden Markov Models (HMMs), Gaussian Mixture Models (GMMs), and Deep Neural Networks (DNNs) are commonly employed for speech recognition tasks.

Sound Localization: Sound localization algorithms estimate the direction and location of sound sources relative to the robot's position. Techniques such as Time Difference of Arrival (TDOA) and Intensity-Based Methods utilize spatial cues from multiple microphones to localize sound sources in three-dimensional space.

Environmental Sound Analysis: Environmental sound analysis algorithms enable robots to recognize and classify sounds from their surroundings, such as footsteps, doorbell rings, or vehicle engines. Machine learning approaches, including Support Vector Machines (SVMs) and Convolutional Neural Networks (CNNs), are utilized for environmental sound classification tasks, allowing robots to infer contextual information about their environment.

Tactile Perception

Tactile perception involves the interpretation of tactile sensations received through touch sensors and tactile arrays, enabling robots to interact with and manipulate objects in their environment. Key algorithms and techniques in tactile perception include:

Texture Recognition: Texture recognition algorithms analyze tactile data to identify and classify surface textures, enabling robots to differentiate between smooth, rough, or irregular surfaces. Techniques such as texture analysis based on statistical features or frequency domain representations are commonly employed for texture recognition tasks.

Shape Recognition: Shape recognition algorithms infer the shape and geometry of objects based on tactile feedback received from touch sensors. By analyzing the distribution of pressure and contact points, robots can identify the shape, size, and orientation of grasped objects, facilitating manipulation and dexterous manipulation tasks.

Haptic Feedback: Haptic feedback algorithms generate tactile sensations or force feedback to simulate the sense of touch in human-robot interaction. By providing haptic feedback during object manipulation or virtual interaction, robots can enhance user experience and improve task performance, enabling intuitive and immersive interaction with robotic systems.

Sensor Fusion

Sensor fusion techniques integrate information from multiple sensory modalities, such as vision, audition, and touch, to form a coherent and comprehensive representation of the robot's environment. By combining complementary sources of sensory information, sensor fusion enhances the robustness and reliability of perception systems, enabling robots to perceive and understand complex and dynamic environments more effectively. Common sensor fusion approaches include Kalman filtering, Particle filtering, and Bayesian inference, which provide mechanisms for integrating noisy sensor data and estimating the state of the environment accurately.

In perception, algorithms and techniques form the cornerstone of intelligent robotic systems, enabling robots to sense, interpret, and understand their environment through visual, auditory, and tactile sensory input. By leveraging advanced algorithms and machine learning techniques, robots can perceive and interact with their surroundings in increasingly sophisticated ways, unlocking new possibilities for applications in fields such as autonomous navigation, human-robot interaction, and assistive robotics.

Real-time Perception Systems

Real-time perception systems play a critical role in enabling robots to interact with and navigate through their environment dynamically. These systems rely on a combination of sensors, algorithms, and computational techniques to rapidly process sensory data and extract meaningful information in real-time. In this section, we will explore the principles, challenges, and applications of real-time perception systems in robotics.

Real-time perception systems are essential components of autonomous robots, allowing them to perceive and understand their surroundings in real-time. Unlike offline processing, which involves analyzing stored data after the fact, real-time perception systems must process sensory input on-the-fly to make timely decisions and respond to changes in the environment. This requires efficient algorithms and hardware capable of processing data with low latency.

Sensors for Real-time Perception

Real-time perception systems rely on a variety of sensors to capture information about the robot's surroundings. These sensors include cameras, LiDAR (Light Detection and Ranging), radar, sonar, and inertial sensors. Each sensor modality has its strengths and limitations, and the choice of sensors depends on the specific application requirements and environmental conditions. For example, cameras provide high-resolution visual information, while LiDAR offers accurate distance measurements in 3D space.

Challenges in Real-time Perception

Real-time perception poses several challenges due to the need for fast and accurate processing of sensor data. One of the primary challenges is processing large volumes of data in real-time while maintaining low latency. This requires efficient algorithms optimized for parallel processing and hardware acceleration. Additionally, real-time perception systems must be robust to sensor noise, occlusions, and changes in lighting conditions, which can affect the reliability of sensory information.

Algorithmic Techniques for Real-time Perception

To achieve real-time performance, perception algorithms must be carefully designed and optimized for efficiency. This often involves leveraging techniques such as parallel processing, algorithmic optimization, and hardware acceleration. Machine learning approaches, such as deep learning, have also shown promise for real-time perception tasks, allowing robots to learn from large datasets and adapt to new environments.

Applications of Real-time Perception Systems

Real-time perception systems have a wide range of applications across various domains, including robotics, autonomous vehicles, augmented reality, and virtual reality. In robotics, real-time perception enables robots to navigate through dynamic environments, interact with humans, and perform complex manipulation tasks. Autonomous vehicles rely on real-time perception for obstacle detection, lane tracking, and object recognition to ensure safe and efficient navigation. In augmented reality and virtual reality, real-time perception enhances the user experience by overlaying digital information onto the physical environment in real-time.

Future Directions and Emerging Technologies

The field of real-time perception is constantly evolving, driven by advancements in sensor technology, algorithm development, and computing hardware. Emerging technologies such as neuromorphic sensors, event-based vision, and edge computing hold promise for further enhancing the capabilities of real-time perception systems. Additionally, the integration of real-time perception with other AI techniques, such as planning and decision-making, will enable robots to perform increasingly complex tasks in real-world environments.

Ethical Considerations

As real-time perception systems become more pervasive in society, it is essential to consider the ethical implications of their deployment. Privacy concerns arise from the potential for real-time surveillance and data collection by autonomous systems. Additionally, biases in perception algorithms can lead to discriminatory outcomes, reinforcing existing social inequalities. Addressing these ethical considerations requires transparent and accountable deployment of real-time perception systems, as well as robust safeguards to protect individual privacy and ensure fairness.

Real-time perception systems are essential for enabling robots and autonomous systems to perceive and interact with their environment in real-time. By leveraging a combination of sensors, algorithms, and computational techniques, these systems enable robots to navigate through dynamic environments, interact with humans, and perform complex tasks autonomously.

As technology continues to advance, the capabilities of real-time perception systems will continue to evolve, opening up new opportunities for innovation and applications across various domains.

Perception and Sensing in Autonomous Systems

The ability to perceive and sense the environment is fundamental to the autonomy of robotic systems. In the realm of robotics, perception refers to the process by which a robot gathers information about its surroundings using various sensors, while sensing encompasses the interpretation and understanding of this sensory data to make informed decisions and take appropriate actions. In this chapter, we delve into the intricacies of perception and sensing in autonomous systems, exploring the underlying principles, sensor modalities, challenges, and applications of these essential components.

Understanding Perception

At the heart of autonomous systems lies the capacity to perceive and interpret the world around them. Perception involves the acquisition, processing, and interpretation of sensory information, enabling robots to sense and understand their environment. Through perception, robots can detect objects, recognize patterns, and navigate complex surroundings with autonomy and precision. Key components of perception include sensors, which serve as the eyes and ears of the robot, and algorithms for processing and analyzing sensory data to extract meaningful insights.

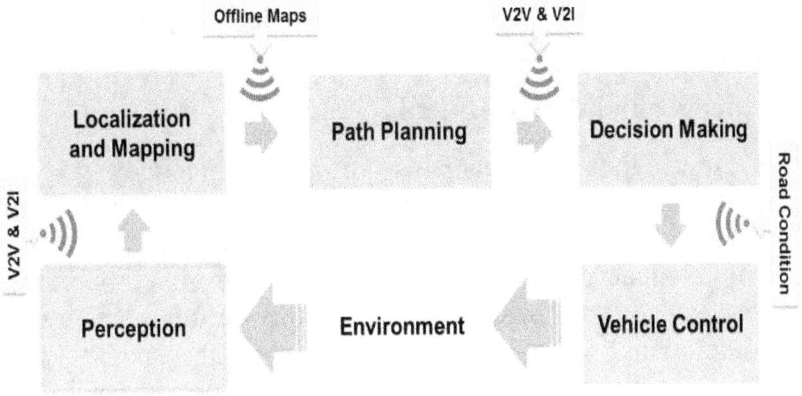

Figure 11. Perception and Sensing in Autonomous Systems

Sensor Modalities

Robotic perception relies on a diverse array of sensor modalities, each offering unique capabilities for capturing different aspects of the environment. Visual perception leverages cameras and vision sensors to capture images and videos, enabling robots to perceive objects, navigate obstacles, and interpret visual cues. Auditory perception utilizes microphones and sound sensors to detect and analyze sound waves, facilitating tasks such as speech recognition, environmental monitoring, and acoustic scene analysis. Tactile perception employs tactile sensors and touch receptors to sense pressure, texture, and temperature, enabling robots to interact with objects and surfaces in their environment.

Sensor Fusion

To enhance perceptual capabilities and achieve robustness in real-world scenarios, autonomous systems often employ sensor fusion techniques. Sensor fusion involves integrating data from multiple sensors to obtain a more comprehensive and accurate representation of the environment. By combining information from different sensory modalities, robots can compensate for the limitations of individual sensors, improve perception in challenging conditions, and enhance overall situational awareness. Common sensor fusion approaches include Kalman filtering, Bayesian inference, and deep learning-based fusion methods.

Challenges and Considerations

Despite the advancements in sensor technology and perception algorithms, robotic perception remains a challenging and evolving field. Challenges such as sensor noise, environmental variability, and occlusions can impede accurate perception and pose obstacles to autonomy. Furthermore, ethical considerations surrounding privacy, consent, and bias in perception algorithms require careful attention to ensure the responsible and ethical use of autonomous systems. Addressing these challenges necessitates interdisciplinary collaboration, innovative research, and a commitment to ethical principles in the design and deployment of autonomous systems.

Applications and Impact

The integration of perception and sensing capabilities has profound implications for a wide range of applications across various industries and domains. In autonomous vehicles, perception enables vehicles to detect and classify objects, navigate complex traffic scenarios, and ensure safe and efficient operation on the road. In industrial automation, robotic perception enhances manufacturing processes by enabling robots to identify and manipulate objects, inspect quality, and adapt to changing environments. In healthcare, perception-driven robots assist with tasks such as patient monitoring, medical imaging, and surgical assistance, improving patient care and outcomes.

Future Directions

As autonomous systems continue to evolve, the future of perception and sensing holds promising avenues for innovation and advancement. Emerging technologies such as neuromorphic sensors, event-based vision, and bio-inspired sensing mechanisms offer new opportunities to enhance perception capabilities and address existing challenges. Additionally, ongoing research in deep learning, reinforcement learning, and cognitive robotics is poised to revolutionize the field of autonomous systems, enabling robots to perceive, reason, and act in increasingly complex and dynamic environments.

Perception and sensing are indispensable components of autonomous systems, enabling robots to perceive, interpret, and interact with their environment autonomously. By harnessing the power of sensor technology, algorithms, and interdisciplinary collaboration, we can unlock new possibilities for innovation and address the challenges of creating intelligent and autonomous systems that can perceive and understand the world around them.

Chapter 3

Robot Control and Navigation

Feedback Control Systems: PID Control

Feedback control systems play a vital role in regulating the behavior of dynamic systems, including robots, by continuously adjusting system inputs based on measured outputs. Among the various control strategies, Proportional-Integral-Derivative (PID) control stands out as one of the most widely used and versatile techniques due to its simplicity, effectiveness, and robustness. In this section, we delve into the principles, components, tuning methods, and applications of PID control in the context of robotic systems.

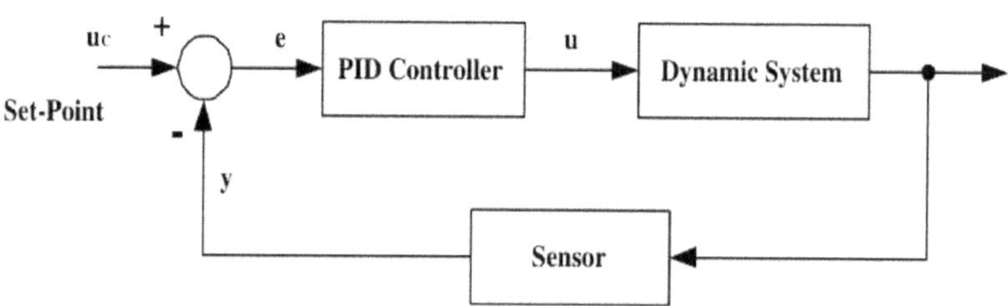

Figure 1. PID Control

Principles of Feedback Control

At the heart of feedback control systems lies the concept of closed-loop control, where the system's output is continuously monitored and fed back to adjust the system's input. The goal of feedback control is to maintain desired system behavior despite disturbances or uncertainties in the system dynamics. In a PID control system, the controller computes an output signal based on three components: Proportional (P), Integral (I), and Derivative (D) terms, each contributing to the control action in different ways.

Proportional Control (P)

The proportional term of a PID controller produces an output signal proportional to the error, which is the difference between the desired setpoint and the actual system output. The proportional gain (Kp) determines the strength of the proportional action, influencing the responsiveness and stability of the control system. Increasing the proportional gain can reduce steady-state error but may lead to overshoot and oscillations if set too high.

Integral Control (I)

The integral term of a PID controller integrates the error signal over time, effectively compensating for steady-state errors and biases in the system. The integral action eliminates any residual error that persists despite the proportional control action. The integral gain (Ki) determines the rate at which accumulated error is corrected, with higher values leading to faster error correction but potentially increasing the risk of instability or oscillations.

Derivative Control (D)

The derivative term of a PID controller provides a corrective action based on the rate of change of the error signal. By anticipating future changes in the error, the derivative action helps dampen oscillations and improve system response time. The derivative gain (Kd) influences the damping characteristics of the control system, with higher values providing stronger damping but also increasing sensitivity to noise and measurement errors.

Tuning Methods for PID Control

The effectiveness of a PID controller hinges on the proper selection of control gains, known as tuning. Tuning a PID controller involves adjusting the proportional, integral, and derivative gains to achieve desired performance specifications such as stability, responsiveness, and robustness. Several tuning methods exist, ranging from manual tuning by experienced engineers to automated methods based on optimization algorithms and system identification techniques. Common tuning methods include Ziegler-Nichols, Cohen-Coon, and trial-and-error tuning.

Applications of PID Control in Robotics

PID control finds widespread applications in various aspects of robotic systems, owing to its simplicity, versatility, and effectiveness. In motion control applications, PID controllers are used to regulate the velocity or position of robotic actuators, enabling precise and smooth motion control in tasks such as robotic arm manipulation, mobile robot navigation, and unmanned aerial vehicle (UAV) stabilization. PID control is also employed in sensor-based feedback loops for tasks such as line following, obstacle avoidance, and target tracking, where the robot's behavior is adjusted based on sensor feedback in real-time.

Challenges and Limitations

Despite its widespread adoption, PID control has certain limitations and challenges that must be addressed in practical applications. One challenge is the need for accurate modeling and characterization of the controlled system, as PID controllers rely on an accurate representation of system dynamics for effective control. Additionally, PID control may struggle to handle nonlinearities, time delays, and uncertainties inherent in real-world systems, requiring advanced control strategies or additional compensatory techniques to overcome these limitations.

Future Directions and Innovations

As robotics and automation continue to advance, new developments and innovations in PID control are poised to further enhance its capabilities and applicability. Research efforts are underway to integrate PID control with advanced sensing, machine learning, and optimization techniques to create more intelligent and adaptive control systems. Additionally, the emergence of distributed and networked control architectures opens up new possibilities for collaborative and decentralized control strategies, leveraging the strengths of PID control in diverse robotic applications.

In PID control stands as a cornerstone of feedback control systems, offering a simple yet powerful approach to regulating the behavior of dynamic systems, including robots. By leveraging proportional, integral, and derivative actions, PID controllers can achieve precise, robust, and adaptive control in a wide range of applications. As robotics continues to evolve, PID control remains a valuable tool for engineers and researchers seeking to design and deploy efficient and reliable robotic systems in diverse real-world environments.

System Modeling and Transfer Functions

In the realm of robotics and control systems, the process of system modeling plays a pivotal role in understanding, analyzing, and designing the behavior of complex systems. By capturing the dynamics and relationships between various components of a system, modeling provides a mathematical framework for predicting system behavior and facilitating the design of control algorithms. In this section, we delve into the fundamentals of system modeling, exploring key concepts such as transfer functions, state-space representations, and the role of modeling in the design of control systems.

Figure 2. Transfer Functions

Fundamentals of System Modeling

At its core, system modeling involves representing the dynamics of a physical system using mathematical equations or models. These models serve as simplified representations of real-world systems, capturing the essential characteristics and relationships between inputs, outputs, and internal states. By abstracting away unnecessary details while retaining critical information about system behavior, models enable engineers to analyze and design control systems with greater efficiency and precision.

Types of System Models

System models can take various forms depending on the complexity of the system and the level of detail required for analysis and design. Linear models, which assume linear relationships between inputs and outputs, are commonly used for analyzing and designing control systems due to their mathematical tractability and simplicity. Nonlinear models, on the other hand, capture nonlinearities and complexities inherent in many real-world systems, allowing for more accurate representations but often requiring more sophisticated analysis techniques.

Transfer Functions

A central concept in system modeling is the transfer function, which describes the relationship between the input and output of a linear time-invariant (LTI) system in the frequency domain. Mathematically, a transfer function is defined as the Laplace transform of the system's output divided by the Laplace transform of its input, assuming zero initial conditions. Transfer functions provide a concise and intuitive representation of system dynamics, allowing engineers to analyze system stability, transient response, and frequency response with ease.

Derivation and Interpretation of Transfer Functions

The process of deriving transfer functions typically involves applying the principles of linear system theory to the differential equations governing the dynamics of the system. By manipulating these equations using techniques such as Laplace transforms, state-space representations, and frequency-domain analysis, engineers can obtain transfer functions that encapsulate the essential characteristics of the system's behavior. Once derived, transfer functions can be interpreted to gain insights into the system's response to different input signals, its stability properties, and its frequency-domain characteristics.

Application of Transfer Functions in Control Systems

Transfer functions play a crucial role in the design and analysis of control systems, providing a mathematical framework for evaluating system performance and designing feedback controllers. By representing the dynamics of the plant (the system being controlled) and the controller in the form of transfer functions, engineers can analyze the closed-loop system's stability, transient response, and steady-state error characteristics using techniques such as root locus analysis, frequency-domain analysis, and pole-zero analysis. Additionally, transfer functions facilitate the design of feedback controllers to achieve desired performance specifications, such as stability, robustness, and transient response.

Challenges and Considerations

While transfer functions offer a powerful tool for system analysis and control design, they also come with certain limitations and challenges. One key limitation is their applicability to linear time-invariant systems, which may not accurately capture the behavior of nonlinear or time-varying systems. Additionally, the accuracy of transfer function models depends on the assumptions made during system modeling and the validity of linearization techniques used to approximate nonlinear dynamics. Addressing these challenges requires careful consideration of system complexity, modeling assumptions, and analysis techniques to ensure that transfer function models provide meaningful insights and accurate predictions of system behavior.

Future Directions and Emerging Trends

As the field of robotics and control systems continues to advance, there is growing interest in developing more sophisticated modeling techniques and tools to address the complexities of modern systems. Emerging trends such as model predictive control (MPC), adaptive control, and data-driven modeling offer new avenues for improving system performance, robustness, and adaptability. Additionally, advancements in computational modeling, simulation, and optimization tools enable engineers to tackle increasingly complex and nonlinear systems with greater precision and efficiency. By embracing these emerging trends and leveraging the power of advanced modeling techniques, researchers and practitioners can unlock new possibilities for innovation and advancement in the field of robotics and control systems.

System modeling and transfer functions are essential tools in the design and analysis of complex systems, providing engineers with a mathematical framework for understanding system behavior, predicting performance, and designing feedback controllers. By capturing the dynamics and relationships between system inputs, outputs, and internal states, transfer functions enable engineers to analyze system stability, transient response, and frequency response with ease. While transfer functions offer a powerful tool for system analysis and control design, they also come with certain limitations and challenges that require careful consideration. Looking ahead, emerging trends such as model predictive control, adaptive control, and data-driven modeling offer new opportunities for improving system performance, robustness, and adaptability in the field of robotics and control systems.

Stability Analysis: Bode Plots and Root Locus

In the realm of control theory, stability analysis is a fundamental aspect of designing and analyzing control systems. Stability refers to the property of a system to maintain its equilibrium or return to a stable state after experiencing disturbances. In this section, we explore two powerful techniques for stability analysis: Bode plots and root locus analysis.

Understanding Stability Analysis

Before delving into specific techniques for stability analysis, it is essential to grasp the concept of stability itself. A system is considered stable if its output remains bounded in response to bounded input signals. Stability analysis involves evaluating the behavior of a system over time and determining whether it exhibits stable, oscillatory, or unstable behavior. Stable systems are desirable in control engineering as they ensure predictable and reliable performance.

Bode Plots

Bode plots are graphical representations of the frequency response of a system, providing valuable insights into its stability and performance characteristics. A Bode plot consists of two graphs: one depicting the magnitude of the system's frequency response and the other showing the phase shift. By examining the magnitude and phase plots across a range of frequencies, engineers can assess the stability, gain margin, phase margin, and bandwidth of the system.

The magnitude plot of a Bode plot reveals the system's gain characteristics, indicating how the system amplifies or attenuates input signals at different frequencies. The phase plot, on the other hand, illustrates the phase shift introduced by the system, which is crucial for analyzing phase relationships and stability margins. By interpreting the behavior of the Bode plot, engineers can identify critical frequencies where the system's performance may degrade or become unstable.

Root Locus Analysis

Root locus analysis is another powerful technique for studying the stability of control systems, particularly in the context of feedback control. Root locus plots depict the trajectories of the system's closed-loop poles as a function of a parameter, typically the gain of a feedback controller. By examining the root locus plot, engineers can visualize how changes in the controller gain impact the stability and behavior of the system.

The key idea behind root locus analysis is to determine the regions of the complex plane where the closed-loop poles reside for different values of the controller gain. By analyzing the root locus plot, engineers can identify the range of controller gains that yield stable closed-loop systems and assess the system's transient response, overshoot, and settling time. Root locus analysis provides valuable insights into the trade-offs between stability and performance in control system design.

Practical Applications

Bode plots and root locus analysis are indispensable tools in the design and analysis of control systems across various engineering disciplines. In aerospace engineering, for example, stability analysis is critical for designing flight control systems that ensure the stability and maneuverability of aircraft. In industrial automation, stability analysis plays a crucial role in optimizing the performance of robotic control systems in manufacturing processes. By leveraging Bode plots and root locus analysis, engineers can design robust and reliable control systems that meet stringent performance requirements.

Challenges and Considerations

While Bode plots and root locus analysis offer powerful insights into the stability and performance of control systems, they are not without limitations. Both techniques require a deep understanding of control theory and mathematical concepts, making them challenging for novice engineers to grasp. Additionally, Bode plots and root locus analysis provide qualitative rather than quantitative assessments of system stability, requiring engineers to complement these techniques with rigorous mathematical analysis and simulation studies.

Future Directions

As technology continues to advance, the field of stability analysis is poised to undergo further innovation and development. Emerging trends such as model-based control, adaptive control, and data-driven approaches offer new avenues for enhancing the accuracy and efficiency of stability analysis techniques. Additionally, advancements in computational tools and simulation software enable engineers to conduct more sophisticated analyses and explore complex control system architectures. By embracing these advancements, engineers can continue to push the boundaries of stability analysis and drive progress in control system design and optimization.

Bode plots and root locus analysis are invaluable tools for stability analysis in control engineering, providing engineers with powerful techniques for assessing the stability and performance of control systems. By leveraging these techniques, engineers can design robust and reliable control systems that meet stringent performance requirements across a wide range of applications.

Frequency Response and Controller Design

Frequency response analysis and controller design play a crucial role in the development of robust and effective control systems for autonomous robots and other dynamic systems. By understanding the frequency characteristics of a system and designing appropriate controllers, engineers can ensure stable and responsive behavior in a wide range of operating conditions. In this section, we delve into the principles of frequency response analysis and controller design, exploring the underlying concepts, methodologies, and practical applications in the realm of robotics and autonomous systems.

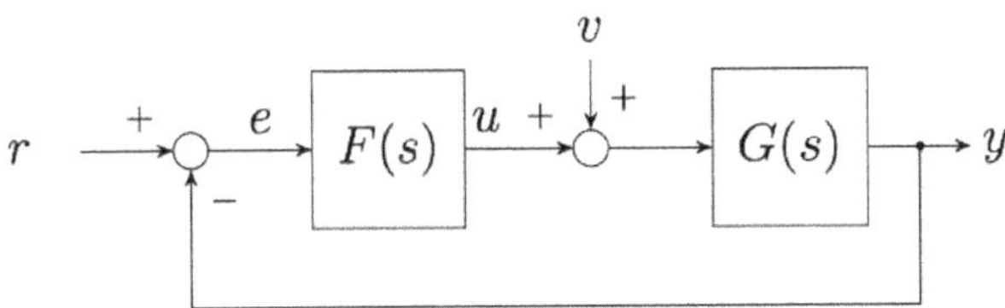

Figure 3. Frequency Response

Understanding Frequency Response

Frequency response analysis is a fundamental technique used to characterize the dynamic behavior of a system in the frequency domain. It involves examining how a system responds to sinusoidal inputs of varying frequencies, revealing insights into its stability, performance, and robustness. The frequency response of a system is typically represented using Bode plots, which depict the magnitude and phase response of the system as a function of frequency. By analyzing the frequency response, engineers can identify resonant frequencies, stability margins, and dynamic behavior that may affect the system's performance.

Controller Design Basics

Controller design is the process of synthesizing control algorithms that regulate the behavior of a dynamic system to achieve desired performance objectives. The choice of controller architecture and design parameters depends on the characteristics of the system, such as its dynamics, input-output behavior, and performance requirements. Proportional-Integral-Derivative (PID) controllers are widely used due to their simplicity and effectiveness in a wide range of applications. PID controllers adjust the control signal based on the error between the desired setpoint and the actual output, using proportional, integral, and derivative terms to achieve stability, accuracy, and responsiveness.

Frequency Response Analysis Techniques

Frequency response analysis encompasses a variety of techniques for characterizing the dynamic behavior of a system in the frequency domain. These techniques include:

Bode Plot Analysis: Bode plots display the magnitude and phase response of a system as a function of frequency, providing insights into its frequency-dependent behavior.

Nyquist Stability Criterion: The Nyquist criterion analyzes the stability of a system by examining the frequency response of its transfer function in the complex plane.

Gain and Phase Margins: Gain and phase margins quantify the stability of a closed-loop system by measuring the amount of gain and phase shift that the system can tolerate before becoming unstable.

Controller Design Methodologies

Controller design methodologies aim to synthesize control algorithms that meet specified performance criteria while ensuring stability and robustness. These methodologies include:

Classical Control Design: Classical control techniques, such as root locus and frequency domain design, are based on analytical methods for designing controllers that achieve desired closed-loop performance specifications.

Modern Control Design: Modern control approaches, such as state-space and optimal control theory, leverage advanced mathematical techniques to design controllers that optimize system performance and robustness.

Practical Applications in Robotics

Frequency response analysis and controller design have numerous practical applications in the field of robotics and autonomous systems. These applications include:

Motion Control: Designing controllers for regulating the motion of robotic manipulators, mobile robots, and autonomous vehicles to achieve accurate and responsive motion trajectories.

Stability Analysis: Analyzing the stability of control systems to ensure safe and reliable operation in dynamic environments.

Adaptive Control: Developing adaptive control algorithms that adjust controller parameters in real-time to accommodate changes in the system dynamics or operating conditions.

Fault Detection and Diagnosis: Using frequency response analysis techniques to detect and diagnose faults in robotic systems by analyzing deviations from expected frequency response characteristics.

Future Directions and Challenges

As robotics and autonomous systems continue to advance, the field of frequency response analysis and controller design faces several challenges and opportunities. These include:

Nonlinear Dynamics: Dealing with the nonlinear dynamics inherent in many robotic systems which may require the development of advanced control techniques capable of handling nonlinearities.

Uncertainty and Variability: Addressing uncertainties and variability in system dynamics, sensor measurements, and environmental conditions to design controllers that are robust to disturbances and uncertainties.

Integration with AI: Exploring the integration of frequency response analysis and controller design with artificial intelligence techniques, such as reinforcement learning and deep learning, to develop adaptive and intelligent control systems.

Frequency response analysis and controller design are essential tools for ensuring the stability, performance, and robustness of robotic and autonomous systems. By understanding the frequency characteristics of a system and designing appropriate control algorithms, engineers can develop control systems that meet stringent performance criteria while adapting to changing operating conditions and environments.

State-Space Representation and Control

In the realm of robotics and autonomous systems, state-space representation and control play a crucial role in modeling, analyzing, and controlling the behavior of dynamic systems. State-space representation provides a concise and comprehensive framework for describing the evolution of a system's state over time, while state-space control enables us to design control strategies to regulate the system's behavior and achieve desired objectives. In this section, we delve into the fundamentals of state-space representation and control, exploring the underlying principles, mathematical formalism, design methodologies, and practical applications in the context of robotics and autonomous systems.

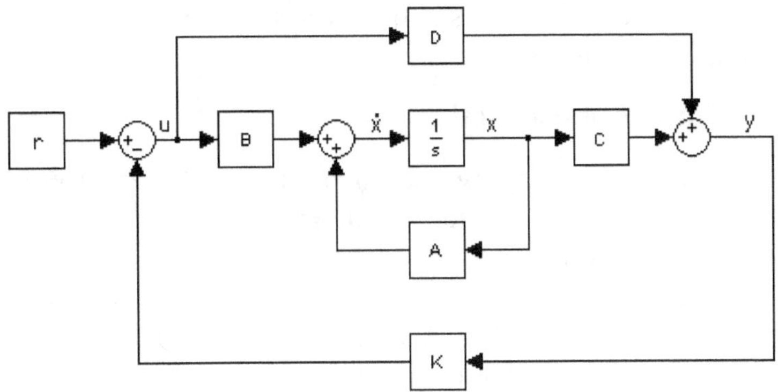

Figure 4. State-Space Representation

Understanding State-Space Representation

At its core, state-space representation offers a mathematical abstraction for describing the behavior of dynamic systems in terms of their internal states, inputs, and outputs. The state of a system encapsulates all the information necessary to predict its future behavior, making it a powerful tool for system analysis and control. In state-space representation, the evolution of the system's state is governed by a set of first-order differential equations, known as state equations, which describe how the state variables change over time in response to inputs and disturbances. By representing a system in state-space form, we can analyze its stability, controllability, and observability and design control strategies to achieve desired performance objectives.

State-Space Representation Formalism

In state-space representation, a dynamic system is typically described by two sets of equations: state equations and output equations. The state equations characterize the evolution of the system's internal states over time, while the output equations relate the system's states to its observable outputs. Mathematically, the state equations are expressed as a set of first-order ordinary differential equations, while the output equations are given by algebraic relations between the system's states and outputs. The combined form of state and output equations constitutes the state-space model of the system, which provides a complete description of its behavior in terms of state trajectories and output responses.

State-Space Control Design

The state-space representation framework offers a powerful platform for designing control strategies to regulate the behavior of dynamic systems. State-space control design involves synthesizing control laws that manipulate the system's inputs to achieve desired performance objectives, such as stability, tracking, and disturbance rejection. One of the key advantages of state-space control is its ability to explicitly account for the system's internal states, allowing for more sophisticated control strategies, such as state feedback and optimal control. By leveraging mathematical tools such as pole placement, eigenvalue assignment, and state observers, we can design control laws that shape the system's behavior and achieve desired performance specifications.

Practical Applications in Robotics and Autonomous Systems

State-space representation and control find wide-ranging applications in robotics and autonomous systems, where precise control of dynamic behavior is essential for achieving autonomy and intelligence. In robotics, state-space control enables us to design control algorithms for manipulator arms, mobile robots, and aerial drones, allowing them to navigate complex environments, manipulate objects, and perform tasks autonomously. In autonomous systems such as self-driving cars and unmanned aerial vehicles (UAVs), state-space control plays a critical role in ensuring safe and efficient operation by regulating vehicle dynamics, trajectory tracking, and obstacle avoidance. By integrating state-space control with perception, planning, and decision-making algorithms, we can create robust and adaptive autonomous systems capable of operating in real-world environments.

Challenges and Future Directions

Despite its power and versatility, state-space representation and control pose several challenges and opportunities for further research and development. One of the key challenges is scalability, particularly in complex systems with high-dimensional state spaces and nonlinear dynamics. Addressing this challenge requires the development of advanced control algorithms capable of handling large-scale systems with efficiency and robustness. Additionally, the integration of state-space control with machine learning and artificial intelligence holds promise for enhancing the autonomy and adaptability of robotic and autonomous systems. Future research directions include the development of learning-based control strategies, adaptive control techniques, and distributed control architectures to address the challenges of autonomy, scalability, and robustness in dynamic systems.

In state-space representation and control provide a powerful framework for modeling, analyzing, and controlling dynamic systems in robotics and autonomous systems. By leveraging mathematical principles and control theory, we can design control strategies that enable robots and autonomous systems to exhibit intelligent behavior, navigate complex environments, and perform tasks autonomously. As we continue to advance the field of robotics and autonomous systems, state-space representation and control will play an increasingly important role in shaping the future of automation, autonomy, and intelligence.

Nonlinear Control Systems

In the realm of robotics and autonomous systems, control theory plays a pivotal role in enabling machines to perform tasks with precision, efficiency, and autonomy. While linear control systems have long been the cornerstone of control engineering, many real-world systems exhibit nonlinear behavior that cannot be accurately modeled or controlled using linear techniques. Nonlinear control systems offer a powerful framework for addressing the complexities of nonlinear dynamics, enabling robots and autonomous systems to navigate uncertain and dynamic environments with agility and robustness. In this section, we delve into the principles, methods, applications, and challenges of nonlinear control systems in the context of robotics and autonomous systems.

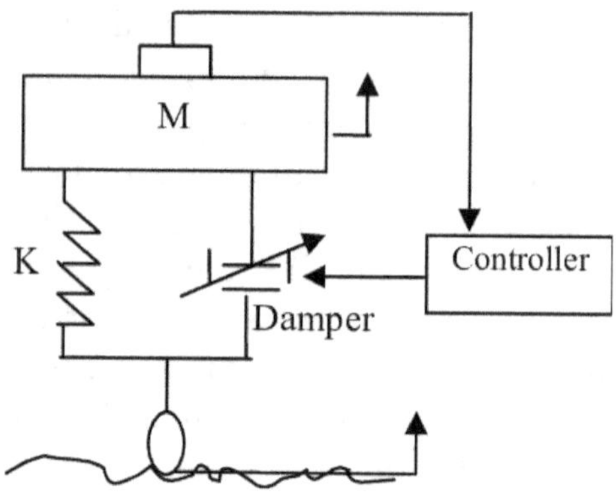

Figure 5. Nonlinear Control Systems

Understanding Nonlinear Dynamics

Nonlinear systems are characterized by complex relationships between inputs and outputs, where small changes in input may lead to disproportionate changes in output. Unlike linear systems, which obey the principle of superposition and satisfy the properties of homogeneity and additivity, nonlinear systems exhibit behaviors such as bifurcation, chaos, and limit cycles. Nonlinear dynamics arise from various sources, including nonlinearities in system components, interactions between system elements, and external disturbances. Understanding and modeling nonlinear dynamics is essential for designing effective control strategies that can stabilize, track, and regulate the behavior of nonlinear systems.

Nonlinear Control Techniques

In contrast to linear control techniques such as PID control and state feedback, nonlinear control techniques offer versatile approaches for addressing the challenges posed by nonlinear dynamics. One widely used approach is feedback linearization, which transforms a nonlinear system into a linear one through a change of coordinates, enabling the application of linear control techniques. Another approach is sliding mode control, which imposes a sliding surface on the system dynamics to achieve robustness to disturbances and uncertainties. Additionally, adaptive control techniques adapt the control law in real-time based on the system's response, enabling adaptation to changing environmental conditions and parameter uncertainties.

Lyapunov Stability Analysis

Central to the analysis and design of nonlinear control systems is the Lyapunov stability theory, which provides a rigorous framework for assessing the stability of dynamical systems. Lyapunov functions serve as candidate energy-like functions that quantify the system's behavior and trajectory convergence properties. By analyzing the time derivative of the Lyapunov function along the system trajectories, stability criteria can be established to ensure asymptotic stability, exponential stability, or robust stability. Lyapunov-based control techniques leverage these stability criteria to design control laws that steer the system towards desired equilibrium points or trajectories while guaranteeing stability in the presence of disturbances and uncertainties.

Applications in Robotics and Autonomous Systems

Nonlinear control systems find wide-ranging applications in robotics and autonomous systems, where precise control and robustness to nonlinear dynamics are paramount. In autonomous vehicles, nonlinear control techniques enable trajectory tracking, obstacle avoidance, and stabilization in dynamic environments. In robotic manipulators, nonlinear control enables precise positioning, trajectory tracking, and interaction with the environment. Nonlinear control is also applied in unmanned aerial vehicles (UAVs), mobile robots, and industrial automation systems, where agility, adaptability, and robustness are essential for accomplishing complex tasks in real-world settings.

Challenges and Future Directions

Despite their effectiveness, nonlinear control systems pose several challenges and limitations that warrant further research and development. Designing Lyapunov functions and stability proofs for complex nonlinear systems can be computationally intensive and require sophisticated mathematical tools. Additionally, the performance of nonlinear control techniques may degrade in the presence of modeling uncertainties, parameter variations, and unmodeled dynamics. Addressing these challenges requires advances in robust control theory, adaptive control techniques, and optimization-based control strategies. Furthermore, integrating nonlinear control systems with artificial intelligence and machine learning approaches holds promise for enhancing the adaptability and autonomy of robotic systems in uncertain and dynamic environments.

Nonlinear control systems offer a powerful framework for addressing the complexities of nonlinear dynamics in robotics and autonomous systems. By leveraging principles from nonlinear dynamics, Lyapunov stability theory, and advanced control techniques, engineers and researchers can design control systems that exhibit robustness, agility, and adaptability in the face of uncertainty and disturbance. As the field of robotics continues to advance, nonlinear control systems will play an increasingly crucial role in enabling machines to navigate, interact, and collaborate with humans in diverse and challenging environments.

Adaptive and Learning Control Systems

In the ever-evolving landscape of robotics and autonomous systems, the ability to adapt to changing environments and learn from experience is paramount. Adaptive and learning control systems empower robots to continuously improve their performance, optimize their behavior, and navigate complex and uncertain environments with agility and efficiency. In this chapter, we explore the principles, algorithms, applications, and implications of adaptive and learning control systems in robotics.

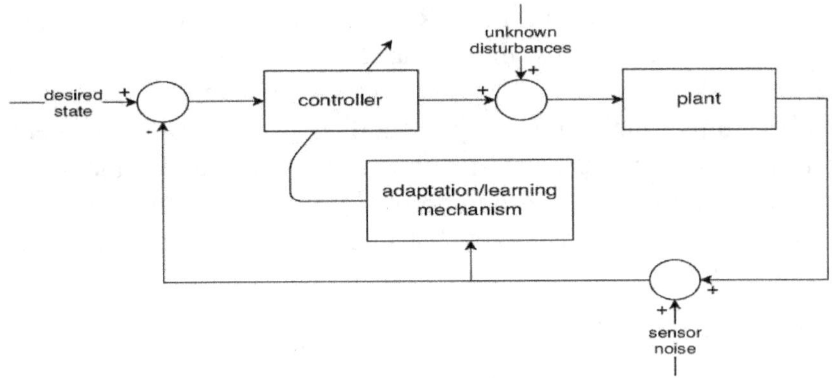

Figure 6. Adaptive and Learning Control System

Fundamentals of Adaptive Control

Adaptive control refers to the ability of a robotic system to adjust its control parameters and strategies in real-time based on feedback from the environment. At its core, adaptive control aims to ensure robustness and stability in the face of uncertainties, disturbances, and variations in the system dynamics. Key components of adaptive control systems include adaptive algorithms, parameter estimation techniques, and online learning mechanisms that enable robots to adapt and react dynamically to changes in their surroundings.

Learning in Robotics

Learning control systems go beyond adaptation by enabling robots to acquire knowledge, skills, and behaviors through experience and interaction with the environment. Learning algorithms allow robots to learn from data, explore different strategies, and refine their actions over time to achieve desired objectives. Whether through supervised learning, reinforcement learning, or unsupervised learning, learning control systems equip robots with the ability to autonomously improve their performance and adapt to new tasks and scenarios.

Adaptive and Learning Algorithms

A variety of algorithms and techniques are employed in adaptive and learning control systems to facilitate adaptation and learning in robots. Adaptive control algorithms, such as model reference adaptive control (MRAC) and adaptive critic designs, enable robots to adjust their control policies based on feedback from the environment and system dynamics. Learning algorithms, including deep neural networks, reinforcement learning algorithms like Q-learning and policy gradient methods, and evolutionary algorithms, provide robots with the ability to acquire and refine complex behaviors through experience and interaction.

Applications in Robotics

Adaptive and learning control systems find diverse applications across various domains of robotics and autonomous systems. In autonomous vehicles, adaptive control algorithms enable vehicles to adapt to changing road conditions, traffic patterns, and vehicle dynamics, enhancing safety and performance. In industrial automation, learning control systems optimize manufacturing processes, adapt to variations in production environments, and improve efficiency and productivity. In healthcare robotics, adaptive and learning algorithms enable robots to personalize care, adapt to patient preferences, and assist with complex medical procedures.

Challenges and Considerations

While adaptive and learning control systems offer significant benefits, they also present challenges and considerations that must be addressed. Challenges include the need for robust and efficient learning algorithms, the integration of learning and adaptation into real-time control systems, and the ethical implications of autonomous learning agents. Furthermore, ensuring safety, reliability, and transparency in adaptive and learning control systems is essential to building trust and acceptance of robotic technologies.

Future Directions

The future of adaptive and learning control systems holds promise for further advancements and innovation in robotics and autonomous systems. Emerging trends such as meta-learning, lifelong learning, and human-in-the-loop learning offer new avenues for enhancing the adaptability, flexibility, and intelligence of robotic systems. Additionally, interdisciplinary research at the intersection of robotics, machine learning, and cognitive science is poised to unlock new capabilities and address existing challenges in adaptive and learning control.

Adaptive and learning control systems play a crucial role in enabling robots to adapt, learn, and thrive in dynamic and uncertain environments. By harnessing the power of adaptation and learning, robotic systems can continuously improve their performance, enhance their capabilities, and contribute to the advancement of robotics and autonomous systems in diverse application domains.

Robust Control Techniques

Robust control techniques play a critical role in ensuring the stability, performance, and reliability of robotic systems in the presence of uncertainties and disturbances. In this section, we explore the principles, methods, and applications of robust control techniques, emphasizing their importance in enhancing the robustness and autonomy of robotic systems.

Understanding Robustness

Robustness is a key property of control systems that refers to their ability to maintain stable and satisfactory performance despite variations in system parameters, disturbances, and uncertainties. In the context of robotic systems, which often operate in dynamic and unpredictable environments, robustness is essential for ensuring safe and effective operation. Robust control techniques aim to design controllers that can handle uncertainties and disturbances while maintaining desired performance objectives, such as tracking accuracy, stability, and response time.

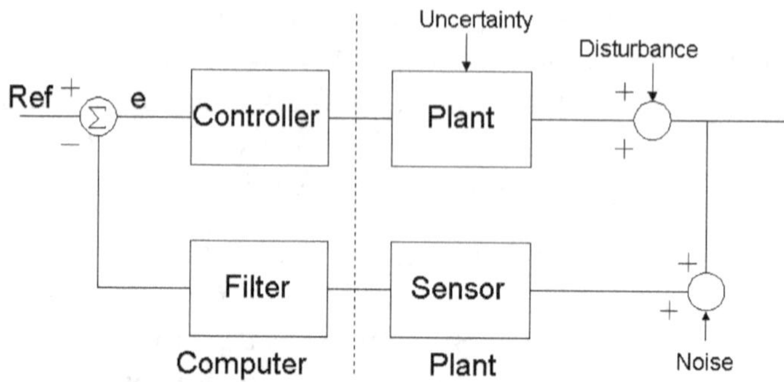

Figure 7. Robust Control

Robust Control Methods

Several robust control methods have been developed to address the challenges of uncertainty and disturbance rejection in robotic systems. One widely used approach is H-infinity control, which seeks to minimize the effect of disturbances on the system by optimizing a performance criterion subject to constraints on the closed-loop system's sensitivity to uncertainties. H-infinity control is particularly well-suited for applications requiring robustness to external disturbances and modeling errors.

Another robust control technique is mu-synthesis, which combines elements of classical control theory with modern optimization methods to design controllers that provide robust performance over a wide range of operating conditions. Mu-synthesis allows engineers to explicitly account for uncertainties in the system model and optimize controller parameters to ensure robust stability and performance.

Applications of Robust Control

Robust control techniques find applications in a variety of robotic systems and domains, including autonomous vehicles, industrial robots, and aerospace systems. In autonomous vehicles, robust control is essential for ensuring safe and stable operation in diverse environmental conditions, such as adverse weather, uneven terrain, and unpredictable traffic scenarios. Industrial robots rely on robust control techniques to achieve precise and reliable motion control in dynamic manufacturing environments, where uncertainties in robot dynamics and external disturbances can affect performance. Aerospace systems, such as aircraft and spacecraft, benefit from robust control techniques to maintain stability and performance in the presence of aerodynamic disturbances, sensor noise, and actuator failures.

Challenges and Considerations

Despite their effectiveness, robust control techniques pose challenges in terms of design complexity, computational requirements, and tuning parameters. Designing robust controllers requires a thorough understanding of system dynamics, uncertainties, and performance requirements, as well as expertise in control theory and optimization methods. Additionally, the implementation of robust control techniques in real-world robotic systems may be limited by constraints such as computational resources, sensor accuracy, and actuator dynamics. Addressing these challenges requires a multidisciplinary approach that integrates expertise from control theory, robotics, and system engineering.

Future Directions

As robotic systems continue to advance in complexity and autonomy, the development of robust control techniques remains an active area of research. Future directions in robust control may involve the integration of machine learning and artificial intelligence techniques to enhance the adaptability and learning capabilities of robotic controllers. Additionally, advances in sensor technology, communication networks, and computational resources hold promise for improving the robustness and performance of robotic systems in real-world applications. By addressing the challenges and leveraging emerging technologies, researchers and engineers can continue to push the boundaries of robust control and unlock new capabilities for autonomous robotic systems.

Robust control techniques play a vital role in ensuring the stability, performance, and reliability of robotic systems in the face of uncertainty and disturbance. By leveraging principles from control theory, optimization, and system engineering, engineers can design controllers that provide robust performance across a wide range of operating conditions. As robotic systems continue to evolve and expand into new domains, the development of robust control techniques will remain essential for enabling safe, efficient, and autonomous operation in diverse environments.

Motion Planning and Trajectory Generation

Motion planning and trajectory generation are fundamental components of robot control systems, enabling autonomous robots to navigate their environment, avoid obstacles, and reach their desired goals. In this section, we delve into the intricacies of motion planning and trajectory generation, exploring the underlying principles, algorithms, challenges, and real-world applications of these essential components of robotic autonomy.

Understanding Motion Planning

Motion planning involves the generation of feasible paths and trajectories for a robot to navigate from its current position to a desired goal while avoiding collisions with obstacles in its environment. At its core, motion planning seeks to answer the fundamental question: "Given a robot and its environment, how can the robot move safely and efficiently to achieve its objectives?" Motion planning algorithms aim to address this question by exploring the configuration space of the robot, considering factors such as geometry, kinematics, dynamics, and environmental constraints.

Types of Motion Planning Problems

Motion planning problems can be classified based on various criteria, including the dimensionality of the robot's configuration space, the presence of static or dynamic obstacles, and the complexity of the robot's motion model. Common types of motion planning problems include:

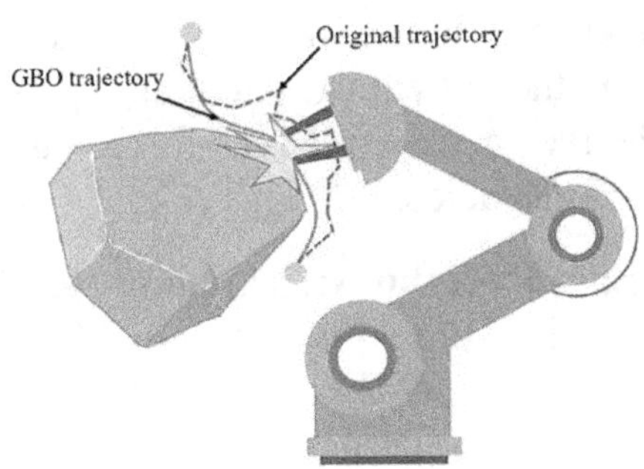

Figure 8. Trajectory Generation

Static Environment Navigation: In this scenario, the robot operates in a static environment with known obstacles and aims to find a collision-free path to its goal.

Dynamic Environment Navigation: In dynamic environments where obstacles or other agents may move unpredictably, motion planning becomes more challenging as the robot must account for dynamic changes in its surroundings.

Manipulation Planning: In addition to navigating through space, robots equipped with manipulators must also plan motions for interacting with objects in their environment, such as grasping, lifting, and manipulating objects.

Trajectory Generation

Trajectory generation involves the generation of smooth and feasible motion trajectories that satisfy constraints imposed by the robot's dynamics, actuator limits, and task requirements. Unlike motion planning, which focuses on high-level path planning, trajectory generation deals with the detailed specification of the robot's motion over time, taking into account factors such as velocity profiles, accelerations, and jerk constraints.

Motion Planning Algorithms

A wide range of algorithms has been developed to address motion planning and trajectory generation problems, each suited to different scenarios and constraints. Some common motion planning algorithms include:

Potential Field Methods: Inspired by concepts from physics, potential field methods treat the robot as a particle moving in a field of attractive and repulsive forces generated by the environment and obstacles.

Sampling-Based Methods: Sampling-based methods, such as Rapidly-exploring Random Trees (RRT) and Probabilistic Roadmap Methods (PRM), randomly sample the robot's configuration space to construct a roadmap of feasible paths.

Optimization-Based Methods: Optimization-based methods formulate motion planning as an optimization problem, seeking to minimize a cost function subject to constraints imposed by the robot's dynamics and environment.

Challenges and Considerations

While motion planning and trajectory generation algorithms have made significant strides in enabling autonomous robot navigation, several challenges and considerations remain:

Complexity: The computational complexity of motion planning algorithms can be prohibitive for real-time applications or environments with high-dimensional configuration spaces.

Dynamic Environments: Adapting to dynamic changes in the environment, such as moving obstacles or other agents, poses challenges for traditional motion planning algorithms.

Uncertainty: Dealing with uncertainty in sensor measurements, robot dynamics, and environmental conditions requires robust planning algorithms capable of handling uncertainty and variability.

Applications and Impact

Motion planning and trajectory generation have broad applications across various domains, including robotics, autonomous vehicles, manufacturing, and healthcare. Some notable applications include:

Autonomous Vehicles: Motion planning enables autonomous vehicles to navigate complex urban environments, avoid collisions with pedestrians and other vehicles, and reach their destinations safely and efficiently.

Warehouse Automation: Robots equipped with manipulators use motion planning to perform tasks such as picking, packing, and palletizing in warehouse and logistics settings, improving efficiency and productivity.

Surgical Robotics: In minimally invasive surgery, robotic systems use trajectory generation to perform precise and dexterous maneuvers, enhancing the capabilities of surgeons and reducing patient risk.

Future Directions

The future of motion planning and trajectory generation holds promising avenues for innovation and advancement. Emerging technologies such as machine learning, reinforcement learning, and artificial intelligence offer new opportunities to address challenges in motion planning and enable more adaptive and robust navigation strategies. Additionally, research in human-robot interaction and collaborative robotics is poised to revolutionize the way robots interact with humans and navigate shared spaces.

Motion planning and trajectory generation are integral components of autonomous robot navigation, enabling robots to navigate complex environments, avoid obstacles, and accomplish tasks autonomously. By harnessing the power of advanced algorithms, interdisciplinary collaboration, and emerging technologies, we can unlock new possibilities for innovation and address the challenges of creating intelligent and autonomous systems capable of safe and efficient navigation in the real world.

Path Following and Collision Avoidance

Path following and collision avoidance are essential components of robot navigation systems, enabling robots to move autonomously in complex and dynamic environments. In this section, we delve into the principles, algorithms, and techniques employed in path following and collision avoidance, highlighting their significance in ensuring safe and efficient robot navigation.

Understanding Path Following

Path following refers to the process by which a robot autonomously follows a predefined trajectory or path while navigating through its environment. Whether navigating along a straight line, a curved path, or a series of waypoints, path-following algorithms enable robots to maintain desired heading and velocity while minimizing deviations from the intended path. Path following is crucial for various applications, including autonomous vehicles, mobile robots, and robotic manipulators, where precise and efficient motion along predefined trajectories is required.

Path Following Techniques

Several techniques are commonly employed for path following in robotic systems, each offering distinct advantages and trade-offs in terms of accuracy, robustness, and computational complexity. Proportional-Integral-Derivative (PID) control is a classical control technique widely used for path following, where feedback control is applied to minimize errors between the desired path and the robot's actual trajectory. Model predictive control (MPC) is another approach that considers future states and control inputs to optimize trajectory tracking, offering improved performance in dynamic environments and non-linear systems. Additionally, optimization-based methods, such as trajectory optimization and spline interpolation, are utilized for generating smooth and efficient paths that minimize control effort and satisfy constraints.

Collision Avoidance Strategies

Collision avoidance is a critical aspect of robot navigation, aimed at preventing collisions with obstacles and ensuring safe traversal through the environment. Collision avoidance strategies involve detecting and avoiding obstacles in real-time, while maintaining progress towards the robot's goal. Reactive methods, such as potential fields and artificial potential fields, utilize repulsive forces to steer the robot away from obstacles while ensuring convergence toward the goal. Voronoi-based methods leverage the concept of free space decomposition to plan collision-free paths through cluttered environments, enabling robots to navigate efficiently while avoiding obstacles. Machine learning approaches, including deep reinforcement learning and neural network-based collision avoidance, are increasingly being explored for learning collision avoidance behaviors from data and improving adaptability to diverse environments and scenarios.

Sensor Technologies for Path Following and Collision Avoidance

Effective path following and collision avoidance relies on accurate and reliable sensor data for environment perception and obstacle detection. Robots employ a variety of sensor technologies, including LIDAR, radar, cameras, and ultrasonic sensors, to perceive their surroundings and make informed navigation decisions. LIDAR sensors provide high-resolution 3D scans of the environment, enabling precise obstacle detection and localization. Radar sensors offer long-range sensing capabilities and are particularly useful for detecting moving obstacles, such as vehicles or pedestrians, in outdoor environments. Cameras are employed for visual perception, enabling object detection, classification, and tracking, while ultrasonic sensors provide proximity sensing for close-range obstacle avoidance. By fusing data from multiple sensors, robots can achieve robust and reliable perception for path following and collision avoidance in diverse and challenging environments.

Challenges and Considerations

Despite the advancements in path following and collision avoidance techniques, several challenges and considerations persist in real-world robotic navigation scenarios. Uncertainty in sensor measurements, environmental variability, and dynamic obstacles pose significant challenges to path following and collision avoidance algorithms, requiring robustness and adaptability to unforeseen conditions. Additionally, real-time constraints and computational complexity present challenges in implementing advanced navigation algorithms on resource-constrained robotic platforms. Ethical considerations surrounding safety, liability, and risk mitigation are also paramount in the design and deployment of autonomous systems, necessitating careful consideration of ethical principles and regulatory frameworks to ensure safe and responsible robot navigation.

Applications and Impact

Path following and collision avoidance have far-reaching applications across various domains, impacting industries such as transportation, logistics, manufacturing, and healthcare. In autonomous vehicles, path following and collision avoidance enable safe and efficient navigation on roads, highways, and urban environments, reducing the risk of accidents and improving traffic flow. In warehouse automation systems, mobile robots utilize path following and collision avoidance to navigate through crowded warehouses, transport goods, and optimize material handling processes. In healthcare settings, robotic assistants employ path following and collision avoidance to navigate hospital corridors, deliver supplies, and assist healthcare professionals, enhancing operational efficiency and patient care.

Future Directions

The future of path following and collision avoidance holds promising avenues for innovation and advancement, driven by emerging technologies and research in robotics and artificial intelligence. Advancements in sensor technology, including the development of more affordable and compact sensors with improved sensing capabilities, will enhance perception and enable more robust path following and collision avoidance. Furthermore, advances in machine learning and reinforcement learning algorithms will enable robots to learn adaptive and context-aware navigation behaviors, improving adaptability to diverse environments and scenarios. Collaborative robotics, swarm robotics, and human-robot collaboration represent emerging trends that will shape the future of robot navigation, enabling robots to work alongside humans in shared spaces and collaborate on complex tasks.

Path following and collision avoidance are fundamental components of robot navigation systems, enabling autonomous robots to navigate safely and efficiently through complex and dynamic environments. By leveraging principles from control theory, optimization, and machine learning, robots can achieve precise trajectory tracking and avoid collisions with obstacles while navigating toward their goals. As we continue to advance the field of robotics, path following and collision avoidance will play a pivotal role in enabling the widespread adoption of autonomous systems across diverse applications and domains, driving innovation, and transforming the way we interact with and perceive the world around us.

Mobile Robot Navigation

Mobile robot navigation is a fundamental aspect of autonomous robotics, enabling robots to traverse and maneuver through complex environments with autonomy and precision. In this section, we delve into the intricacies of mobile robot navigation, exploring the underlying principles, navigation algorithms, sensor-based techniques, challenges, and real-world applications of this essential component of robotic autonomy.

Understanding Mobile Robot Navigation

Mobile robot navigation involves the ability of robots to plan and execute trajectories while avoiding obstacles and reaching desired destinations autonomously. Unlike stationary robots, mobile robots possess the capability to move freely in their environment, necessitating robust navigation algorithms and sensing capabilities to ensure safe and efficient movement. Mobile robot navigation encompasses various subdomains, including localization, mapping, path planning, and motion control, all of which are essential for enabling autonomous navigation in dynamic and unstructured environments.

Localization Techniques

Localization is the process by which a robot determines its position and orientation relative to its surroundings. Mobile robots employ various localization techniques, including odometry, GPS, and inertial navigation, to estimate their pose accurately. Odometry relies on wheel encoders to track the robot's motion and estimate its position based on wheel rotations. GPS utilizes satellite signals to determine the robot's global position, while inertial navigation relies on accelerometers and gyroscopes to track changes in the robot's velocity and orientation. Integration of multiple localization methods, known as sensor fusion, enhances accuracy and reliability, particularly in environments where individual sensors may be prone to errors.

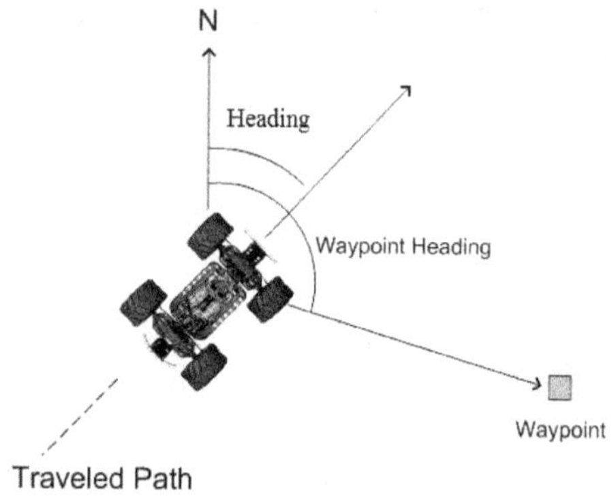

Figure 9. Mobile Robot Navigation

Mapping Algorithms

Mapping is the process of creating a representation of the robot's environment to facilitate navigation and decision-making. Mobile robots employ mapping algorithms to construct maps of their surroundings using sensor data, such as LIDAR, radar, and sonar measurements. Simultaneous Localization and Mapping (SLAM) algorithms enable robots to simultaneously localize themselves and map their environment in real-time, even in unknown or dynamically changing environments. SLAM algorithms leverage probabilistic techniques, such as particle filters and extended Kalman filters, to fuse sensor data and estimate the robot's trajectory and the locations of surrounding landmarks.

Path Planning Strategies

Path planning involves the generation of a collision-free trajectory from the robot's current position to a desired goal location while avoiding obstacles. Mobile robots utilize various path planning strategies, including graph-based algorithms such as Dijkstra's algorithm and A, probabilistic sampling-based methods such as Rapidly-exploring Random Trees (RRT), and potential field approaches. Dijkstra's algorithm and A search are deterministic algorithms that search for the shortest path in a predefined map, while RRTs randomly sample the configuration space to efficiently explore the search space and find feasible paths. Potential field methods generate artificial potential fields to guide the robot away from obstacles and toward the goal location, enabling reactive navigation in dynamic environments.

Sensor-Based Navigation

Sensor-based navigation leverages sensor data to enable mobile robots to navigate autonomously in their environment. Mobile robots are equipped with various sensors, including LIDAR, cameras, and ultrasonic sensors, to perceive their surroundings and make informed navigation decisions. Sensor fusion techniques integrate data from multiple sensors to enhance perception and localization accuracy, enabling robust navigation in diverse and challenging environments. Reactive navigation algorithms utilize sensor data to generate real-time control commands, allowing robots to respond quickly to changes in their environment and avoid obstacles while following a desired trajectory.

Challenges and Considerations

Despite advancements in mobile robot navigation technology, several challenges and considerations remain. Mobile robots must navigate in dynamic and unpredictable environments, where obstacles may appear suddenly and conditions may change rapidly. Uncertainty in sensor measurements and environmental conditions can pose challenges to localization and mapping accuracy, requiring robust sensor fusion and localization algorithms. Real-time constraints and computational complexity impose limitations on path planning and navigation algorithms, necessitating efficient and scalable solutions for deployment on resource-constrained robotic platforms.

Applications and Real-World Examples

Mobile robot navigation has diverse applications across various industries and domains. Autonomous vehicles utilize navigation technology to navigate safely and efficiently on roads, enabling tasks such as transportation and delivery. Warehouse robots employ navigation algorithms to navigate through cluttered environments and transport goods between storage locations, improving efficiency and productivity in logistics operations. Search and rescue robots utilize navigation capabilities to navigate through hazardous environments and locate survivors in disaster scenarios, enhancing the effectiveness of rescue missions.

Future Directions and Implications

The future of mobile robot navigation holds promising opportunities for innovation and advancement. Emerging technologies, such as advanced sensor fusion techniques, AI-driven navigation algorithms, and swarm robotics, offer new avenues for enhancing navigation capabilities and addressing existing challenges. Furthermore, ongoing research in human-robot interaction and collaborative navigation paves the way for new applications and interactions between mobile robots and humans. As mobile robot navigation continues to evolve, it will play an increasingly integral role in enabling autonomous systems to navigate and operate effectively in diverse and dynamic environments.

In mobile robots navigation is a critical component of autonomous robotics, enabling robots to traverse and maneuver through complex environments with autonomy and precision. By leveraging localization, mapping, path planning, and sensor-based navigation techniques, mobile robots can navigate safely and efficiently in diverse and challenging environments, unlocking new possibilities for applications in transportation, logistics, search and rescue, and beyond.

Localization and Mapping Algorithms

Localization and mapping are essential components of autonomous systems, enabling robots to understand their position and orientation in the environment and create maps of their surroundings. In this section, we delve into the intricacies of localization and mapping algorithms, exploring the underlying principles, techniques, challenges, and applications of these fundamental components in robotics.

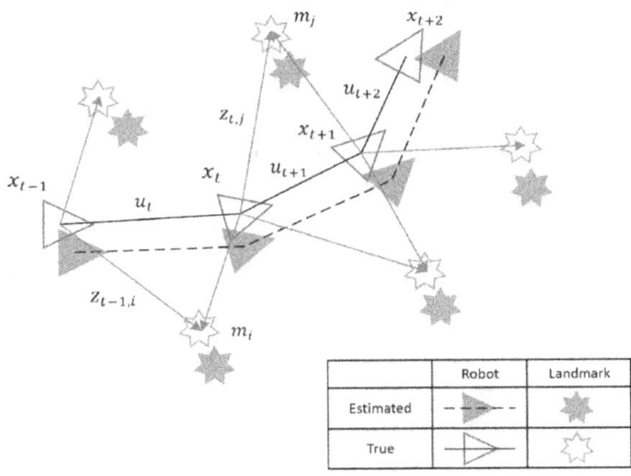

	Robot	Landmark
Estimated		
True		

Figure 10. Localization and Mapping

Understanding Localization

Localization, often referred to as "position estimation," is the process by which a robot determines its position and orientation relative to a known coordinate system or map of the environment. The goal of localization is to accurately estimate the robot's pose (position and orientation) despite uncertainties in sensor measurements and environmental conditions. By knowing its precise location, a robot can navigate autonomously and execute tasks with precision and efficiency.

Techniques for Localization

Several techniques exist for robot localization, each with its advantages and limitations. Odometry is a common method used in mobile robots, where wheel encoders measure the distance traveled by the wheels to estimate the robot's position relative to its starting point. However, odometry suffers from cumulative error over time and is prone to drift. Inertial navigation systems (INS) utilize gyroscopes and accelerometers to track the robot's motion and estimate its position and orientation. Global Positioning System (GPS) receivers provide absolute positioning information based on satellite signals, but they may not be available or accurate in indoor or urban environments.

Simultaneous Localization and Mapping (SLAM)

Simultaneous Localization and Mapping (SLAM) is a fundamental problem in robotics that addresses the challenge of building a map of an unknown environment while simultaneously estimating the robot's pose within that map. SLAM algorithms leverage sensor data, such as odometry, laser rangefinders, and cameras, to construct a map of the environment and localize the robot within it. Popular SLAM approaches include feature-based SLAM, which detects and tracks distinctive features in the environment, and grid-based SLAM, which represents the environment as a grid map and estimates the robot's pose using probabilistic methods such as particle filters or extended Kalman filters.

Challenges in Localization and Mapping

Despite significant advancements in localization and mapping algorithms, several challenges persist in real-world robotic applications. Sensor noise and uncertainty can lead to inaccuracies in pose estimation and map creation, especially in dynamic and cluttered environments. Loop closure detection, the process of identifying previously visited locations to correct drift errors, remains a challenging problem in SLAM. Additionally, computational complexity and memory requirements pose constraints on real-time performance, particularly in resource-constrained robotic platforms.

Applications of Localization and Mapping

Localization and mapping algorithms find applications across various domains, including autonomous vehicles, mobile robotics, and augmented reality. In autonomous vehicles, accurate localization is critical for navigation and obstacle avoidance, enabling vehicles to operate safely and efficiently in dynamic traffic environments. In mobile robotics, SLAM enables robots to explore and map unknown environments and perform tasks such as exploration, surveillance, and search and rescue operations. In augmented reality applications, localization and mapping techniques are used to overlay digital information onto the physical world, enhancing user experiences in gaming, navigation, and education.

Future Directions

The future of localization and mapping in robotics holds exciting possibilities for innovation and advancement. Emerging technologies such as advanced sensor fusion techniques, deep learning-based approaches, and distributed SLAM algorithms offer new avenues for improving accuracy, robustness, and scalability in localization and mapping. Furthermore, interdisciplinary research in areas such as computer vision, sensor networks, and cognitive robotics promises to push the boundaries of what is possible in autonomous systems.

Localization and mapping algorithms are foundational components of autonomous systems, enabling robots to navigate and interact with their environment autonomously. By leveraging sensor data, probabilistic methods, and computational techniques, localization and mapping algorithms empower robots to understand their surroundings, make informed decisions, and execute tasks with precision and efficiency.

Sensor-Based Control Systems

Sensor-based control systems play a pivotal role in enabling autonomy and intelligence in robotic systems. By leveraging data from various sensors, these systems enable robots to perceive, interpret, and respond to their environment in real-time. In this section, we delve into the principles, components, algorithms, applications, and challenges of sensor-based control systems, exploring their significance in the field of robotics and autonomous systems.

Principles of Sensor-Based Control

At the core of sensor-based control systems lies the principle of closed-loop feedback, wherein sensors provide real-time feedback to the control system, enabling it to adjust and modulate robot behavior based on the observed environmental conditions. This closed-loop architecture enables robots to adapt to dynamic environments, compensate for disturbances, and achieve desired objectives with precision and efficiency. Key components of sensor-based control systems include sensors for perception, actuators for action, and a control algorithm for decision-making.

Components of Sensor-Based Control Systems

Sensor-based control systems consist of a diverse array of sensors, each serving a specific purpose in gathering information about the robot's surroundings. Common sensors used in sensor-based control systems include:

Vision sensors: Cameras and depth sensors for visual perception

Range sensors: LIDAR, radar, and sonar sensors for distance measurement

Inertial sensors: Gyroscopes and accelerometers for measuring orientation and acceleration

Tactile sensors: Pressure sensors and force/torque sensors for touch feedback

Environmental sensors: Temperature, humidity, and gas sensors for environmental monitoring

Algorithms for Sensor-Based Control

The effectiveness of sensor-based control systems relies on the design and implementation of robust control algorithms that can interpret sensor data and generate appropriate control signals to achieve desired behavior. Common control algorithms used in sensor-based control systems include:

Proportional-Integral-Derivative (PID) control: A classic control algorithm that adjusts the control signal based on the error between the desired and measured sensor values.

Model predictive control (MPC): A predictive control algorithm that optimizes control actions over a finite time horizon based on a dynamic model of the system and sensor feedback.

Reactive control: A rule-based control strategy that generates immediate responses to sensor inputs, such as obstacle avoidance or target tracking.

Applications of Sensor-Based Control Systems

Sensor-based control systems find applications across a wide range of domains and industries, including:

Autonomous vehicles: Sensor-based control systems enable autonomous vehicles to perceive their environment, detect obstacles, and navigate safely and efficiently.

Industrial automation: Robots equipped with sensor-based control systems can perform tasks such as pick-and-place operations, assembly, and quality inspection in manufacturing environments.

Healthcare robotics: Sensor-based control systems facilitate precise and delicate tasks in medical robotics, such as surgical assistance, patient monitoring, and rehabilitation.

Environmental monitoring: Autonomous drones equipped with sensor-based control systems can monitor environmental parameters, such as air quality, temperature, and pollution levels, for applications in agriculture, disaster response, and conservation.

Challenges and Considerations

Despite the advancements in sensor technology and control algorithms, sensor-based control systems face several challenges and considerations, including:

Sensor noise and uncertainty: Sensors may produce noisy or inaccurate measurements, leading to errors in perception and control.

Sensor fusion: Integrating data from multiple sensors to achieve robust perception and control requires sophisticated fusion algorithms and calibration techniques.

Real-time processing: Sensor-based control systems must process sensor data and generate control signals in real-time to ensure timely and responsive behavior.

Ethical considerations: Sensor-based control systems raise ethical questions regarding privacy, data security, and algorithmic bias, requiring careful consideration and ethical guidelines in their design and deployment.

Future Directions

The future of sensor-based control systems holds promise for continued innovation and advancement, driven by emerging technologies such as:

Advanced sensor fusion techniques: Fusion of data from heterogeneous sensors, such as vision, LIDAR, and inertial sensors, to achieve robust perception and control in complex environments.

AI-driven control systems: Integration of machine learning and artificial intelligence techniques to enable adaptive and autonomous control behavior based on sensor feedback and environmental dynamics.

Bio-inspired sensing and control: Drawing inspiration from biological systems to develop sensors and control algorithms that are more robust, adaptive, and energy-efficient.

In sensor-based control systems are integral to the development of autonomous and intelligent robotic systems, enabling robots to perceive, interpret, and respond to their environment in real-time. By harnessing the power of sensor technology, control algorithms, and interdisciplinary research, we can unlock new possibilities for innovation and address the challenges of creating autonomous systems that are safe, efficient, and ethically responsible.

Control System Design for Robots

Control system design lies at the heart of robotics, enabling robots to perform tasks autonomously and with precision. In this section, we explore the principles, methodologies, and techniques involved in designing control systems for robots, encompassing both theoretical foundations and practical implementation considerations.

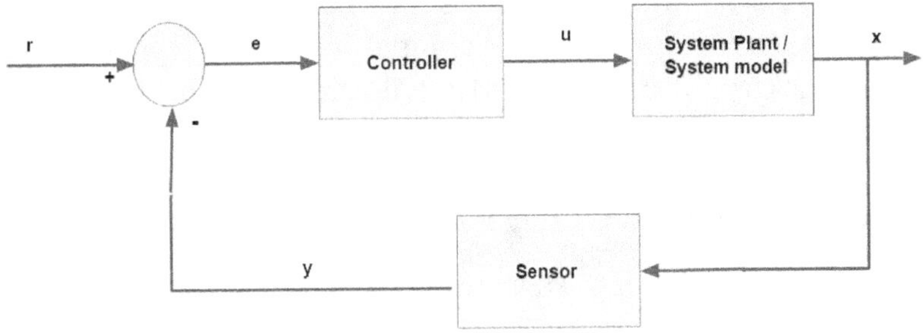

Figure 11. Control System

Understanding Control Systems

A control system is a set of components that work together to regulate the behavior of a dynamic system, such as a robotic manipulator or a mobile robot. The primary objective of a control system is to ensure that the system's output (e.g., position, velocity, or trajectory) follows a desired reference or setpoint while accounting for disturbances and uncertainties. Control systems play a crucial role in enabling robots to achieve desired tasks, ranging from simple point-to-point movements to complex manipulation and navigation tasks in dynamic environments.

Control System Components

A typical control system for a robot comprises several key components, each serving a specific function in regulating the system's behavior:

Actuators: Actuators are responsible for converting control signals into physical motion or force. Common types of actuators used in robotics include electric motors, hydraulic actuators, and pneumatic actuators.

Sensors: Sensors provide feedback on the system's state and environment, enabling closed-loop control. Sensors used in robotics include encoders for measuring joint angles, accelerometers for detecting acceleration, and proximity sensors for detecting obstacles.

Controller: The controller is the core component of the control system, responsible for computing control signals based on feedback from sensors and desired setpoints. Controllers can range from simple proportional-derivative (PD) controllers to more sophisticated model-based controllers such as model predictive control (MPC) and adaptive control.

Control System Design Methodologies

The design of a control system for a robot involves several iterative steps aimed at achieving desired performance specifications while accounting for system dynamics, actuator constraints, and environmental factors:

System Modeling: The first step in control system design is to develop mathematical models of the robot's dynamics, including its kinematics, dynamics, and sensor characteristics. These models serve as the basis for controller design and performance analysis.

Controller Selection: Based on the system model and performance requirements, an appropriate control strategy is selected. This may involve choosing between feedback and feedforward control, as well as determining the structure and parameters of the controller.

Controller Tuning: Once the controller structure is selected, its parameters are tuned to achieve desired performance specifications, such as stability, tracking accuracy, and robustness to disturbances. Controller tuning may involve manual adjustment or automated methods such as auto-tuning algorithms.

Simulation and Analysis: The designed control system is then validated through simulation using software tools or hardware-in-the-loop (HIL) simulations. Simulation allows for the evaluation of the control system's performance under various operating conditions and the identification of potential issues or limitations.

Implementation and Testing: Once validated, the control system is implemented on the robot's hardware platform. Extensive testing is conducted to verify the system's performance in real-world conditions and to fine-tune controller parameters as needed.

Control System Architectures

Control system architectures for robots can vary depending on the specific application requirements and system complexity. Common architectures include:

Centralized Control: In centralized control architectures, a single controller is responsible for coordinating the behavior of all system components. This approach simplifies system design but may suffer from scalability and single-point-of-failure issues.

Decentralized Control: Decentralized control architectures distribute control tasks among multiple controllers, each responsible for a subset of system components. This approach offers improved scalability and fault tolerance but may require additional communication and coordination overhead.

Hierarchical Control: Hierarchical control architectures organize control tasks into multiple levels of abstraction, with higher-level controllers providing supervisory control and coordination while lower-level controllers handle low-level details such as trajectory tracking and actuator control.

Challenges and Considerations

Designing control systems for robots poses several challenges and considerations that must be addressed to ensure successful system operation:

Nonlinear Dynamics: Robot dynamics are often nonlinear and subject to uncertainties, requiring the use of advanced control techniques such as nonlinear control and adaptive control.

Real-time Constraints: Control systems for robots must operate in real-time to ensure timely response to changes in the environment and system conditions. This requires efficient implementation and optimization of control algorithms to meet stringent timing requirements.

Actuator Limitations: The performance of a control system is limited by the capabilities of the actuators used to drive the robot's motion. Control system design must account for actuator dynamics, saturation limits, and other physical constraints.

Robustness to Uncertainty: Control systems for robots must be robust to uncertainties in the environment, sensor measurements, and model inaccuracies. Robust control techniques such as H-infinity control and robust MPC are used to mitigate the effects of uncertainty.

Case Studies and Applications

Control system design plays a critical role in enabling a wide range of robotic applications across various domains:

Manipulation: Control systems for robotic arms enable precise manipulation of objects in manufacturing, assembly, and surgical applications.

Navigation: Control systems for mobile robots enable autonomous navigation in dynamic environments, such as warehouses, factories, and outdoor environments.

Aerial Robotics: Control systems for drones enable stable flight, autonomous navigation, and aerial surveillance in applications ranging from agriculture to disaster response.

Future Directions

The future of control system design for robots holds exciting opportunities for innovation and advancement:

Machine Learning: Integration of machine learning techniques such as reinforcement learning and deep learning into control system design to enable adaptive and autonomous behavior.

Distributed Control: Development of distributed control architectures for multi-robot systems to enable scalable and decentralized coordination.

Human-Robot Interaction: Design of control systems that enable intuitive and natural interaction between humans and robots, enabling collaborative and assistive robotics applications.

In control system design is a cornerstone of robotics, enabling robots to perform tasks autonomously and with precision. By leveraging principles from control theory, robotics, and computer science, researchers and engineers continue to push the boundaries of what is possible in robotics, paving the way for a future where robots play increasingly significant roles in our daily lives.

Control Strategies for Robotic Manipulators

Robotic manipulators are versatile machines designed to manipulate objects with precision and dexterity, performing tasks ranging from assembly and manufacturing to surgery and exploration. Control strategies play a crucial role in governing the motion and behavior of robotic manipulators, enabling them to execute complex tasks with efficiency and accuracy. In this section, we explore the various control strategies employed in robotic manipulators, encompassing both classical and modern approaches, along with their applications, challenges, and future directions.

Classical Control Strategies

Classical control strategies form the foundation of robotic manipulator control, providing robust and reliable solutions for basic manipulation tasks. Proportional-Integral-Derivative (PID) control is one of the most widely used classical control techniques, leveraging feedback mechanisms to regulate the position, velocity, and torque of robotic joints. PID controllers offer simplicity and stability, making them suitable for applications requiring precise position control, such as pick-and-place operations and trajectory tracking.

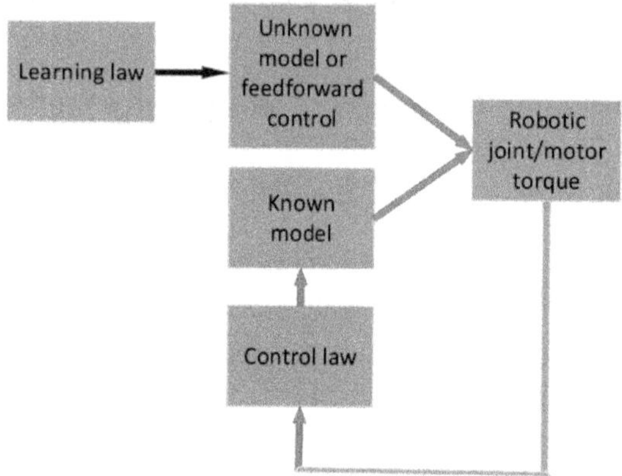

Figure 12. Robotic Manipulators

Kinematic Control

Kinematic control focuses on regulating the position and orientation of robotic manipulators by manipulating their joint angles or end-effector coordinates. Forward kinematics enables the calculation of the end-effector pose from the joint angles, while inverse kinematics determines the joint angles required to achieve a desired end-effector pose. These kinematic models serve as the basis for kinematic control strategies, allowing robots to perform tasks such as reaching specific points in space, following predefined trajectories, and orienting objects with precision.

Dynamic Control

Dynamic control strategies consider the dynamic interactions between the robotic manipulator and its environment, accounting for factors such as inertia, gravity, friction, and external forces. Dynamic models describe the motion and behavior of robotic manipulators under the influence of these forces, enabling the development of dynamic control algorithms for tasks requiring accurate trajectory tracking, robust manipulation, and compliance with external disturbances. Advanced dynamic control techniques, such as computed torque control and model predictive control, offer superior performance in dynamic and uncertain environments.

Force and Impedance Control

Force and impedance control strategies enable robotic manipulators to interact with objects and environments with compliance and adaptability, mimicking the behavior of human operators. Force control regulates the interaction forces between the robot and its surroundings, allowing for delicate manipulation tasks such as object grasping, insertion, and assembly. Impedance control modulates the stiffness and damping properties of the robot's end-effector, enabling it to respond appropriately to external forces and disturbances while maintaining stability and precision in contact tasks.

Hybrid Control Architectures

Hybrid control architectures combine multiple control strategies to leverage their respective strengths and address the limitations of individual approaches. Hierarchical control architectures integrate kinematic, dynamic, and task-level controllers to enable complex manipulation tasks involving both position and force control. Behavior-based control architectures employ a set of predefined behaviors or modules, each implementing a specific control strategy and combining them dynamically based on the task requirements and environmental conditions. These hybrid control architectures offer flexibility, adaptability, and robustness, making them well-suited for real-world applications with diverse manipulation challenges.

Applications and Case Studies

Control strategies for robotic manipulators find applications across various industries and domains, including manufacturing, healthcare, agriculture, and space exploration. In manufacturing, robotic manipulators are employed for tasks such as assembly, welding, painting, and material handling, improving efficiency, quality, and safety in production processes. In healthcare, surgical robots perform minimally invasive procedures with precision and accuracy, reducing patient trauma and recovery times. In agriculture, robotic manipulators assist with tasks such as fruit harvesting, crop spraying, and weed control, enhancing productivity and sustainability in farming practices.

Challenges and Future Directions

Despite the advancements in control strategies for robotic manipulators, several challenges remain to be addressed to unlock their full potential. These challenges include the need for robustness in dynamic and uncertain environments, the integration of sensory feedback for adaptive control, the development of intuitive human-robot interfaces, and the ethical considerations surrounding autonomous manipulation systems. Future directions in control strategies for robotic manipulators include the integration of artificial intelligence and machine learning techniques, the development of bio-inspired control paradigms, and the exploration of collaborative and cooperative manipulation strategies in multi-robot systems.

In control, strategies play a central role in shaping the behavior and capabilities of robotic manipulators, enabling them to perform a wide range of manipulation tasks with precision, adaptability, and efficiency. By leveraging a combination of classical and modern control techniques, robotic manipulators can navigate complex environments, interact with objects and humans, and contribute to advancements in various fields and industries.

Chapter 4

Machine Learning for Robotics

Introduction to Machine Learning

Machine learning (ML) is a subfield of artificial intelligence (AI) that focuses on the development of algorithms and models that enable computers to learn from data and make predictions or decisions without being explicitly programmed. Over the past few decades, machine learning has emerged as a powerful tool with diverse applications in various domains, including robotics, healthcare, finance, and natural language processing. In this section, we provide an introduction to machine learning, exploring its fundamental concepts, historical background, and key principles.

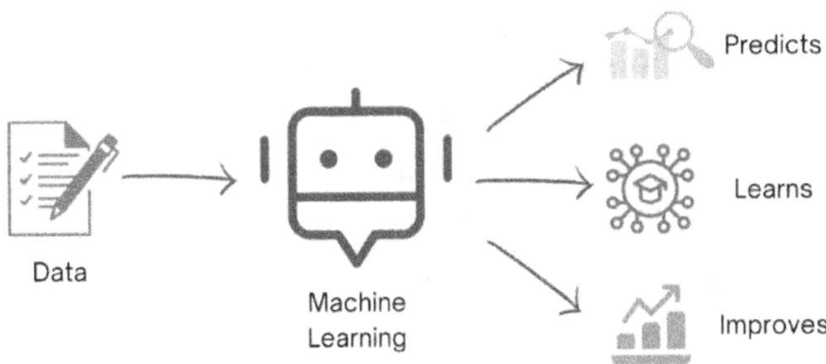

Figure 1. Machine Learning

Historical Background

The roots of machine learning can be traced back to the mid-20th century, with the emergence of early computational models and algorithms aimed at simulating human learning processes. The term "machine learning" was coined by Arthur Samuel in 1959, who defined it as the field of study that gives computers the ability to learn without being explicitly programmed. In the following decades, researchers made significant strides in developing machine learning algorithms and techniques, leading to the establishment of key concepts and methodologies that form the foundation of modern machine learning.

Key Concepts

At the heart of machine learning are several key concepts and principles that underpin its methodology and approach:

Supervised Learning: In supervised learning, the algorithm learns from labeled data, where each input example is associated with a corresponding output label or target. The goal is to learn a mapping from inputs to outputs, enabling the algorithm to make predictions on new, unseen data.

Unsupervised Learning: Unsupervised learning involves learning from unlabeled data, where the algorithm aims to discover hidden patterns or structures within the data. Common tasks in unsupervised learning include clustering, dimensionality reduction, and density estimation.

Reinforcement Learning: Reinforcement learning (RL) is a learning paradigm inspired by behavioral psychology, where an agent learns to interact with an environment through trial and error, receiving feedback in the form of rewards or penalties. The goal of reinforcement learning is to learn a policy that maximizes cumulative reward over time.

Feature Representation: Feature representation refers to the process of transforming raw data into a suitable format for learning. Feature engineering involves selecting and extracting relevant features from the data, while feature learning involves automatically learning informative representations directly from the data.

Model Evaluation and Generalization: Evaluating the performance of machine learning models is essential to assess their effectiveness and robustness. Model evaluation involves measuring performance metrics such as accuracy, precision, recall, and F1-score. Generalization refers to the ability of a model to perform well on unseen data, indicating its ability to capture underlying patterns in the data rather than memorizing specific examples.

Fundamental Principles

Several fundamental principles guide the design and development of machine learning algorithms:

Occam's Razor: The principle of Occam's Razor states that among competing hypotheses, the simplest explanation is usually the correct one. In the context of machine learning, this principle encourages simplicity and parsimony in model design, favoring models with fewer parameters and complexity.

Bias-Variance Trade-off: The bias-variance trade-off refers to the balance between model bias (error due to overly simplistic assumptions) and variance (error due to sensitivity to fluctuations in the training data). Finding the optimal trade-off involves minimizing both bias and variance to achieve good generalization performance.

Overfitting and Underfitting: Overfitting occurs when a model learns to memorize the training data rather than capturing underlying patterns, leading to poor generalization on unseen data. Underfitting, on the other hand, occurs when a model is too simplistic to capture the underlying structure of the data. Balancing the trade-off between overfitting and underfitting is essential for building models that generalize well to new data.

Cross-validation: Cross-validation is a technique used to assess the performance of machine learning models by partitioning the data into multiple subsets, training the model on one subset, and evaluating it on the remaining subsets. Cross-validation helps to obtain a more accurate estimate of a model's performance and detect issues such as overfitting.

In machine learning is a powerful and versatile approach to artificial intelligence that enables computers to learn from data and make predictions or decisions without explicit programming. By leveraging key concepts such as supervised learning, unsupervised learning, and reinforcement learning, along with fundamental principles such as Occam's Razor and the bias-variance trade-off, machine learning algorithms can tackle a wide range of tasks across diverse domains. As we delve deeper into the field of machine learning, it is essential to understand its historical roots, fundamental concepts, and guiding principles to develop effective and robust learning systems that can address real-world challenges and opportunities.

Supervised Learning Algorithms

Supervised learning is a fundamental paradigm in machine learning where the model learns to map input data to output labels based on labeled training examples. In this section, we delve into various supervised learning algorithms, their principles, applications, and challenges, elucidating their role in solving real-world problems in robotics and beyond.

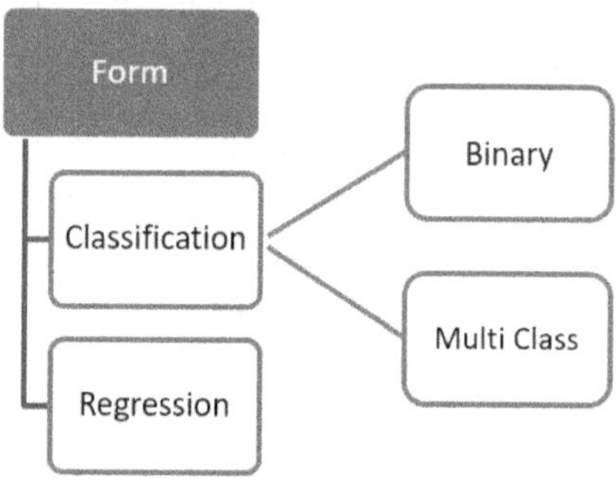

Figure 2. Supervised Learning Algorithm

Linear Regression

Linear regression is one of the simplest and most widely used supervised learning algorithms. It models the relationship between input features and continuous output labels using a linear equation. The goal of linear regression is to find the best-fitting line that minimizes the difference between the predicted and actual values. Applications of linear regression in robotics include pose estimation, trajectory prediction, and sensor calibration.

Logistic Regression

Logistic regression is a binary classification algorithm that models the probability of a binary outcome based on input features. It utilizes the logistic sigmoid function to map input data to a probability score between 0 and 1, which is then thresholded to make binary predictions. Logistic regression is commonly used in robotics for tasks such as object detection, gesture recognition, and anomaly detection.

Decision Trees

Decision trees are versatile supervised learning algorithms that recursively partition the input space into disjoint regions based on the feature values. Each internal node represents a decision based on a feature, and each leaf node corresponds to a class label or regression value. Decision trees are interpretable, easy to visualize, and robust to noisy data. They find applications in robotics for tasks such as object recognition, path planning, and fault diagnosis.

Random Forests

Random forests are ensemble learning algorithms that combine multiple decision trees to improve predictive performance and generalization. Each tree in the forest is trained on a bootstrap sample of the training data, and random feature subsets are considered at each split to decorrelate the trees. Random forests are robust to overfitting and noisy data and can handle high-dimensional input spaces. They are used in robotics for tasks such as sensor fusion, object detection, and classification.

Support Vector Machines (SVM)

Support vector machines (SVM) are powerful supervised learning algorithms for classification and regression tasks. SVMs find the optimal hyperplane that separates the input data into different classes or predicts continuous output values. They maximize the margin between the decision boundary and the closest data points, leading to better generalization. SVMs are used in robotics for tasks such as object classification, pose estimation, and anomaly detection.

Applications and Case Studies

Supervised learning algorithms find myriad applications in robotics, enabling robots to perceive, reason, and act in complex environments. For example, in autonomous vehicles, linear regression and SVMs are used for road lane detection and vehicle trajectory prediction. Logistic regression and decision trees are employed in robotic manipulation tasks for object recognition and grasp planning. Random forests are utilized in robot localization and mapping applications to fuse sensor data and estimate the robot's position and orientation accurately.

Challenges and Considerations

While supervised learning algorithms offer powerful tools for solving a wide range of problems in robotics, they are not without challenges. Challenges include the need for labeled training data, the curse of dimensionality in high-dimensional feature spaces, and the risk of overfitting to noisy or biased data. Additionally, deploying supervised learning models on real-world robotic systems requires considerations such as computational efficiency, real-time performance, and robustness to environmental variability and uncertainty.

Future Directions and Trends

Future research directions in supervised learning for robotics include the development of scalable algorithms for handling large-scale and streaming data, the integration of uncertainty estimation and probabilistic reasoning into learning models, and the exploration of meta-learning techniques for adaptive and lifelong learning in dynamic environments. Addressing these challenges and advancing the state-of-the-art in supervised learning will pave the way for more intelligent, adaptive, and autonomous robotic systems in the future.

In supervised learning algorithms are indispensable tools in the arsenal of machine learning techniques for robotics, enabling robots to learn from labeled data and make informed decisions in real-world environments. By leveraging the principles and algorithms of supervised learning, researchers and practitioners can tackle a wide range of challenges and unlock new capabilities in robotics, ultimately advancing the field towards more intelligent and autonomous robotic systems.

Unsupervised Learning Techniques

Unsupervised learning is a branch of machine learning that aims to uncover hidden patterns, structures, and relationships within data without the need for explicit labels or supervision. Unlike supervised learning, where the algorithm is provided with labeled examples to learn from, unsupervised learning algorithms operate on unlabeled data, making it a powerful tool for discovering intrinsic characteristics and organizing information in a variety of domains. In this section, we delve into the principles, algorithms, applications, and challenges of unsupervised learning techniques, exploring their utility and potential in the context of robotics and autonomous systems.

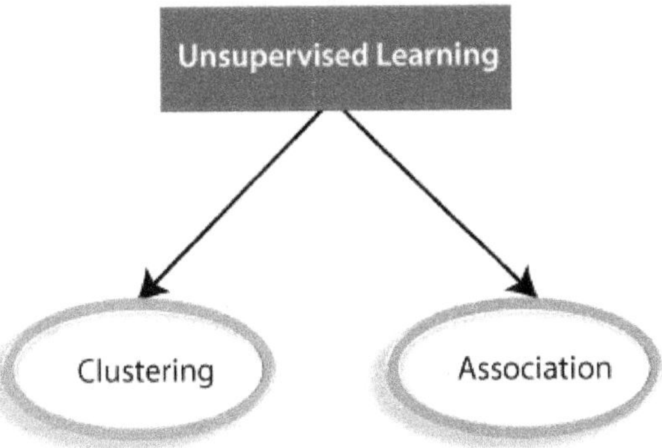

Figure 3. Unsupervised Learning

Principles of Unsupervised Learning

At the core of unsupervised learning lies the principle of discovering underlying structures and patterns within data without explicit guidance or supervision. Unsupervised learning algorithms aim to extract meaningful representations or features from raw data by identifying similarities, differences, and relationships between data points. By clustering similar data points together or reducing the dimensionality of the data while preserving essential information, unsupervised learning techniques enable the exploration and organization of complex datasets, facilitating subsequent analysis and decision-making tasks.

Clustering Algorithms

Clustering is a fundamental task in unsupervised learning that involves grouping similar data points together into clusters or segments based on their intrinsic properties. Clustering algorithms partition the data space into clusters such that data points within the same cluster are more similar to each other than to those in other clusters. K-means clustering is one of the most widely used clustering algorithms, where the goal is to partition the data into K clusters by iteratively assigning data points to the nearest cluster centroids and updating the centroids based on the mean of the data points assigned to each cluster. Other clustering algorithms include hierarchical clustering, density-based clustering (e.g., DBSCAN), and Gaussian mixture models (GMM), each with its own strengths and limitations in different applications.

Dimensionality Reduction Techniques

Dimensionality reduction is another key task in unsupervised learning aimed at reducing the complexity of high-dimensional data while preserving essential information and structures. By transforming the data into a lower-dimensional space, dimensionality reduction techniques facilitate visualization, interpretation, and analysis of data, as well as improve computational efficiency and alleviate the curse of dimensionality. Principal Component Analysis (PCA) is one of the most commonly used dimensionality reduction techniques, which identifies the orthogonal directions (principal components) that capture the maximum variance in the data and projects the data onto these components. Other dimensionality reduction methods include t-distributed Stochastic Neighbor Embedding (t-SNE), Isomap, and autoencoders, each with its own approach to capturing and preserving the underlying structure of the data in a reduced space.

Applications in Robotics and Autonomous Systems

Unsupervised learning techniques find diverse applications in robotics and autonomous systems, enabling robots to analyze, interpret, and respond to complex environments and data streams autonomously. In perception tasks, unsupervised learning algorithms can be used to cluster sensory data (e.g., images, point clouds) into meaningful categories or representations, facilitating object recognition, scene understanding, and anomaly detection. In navigation and mapping, dimensionality reduction techniques can help robots extract salient features from sensor data (e.g., lidar scans, camera images) and construct compact representations of the environment for localization, mapping, and path planning. In human-robot interaction, clustering algorithms can aid in segmenting and clustering human gestures, expressions, and behaviors, enabling robots to understand and respond to human intentions and emotions in natural and intuitive ways.

Challenges and Considerations

Despite their utility and potential, unsupervised learning techniques pose several challenges and considerations in the context of robotics and autonomous systems. One of the main challenges is the interpretation and evaluation of unsupervised learning results, as the absence of explicit labels makes it difficult to assess the quality and relevance of the learned representations or clusters. Additionally, unsupervised learning algorithms may suffer from issues such as sensitivity to initialization, scalability to large datasets, and robustness to noisy or ambiguous data. Moreover, the application of unsupervised learning techniques in real-world robotic systems requires careful consideration of computational resources, memory constraints, and real-time performance requirements, as well as ethical considerations regarding data privacy, security, and bias.

Future Directions and Opportunities

Despite these challenges, unsupervised learning techniques offer promising opportunities for advancing robotics and autonomous systems in the future. Emerging research directions such as self-supervised learning, semi-supervised learning, and unsupervised domain adaptation aim to bridge the gap between unsupervised and supervised learning, leveraging additional sources of information (e.g., temporal coherence, auxiliary tasks, domain knowledge) to improve the quality and generalization of unsupervised representations. Furthermore, the integration of unsupervised learning with reinforcement learning and imitation learning techniques opens up new possibilities for end-to-end learning of complex robotic behaviors and skills, enabling robots to acquire and adapt to new tasks and environments autonomously.

In unsupervised learning techniques play a vital role in uncovering hidden patterns, structures, and relationships within data, offering valuable insights and representations for analysis, interpretation, and decision-making in robotics and autonomous systems. By leveraging clustering algorithms and dimensionality reduction techniques, robots can autonomously explore and understand complex environments, adapt to changing conditions, and interact with humans and the world in more intelligent and adaptive ways.

Reinforcement Learning Basics

Reinforcement learning (RL) is a powerful paradigm in machine learning that enables agents to learn how to make sequential decisions by interacting with an environment. Unlike supervised learning, where the agent is provided with labeled examples, or unsupervised learning, where the agent learns patterns from unlabeled data, reinforcement learning relies on a reward signal to guide the agent's behavior towards achieving a desired goal. In this section, we delve into the fundamentals of reinforcement learning, exploring its key components, algorithms, and applications in the context of robotics and autonomous systems.

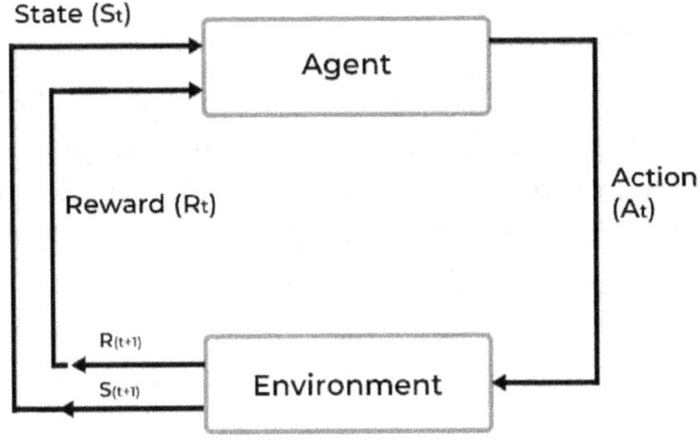

Figure 4. Reinforcement Learning

The RL Framework

At the core of reinforcement learning lies the RL framework, which consists of three main components: the agent, the environment, and the reward signal. The agent is the learner or decision-maker that interacts with the environment, taking actions and receiving feedback in the form of rewards. The environment represents the external system with which the agent interacts, encompassing all possible states, actions, and transitions. The reward signal is a scalar value that provides feedback to the agent, indicating the desirability of its actions and guiding its learning process.

Markov Decision Processes (MDPs)

Reinforcement learning problems are formalized as Markov Decision Processes (MDPs), which provide a mathematical framework for modeling sequential decision-making under uncertainty. An MDP consists of a set of states S, a set of actions A, transition probabilities P that describe the dynamics of the environment, a reward function R that specifies the immediate rewards obtained by the agent, and a discount factor γ that controls the influence of future rewards. The goal of the agent in an MDP is to learn a policy π that maps states to actions, maximizing the expected cumulative reward over time.

Policy Optimization

A policy in reinforcement learning represents the agent's strategy or behavior, specifying the action to be taken in each state. Policy optimization is the process of finding the optimal policy that maximizes the expected cumulative reward. Different approaches can be used to optimize policies, including value-based methods, policy gradient methods, and actor-critic methods. Value-based methods estimate the value of states or state-action pairs and derive policies from these value estimates. Policy gradient methods directly optimize the policy parameters to maximize the expected reward, typically using gradient ascent algorithms. Actor-critic methods combine value-based and policy-based approaches, with an actor network learning the policy and a critic network learning the value function.

Exploration vs. Exploitation

One of the key challenges in reinforcement learning is the exploration-exploitation trade-off. Exploration involves trying out different actions to discover the optimal policy, while exploitation involves selecting actions that are known to yield high rewards based on current knowledge. Balancing exploration and exploitation is essential for effective learning, as overly conservative policies may lead to suboptimal solutions, while overly aggressive policies may result in poor performance. Various exploration strategies, such as ϵ-greedy exploration, softmax exploration, and optimistic initialization, can be employed to encourage exploration while ensuring that the agent converges to a near-optimal policy.

Temporal-Difference Learning

Temporal-difference (TD) learning is a fundamental concept in reinforcement learning, referring to the method of updating value estimates based on the discrepancy between predicted and observed rewards. TD methods combine ideas from dynamic programming and Monte Carlo methods, allowing agents to learn from incomplete sequences of experiences without requiring a model of the environment. One of the most well-known TD algorithms is Q-learning, which estimates the value of state-action pairs and iteratively updates the Q-values using the Bellman equation. Q-learning is particularly effective for discrete action spaces and can be extended to handle continuous action spaces using function approximation techniques.

Deep Reinforcement Learning (DRL)

Deep reinforcement learning (DRL) extends reinforcement learning to handle high-dimensional state and action spaces using deep neural networks. DRL algorithms, such as deep Q-networks (DQN), deep deterministic policy gradients (DDPG), and proximal policy optimization (PPO), leverage deep learning architectures to approximate value functions and policies, enabling agents to learn directly from raw sensory inputs, such as images or sensor data. DRL has achieved remarkable success in a variety of domains, including video games, robotics, and autonomous vehicles, demonstrating the potential of combining deep learning with reinforcement learning for complex decision-making tasks.

Applications in Robotics and Autonomous Systems

Reinforcement learning has a wide range of applications in robotics and autonomous systems, enabling agents to acquire skills and behaviors through trial and error. In robotics, reinforcement learning is used for tasks such as robot manipulation, locomotion, navigation, and control. Agents learn to grasp objects, navigate through cluttered environments, and adapt to changing conditions, leveraging reinforcement learning algorithms to optimize their policies and improve performance over time. Autonomous systems, such as autonomous vehicles and drones, also benefit from reinforcement learning techniques for tasks such as path planning, obstacle avoidance, and decision-making in dynamic environments.

Challenges and Future Directions

While reinforcement learning has shown great promise in robotics and autonomous systems, several challenges remain to be addressed to unlock its full potential. These challenges include sample efficiency, scalability to high-dimensional state and action spaces, safety and robustness in real-world settings, and the integration of human knowledge and preferences into learning algorithms. Future directions in reinforcement learning for robotics include the development of algorithms that can learn from limited data, transfer knowledge across tasks and domains, and interact safely and intelligently with humans in collaborative environments.

Reinforcement learning provides a powerful framework for autonomous agents to learn from experience and optimize their behavior in complex and uncertain environments. By leveraging the principles of exploration, exploitation, and temporal-difference learning, agents can acquire skills and knowledge through trial and error, gradually improving their performance over time. In robotics and autonomous systems, reinforcement learning offers exciting opportunities for developing adaptive, intelligent, and autonomous agents capable of performing a wide range of tasks with efficiency and robustness.

Deep Learning Architectures

Deep learning has emerged as a powerful paradigm for solving complex problems in various domains, including computer vision, natural language processing, and robotics. Deep learning architectures, composed of multiple layers of interconnected neurons, enable machines to learn intricate patterns and representations from large volumes of data. In this section, we delve into the fundamental principles, key architectures, and applications of deep learning in robotics and autonomous systems.

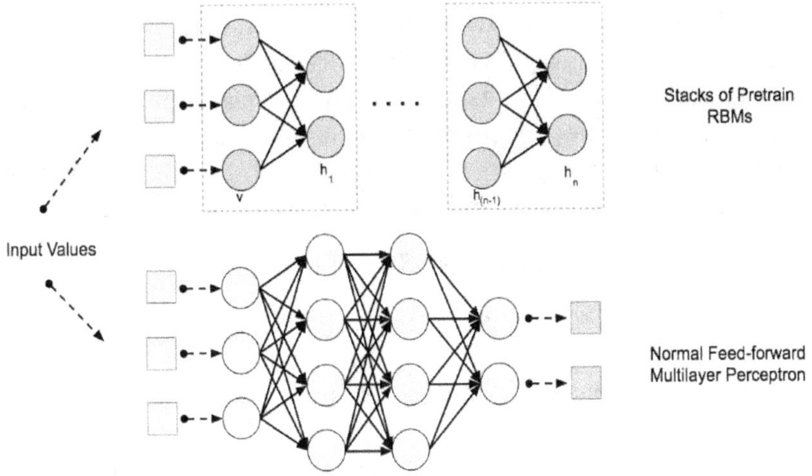

Figure 5. Deep Learning

Understanding Deep Learning

At the core of deep learning lies the concept of artificial neural networks inspired by the structure and function of the human brain. Neural networks consist of interconnected nodes, or neurons, organized into layers, with each layer responsible for extracting and transforming specific features from the input data. Deep learning extends this idea by introducing multiple layers of neurons, allowing for the automatic learning of hierarchical representations from raw data. Through a process known as backpropagation, deep neural networks adjust their internal parameters iteratively to minimize the difference between predicted and actual outputs, thereby learning to perform complex tasks such as image classification, speech recognition, and decision-making.

Convolutional Neural Networks (CNNs)

Convolutional Neural Networks (CNNs) have revolutionized the field of computer vision by enabling machines to extract spatial hierarchies of features from images. CNNs consist of alternating layers of convolutional, pooling, and fully connected layers, with convolutional layers performing local feature extraction through convolutions with learnable filters. Pooling layers downsample the feature maps to reduce computational complexity and increase translation invariance, while fully connected layers integrate the extracted features for classification or regression tasks. CNNs have achieved remarkable success in tasks such as object recognition, semantic segmentation, and facial recognition, making them indispensable tools in robotics for perception and scene understanding.

Recurrent Neural Networks (RNNs)

Recurrent Neural Networks (RNNs) are specialized architectures designed to model sequential data and capture temporal dependencies. Unlike feedforward neural networks, which process input data in a single pass, RNNs maintain an internal state, or memory, to store information about past inputs. This recurrent connectivity allows RNNs to model dynamic processes and sequences of varying lengths, making them well-suited for tasks such as time series prediction, language modeling, and speech synthesis. However, traditional RNNs suffer from the vanishing gradient problem, limiting their ability to capture long-range dependencies. To address this issue, variants such as Long Short-Term Memory (LSTM) and Gated Recurrent Unit (GRU) architectures have been developed, which introduce gating mechanisms to regulate the flow of information and alleviate gradient vanishing.

Deep Reinforcement Learning (DRL)

Deep Reinforcement Learning (DRL) combines deep learning with reinforcement learning principles to enable machines to learn complex behaviors through interaction with their environment. In DRL, an agent learns to maximize cumulative rewards by taking actions in an environment and observing the resulting states and rewards. Deep neural networks are used to approximate the value function or policy of the agent, enabling it to learn directly from raw sensory inputs. DRL has achieved remarkable success in challenging domains such as game playing, robotic manipulation, and autonomous navigation. Applications of DRL in robotics include robotic control, path planning, and task execution, where agents learn to perform tasks autonomously through trial and error.

Transfer Learning and Domain Adaptation

Transfer learning and domain adaptation techniques enable the transfer of knowledge learned from one domain or task to another, facilitating the training of deep learning models with limited data or in new environments. In transfer learning, pre-trained models trained on large-scale datasets are fine-tuned on target tasks with limited labeled data, leveraging the learned representations to bootstrap learning. Domain adaptation techniques aim to align the feature distributions between the source and target domains, enabling models trained on source data to generalize to new domains with different characteristics. Transfer learning and domain adaptation are particularly useful in robotics applications where labeled data may be scarce or where robots need to adapt to diverse and changing environments.

Challenges and Considerations

Despite their remarkable success, deep learning architectures pose several challenges and considerations in the context of robotics and autonomous systems. These include the need for large amounts of labeled data for training, the computational complexity and resource requirements of deep models, the interpretability and explainability of learned representations, and the safety and robustness of deep learning systems in real-world scenarios. Addressing these challenges requires interdisciplinary collaboration and research efforts focused on developing scalable, efficient, and trustworthy deep learning solutions tailored to the unique requirements of robotics applications.

Future Directions and Trends

The future of deep learning in robotics holds promising opportunities for innovation and advancement. Emerging trends and research directions include the development of more efficient and scalable deep learning architectures, the integration of deep learning with symbolic reasoning and planning techniques, the exploration of lifelong learning and continual adaptation mechanisms, and the pursuit of interpretable and explainable AI for enhanced human-robot collaboration and trust. Additionally, ongoing efforts to democratize access to deep learning tools and resources and to address ethical considerations surrounding the deployment of deep learning systems will play a crucial role in shaping the future of robotics and autonomous systems.

In deep learning, architectures have revolutionized the field of robotics by enabling machines to learn complex patterns and behaviors from data. From convolutional neural networks for perception to recurrent neural networks for sequential data processing and deep reinforcement learning for autonomous decision-making, deep learning has empowered robots to perceive, understand, and interact with their environment autonomously. By addressing challenges, exploring new directions, and embracing interdisciplinary collaboration, deep learning will continue to drive innovation and shape the future of robotics and autonomous systems.

Neural Networks for Robotics

Neural networks, inspired by the structure and function of the human brain, have emerged as powerful tools for addressing complex problems in robotics. Their ability to learn from data and extract patterns makes them well-suited for a wide range of tasks, from perception and control to planning and decision-making. In this section, we explore the principles, architectures, applications, challenges, and future directions of neural networks in robotics.

Principles of Neural Networks

Neural networks are computational models composed of interconnected nodes, or neurons, organized into layers. Each neuron receives input signals, performs a computation based on weighted connections, and produces an output signal. Through a process known as training, neural networks learn to adjust their weights and biases to minimize a predefined loss function, thereby optimizing their performance on a given task. Common types of neural networks used in robotics include feedforward neural networks, recurrent neural networks, convolutional neural networks, and deep neural networks.

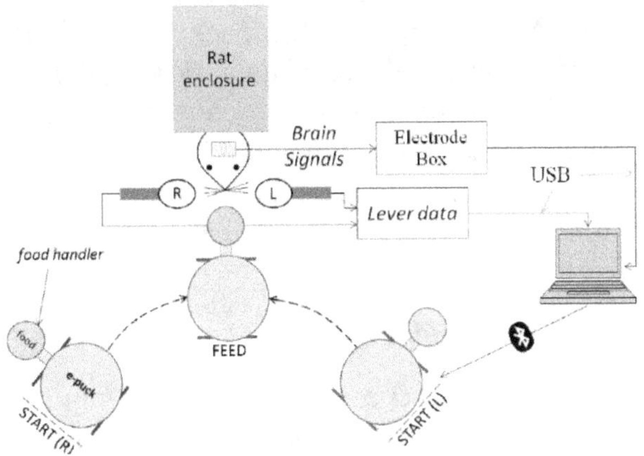

Figure 6. Neural Networks

Applications of Neural Networks in Robotics

Neural networks find applications across various domains of robotics, contributing to advancements in perception, control, planning, and decision-making. In perception tasks, convolutional neural networks (CNNs) are widely used for image classification, object detection, and scene understanding, enabling robots to interpret visual information and navigate complex environments. Recurrent neural networks (RNNs) are employed for sequential data processing, facilitating tasks such as speech recognition, gesture recognition, and time-series prediction. In control and planning, neural networks are used to learn inverse kinematics and dynamics models, enabling robots to manipulate objects with precision and adapt to dynamic environments. Additionally, reinforcement learning techniques leverage neural networks to enable robots to learn optimal control policies through trial and error, achieving autonomy in decision-making and task execution.

Architectures of Neural Networks

Neural network architectures in robotics are tailored to the specific requirements of the task at hand, ranging from shallow feedforward networks to deep hierarchical networks.

Convolutional neural networks (CNNs) are designed for spatial data processing, leveraging shared weights and local connectivity to capture spatial hierarchies in input data. Recurrent neural networks (RNNs) incorporate feedback connections to enable temporal processing of sequential data, making them suitable for tasks involving time-series data or sequential decision-making. Deep neural networks, comprising multiple layers of neurons, are capable of learning hierarchical representations of complex data, enabling robots to extract abstract features and patterns from high-dimensional sensor data.

Challenges and Considerations

Despite their effectiveness, neural networks in robotics pose several challenges and considerations that must be addressed to ensure their practical applicability and reliability. One challenge is the need for large amounts of annotated data for training, which may be expensive or impractical to obtain in real-world robotic applications. Additionally, neural networks are susceptible to adversarial attacks, where small perturbations to input data can lead to erroneous predictions or behaviors. Robustness to environmental variability, uncertainty, and sensor noise is another challenge, requiring techniques such as data augmentation, regularization, and uncertainty estimation to improve generalization and robustness. Ethical considerations surrounding the use of neural networks in robotics, such as bias, transparency, and accountability, also necessitate careful attention to ensure responsible and ethical deployment of autonomous systems.

Future Directions and Trends

Despite the challenges, neural networks hold immense potential for shaping the future of robotics, enabling robots to perceive, reason, and act in increasingly complex and dynamic environments. Future directions in neural networks for robotics include the integration of multimodal sensory data, enabling robots to learn from diverse sources of information and improve their understanding of the environment. Additionally, research efforts are focused on developing explainable and interpretable neural network models, enabling humans to understand and trust the decisions made by autonomous systems. Continual learning and lifelong adaptation are also emerging research directions, enabling robots to learn and evolve over time in response to changing tasks and environments.

Neural networks have revolutionized robotics, enabling robots to perform tasks with unprecedented levels of autonomy, adaptability, and intelligence. By leveraging the principles of neural computation, robots can perceive the world, learn from experience, and make decisions in real-time, unlocking new possibilities for automation, exploration, and collaboration. As research in neural networks continues to advance, the future holds promise for a new generation of intelligent robotic systems capable of addressing the most challenging problems facing society.

Reinforcement Learning in Robotics

Reinforcement learning (RL) stands as a powerful paradigm within the realm of artificial intelligence, offering the potential for robots to learn and adapt to complex environments through interaction and feedback. In the context of robotics, reinforcement learning serves as a promising approach to enable autonomous decision-making, skill acquisition, and task optimization. In this section, we explore the principles, methods, applications, challenges, and future directions of reinforcement learning in robotics, highlighting its transformative potential in shaping the capabilities of robotic systems.

Principles of Reinforcement Learning

At its core, reinforcement learning revolves around the notion of an agent interacting with an environment, receiving feedback in the form of rewards or penalties based on its actions, and learning to maximize cumulative rewards over time. Formally, reinforcement learning can be framed as a Markov decision process (MDP), where the agent seeks to learn an optimal policy that maps states to actions to maximize long-term rewards. Key components of reinforcement learning include:

State: The current configuration or situation of the environment.

Action: The decision or choice made by the agent in response to the current state.

Reward: The feedback signal provided to the agent indicates the desirability of its action in a given state.

Policy: The strategy or rule employed by the agent to select actions based on states.

Value function: An estimate of the expected cumulative reward associated with being in a particular state or taking a specific action.

Reinforcement Learning Algorithms

Reinforcement learning encompasses a variety of algorithms and techniques for learning optimal policies in different settings and environments. Some of the most prominent reinforcement learning algorithms include:

Q-Learning: A model-free, value-based algorithm that iteratively learns the optimal action-value function by updating Q-values based on observed rewards and transitions.

Deep Q-Networks (DQN): A deep learning-based extension of Q-learning that employs neural networks to approximate the action-value function, enabling RL in high-dimensional state spaces.

Policy Gradient Methods: Model-free algorithms that directly optimize the policy parameters to maximize expected rewards, such as the REINFORCE algorithm and actor-critic methods.

Deep Deterministic Policy Gradient (DDPG): A model-free, actor-critic algorithm that combines deep learning with deterministic policy gradients to learn continuous control policies.

Proximal Policy Optimization (PPO): A policy gradient algorithm that optimizes policy updates while ensuring sample efficiency and stability through clipped surrogate objectives.

Applications in Robotics

Reinforcement learning holds immense potential for empowering robots to acquire complex skills, adapt to dynamic environments, and autonomously solve tasks. In robotics, reinforcement learning finds applications across various domains, including:

Robot Navigation: Reinforcement learning enables robots to learn navigation policies for autonomous exploration, obstacle avoidance, and path planning in dynamic environments.

Manipulation and Grasping: Robots can learn manipulation skills, such as grasping objects of different shapes and sizes, through reinforcement learning, improving efficiency and adaptability in manufacturing and logistics.

Autonomous Vehicles: Reinforcement learning algorithms facilitate the training of autonomous driving policies, enabling vehicles to navigate traffic, handle complex road scenarios, and optimize driving behavior.

Robotics Surgery: Reinforcement learning techniques are utilized to train surgical robots for precise and dexterous manipulation during minimally invasive procedures, enhancing surgical outcomes and patient safety.

Challenges and Considerations

Despite its promise, reinforcement learning in robotics poses several challenges and considerations that must be addressed to realize its full potential:

Sample Efficiency: RL algorithms often require a large number of interactions with the environment to learn effective policies, which can be impractical or costly in real-world robotics settings.

Safety and Robustness: Learning policies through trial and error may lead to unsafe or undesirable behavior, necessitating the development of mechanisms for ensuring safety and robustness in RL-based systems.

Transfer Learning: Generalizing learned policies to new tasks or environments remains a significant challenge in reinforcement learning, requiring techniques for transfer learning, domain adaptation, and continual learning.

Ethical and Societal Implications: As robots learn from their interactions with the environment, ethical considerations surrounding fairness, transparency, and accountability in decision-making become increasingly important, warranting careful scrutiny and regulation.

Future Directions and Outlook

Despite the challenges, reinforcement learning continues to advance rapidly, driven by innovations in algorithms, hardware, and application domains. Future directions in reinforcement learning for robotics include:

Meta-Learning and Multi-Task Learning: Techniques for meta-learning and multi-task learning enable robots to learn efficient learning algorithms and generalize knowledge across diverse tasks and environments.

Hierarchical Reinforcement Learning: Hierarchical reinforcement learning architectures allow robots to learn and execute complex tasks by decomposing them into hierarchies of subtasks, facilitating efficient exploration and planning.

Interactive and Imitation Learning: Interactive and imitation learning methods enable robots to leverage human guidance and demonstrations to accelerate learning and acquire complex skills in real-world settings.

Ethical and Responsible AI: As reinforcement learning-based systems become increasingly autonomous and capable, addressing ethical, legal, and societal considerations surrounding their deployment and impact remains paramount, requiring interdisciplinary collaboration and ethical frameworks.

Reinforcement learning stands as a transformative paradigm for advancing the capabilities of robotic systems, enabling them to learn, adapt, and interact intelligently with their environments. By leveraging principles and techniques from reinforcement learning, robots can acquire complex skills, navigate dynamic environments, and autonomously solve tasks in diverse application domains. As research in reinforcement learning continues to evolve, the integration of ethical, safety, and societal considerations remains essential to ensuring the responsible and beneficial deployment of RL-based robotics systems.

Transfer Learning in Robotics

Transfer learning has emerged as a powerful technique in machine learning, enabling models trained on one task or domain to be leveraged for related tasks or domains with limited data. In the context of robotics, transfer learning holds significant promise for accelerating learning, improving generalization, and addressing the challenges of data scarcity and domain shift. In this section, we delve into the principles, methods, applications, and challenges of transfer learning in robotics, exploring its potential to enhance the capabilities of robotic systems across various domains and applications.

Understanding Transfer Learning

Transfer learning refers to the process of transferring knowledge from a source domain or task to a target domain or task, where the target domain may have limited or different data availability compared to the source domain. The goal of transfer learning is to leverage the knowledge learned from the source domain to facilitate learning in the target domain, thereby reducing the need for extensive labeled data and accelerating the learning process. By transferring knowledge across related tasks or domains, transfer learning enables models to generalize better and adapt more quickly to new environments or tasks.

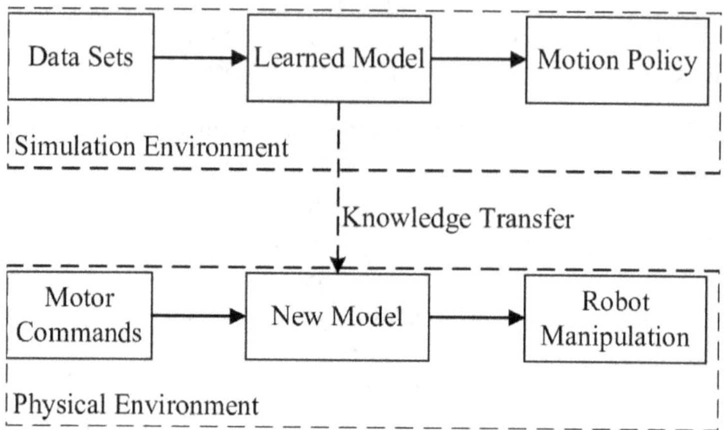

Figure 7. Transfer Learning

Types of Transfer Learning

Transfer learning in robotics can be categorized into several types based on the relationship between the source and target domains or tasks:

Inductive Transfer Learning: In inductive transfer learning, knowledge is transferred from a source domain with ample data to a target domain with limited data. The goal is to improve the performance of the target task by leveraging the learned representations or features from the source domain.

Transductive Transfer Learning: Transductive transfer learning focuses on transferring knowledge from a specific set of source instances to related instances in the target domain. The goal is to improve the generalization performance of the target model by leveraging the similarities between the source and target instances.

Unsupervised Transfer Learning: Unsupervised transfer learning aims to transfer knowledge from a labeled source domain to an unlabeled target domain. By leveraging the labeled data from the source domain, the model can learn useful representations or features that improve its performance on the target task without requiring labeled data in the target domain.

Methods and Techniques

Several techniques have been developed to facilitate transfer learning in robotics, including:

Feature Extraction: Pre-trained neural network models, such as convolutional neural networks (CNNs) trained on large-scale image datasets (e.g., ImageNet), can be used as feature extractors for tasks such as object recognition, scene understanding, and localization. By leveraging the learned representations from these models, robotic systems can achieve better performance with limited labeled data.

Fine-tuning: Fine-tuning involves retraining a pre-trained model on a target task or domain using a small amount of labeled data. By initializing the model with the learned weights from the pre-trained model and fine-tuning them on the target task, the model can adapt to the specific characteristics of the target domain more effectively.

Domain Adaptation: Domain adaptation techniques aim to align the distributions of the source and target domains to mitigate the effects of domain shift. This can be achieved through methods such as adversarial training, where a domain discriminator is trained to distinguish between source and target domain instances, and the model is optimized to minimize this domain-discriminator loss.

Model Ensembles: Model ensembles combine multiple models trained on different source domains or tasks to improve robustness and generalization performance. By leveraging the diverse knowledge encoded in the ensemble members, the model can achieve better performance across a range of target tasks or domains.

Applications in Robotics

Transfer learning has found applications in various domains of robotics, including:

Perception: Transfer learning enables robotic systems to leverage pre-trained models for tasks such as object recognition, semantic segmentation, and depth estimation, thereby improving their perception capabilities in new environments or domains.

Manipulation: In robotic manipulation tasks such as grasping, transfer learning can be used to transfer knowledge from simulated or pre-collected datasets to real-world scenarios, reducing the need for extensive real-world data collection and labeling.

Navigation: Transfer learning facilitates the adaptation of navigation policies learned in simulation to real-world environments, enabling robots to navigate autonomously in complex and dynamic environments with limited real-world experience.

Human-Robot Interaction: In applications involving human-robot interaction, transfer learning can be used to transfer knowledge from human demonstrations to robotic policies, enabling robots to learn from human feedback and demonstrations to perform tasks such as gesture recognition and collaborative manipulation.

Challenges and Considerations

Despite its potential benefits, transfer learning in robotics poses several challenges and considerations:

Domain Shift: Differences in the distributions of the source and target domains can lead to domain shift, where the learned knowledge may not generalize well to the target domain. Addressing domain shift requires robust domain adaptation techniques that can align the distributions of the source and target domains effectively.

Data Efficiency: While transfer learning aims to improve data efficiency by leveraging knowledge from related tasks or domains, it still requires access to relevant labeled data in the source domain. Ensuring the availability and quality of source domain data is essential for effective transfer learning.

Generalization: Transfer learning models must generalize well to unseen instances in the target domain to be effective.

Ensuring robust generalization requires careful selection of source domains, appropriate transfer learning techniques, and a thorough evaluation of target domain data.

Ethical Considerations: Transfer learning models trained on biased or unrepresentative data in the source domain may perpetuate biases or unfairness in the target domain. Ensuring fairness and equity in transfer learning models requires careful attention to data selection, model training, and evaluation methodologies.

Future Directions

Future research directions in transfer learning for robotics include:

Adaptive Transfer Learning: Developing adaptive transfer learning techniques that can continuously adapt and update the learned representations or models based on feedback from the target domain, enabling lifelong learning and adaptation in robotic systems.

Incremental Transfer Learning: Exploring incremental transfer learning techniques that can incrementally incorporate new knowledge from the target domain while retaining the previously learned knowledge, allowing robotic systems to adapt to changing environments and tasks over time.

Multi-Modal Transfer Learning: Extending transfer learning techniques to handle multi-modal data sources, such as vision, language, and sensor data, enabling robotic systems to learn from diverse sources of information and achieve robust perception and interaction capabilities.

Robustness and Safety: Addressing the challenges of robustness and safety in transfer learning for robotics, ensuring that transfer learning models can operate reliably and safely in real-world environments while minimizing the risk of unintended behaviors or failures.

Transfer learning holds immense potential for enhancing the capabilities of robotic systems by leveraging knowledge from related tasks or domains to improve learning efficiency, generalization, and adaptation to new environments. By addressing the challenges and considerations associated with transfer learning, robotic systems can benefit from the rich knowledge encoded in pre-trained models and datasets, accelerating progress and innovation in robotics and autonomous systems.

Machine Learning for Perception

Perception, the ability to interpret sensory information and extract meaningful insights about the surrounding environment, forms the cornerstone of robotic intelligence. Machine learning (ML) techniques have revolutionized perception in robotics, enabling robots to perceive and understand the world with unprecedented accuracy and efficiency. In this section, we explore the role of machine learning in enhancing perception capabilities in robotics, covering key concepts, algorithms, applications, challenges, and future directions.

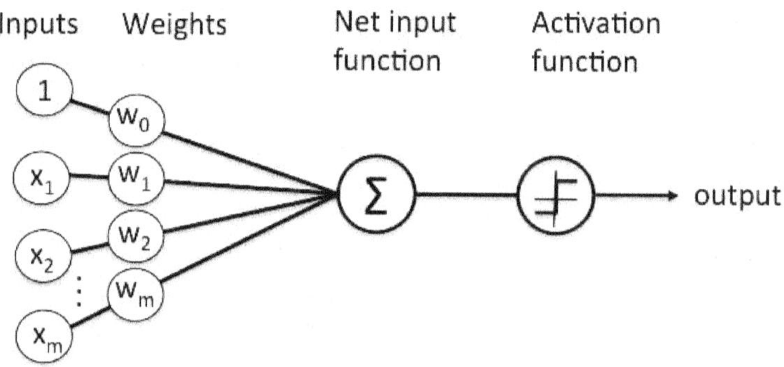

Figure 8. Machine Learning for Perception

Understanding Perception in Robotics

Perception in robotics involves the interpretation of sensor data to extract information about the environment, including objects, obstacles, and spatial relationships. Traditional perception methods often relied on handcrafted algorithms and heuristics to process sensory inputs, leading to limited flexibility and scalability. Machine learning offers a paradigm shift in perception by allowing robots to learn patterns and relationships directly from data, enabling them to adapt to diverse environments and tasks.

Fundamentals of Machine Learning for Perception

Machine learning algorithms for perception can be broadly categorized into supervised, unsupervised, and reinforcement learning paradigms. Supervised learning involves training models on labeled datasets, where the correct outputs are provided for training examples. Unsupervised learning focuses on discovering patterns and structures in unlabeled data without explicit supervision. Reinforcement learning entails learning through interaction with the environment, with the agent receiving feedback in the form of rewards or penalties based on its actions.

Applications of Machine Learning in Perception

Machine learning techniques have been applied to various perception tasks in robotics, including:

Object recognition and classification: ML models can learn to identify objects in images or point clouds, enabling robots to perceive their surroundings and interact with objects autonomously.

Scene understanding: ML algorithms can infer semantic information from sensor data, such as identifying different types of terrain or obstacles in the robot's path.

Gesture recognition: ML models can interpret human gestures from camera or depth sensor data, facilitating intuitive human-robot interaction.

Emotion detection: ML techniques can analyze facial expressions or vocal cues to infer human emotions, enhancing social robotics applications.

Deep Learning for Perception

Deep learning, a subfield of machine learning focused on neural network architectures with multiple layers, has emerged as a powerful tool for perception in robotics. Convolutional neural networks (CNNs) are particularly well-suited for visual perception tasks, such as image classification and object detection. Recurrent neural networks (RNNs) are effective for sequential data processing, making them useful for tasks like natural language understanding or time-series analysis. Deep reinforcement learning combines deep learning with reinforcement learning principles, enabling agents to learn complex behaviors directly from raw sensory inputs.

Challenges and Considerations

Despite the remarkable progress in machine learning for perception, several challenges remain to be addressed:

Data scarcity and quality: Obtaining labeled datasets for training perception models can be challenging, particularly in robotics domains with limited availability of annotated data.

Robustness to real-world variability: ML models trained on synthetic or controlled datasets may struggle to generalize to diverse real-world environments with varying lighting conditions, backgrounds, and object appearances.

Safety and ethical considerations: Perception errors or biases in ML models can have serious consequences in safety-critical applications, highlighting the importance of robustness, fairness, and transparency in perception algorithms.

Future Directions and Opportunities

The future of machine learning for perception in robotics holds promising avenues for innovation and advancement:

Continual learning and lifelong adaptation: Developing ML models that can learn from new experiences and adapt to changing environments over time.

Interpretable and explainable AI: Enhancing the transparency and interpretability of perception models to facilitate human understanding and trust.

Human-centered machine learning: Designing perception systems that prioritize human preferences, values, and safety in human-robot interaction scenarios.

Machine learning has transformed perception in robotics, empowering robots with the ability to perceive and understand the world in ways previously thought impossible. By leveraging ML techniques such as deep learning, robots can interpret complex sensory inputs, recognize objects and patterns, and interact intelligently with their environment and human users. As we continue to advance the field of machine learning for perception, the possibilities for enhancing robotic intelligence and autonomy are limitless, paving the way for a future where robots seamlessly integrate into our daily lives and contribute to a wide range of applications across industries and domains.

Machine Learning for Control

Machine learning (ML) techniques have emerged as powerful tools for addressing complex control problems in robotics and automation. By leveraging data-driven approaches, machine learning enables the development of control strategies that adapt to changing environments, learn from experience, and achieve high-performance control in diverse and uncertain scenarios. In this section, we explore the applications, algorithms, challenges, and future directions of machine learning for control in robotics.

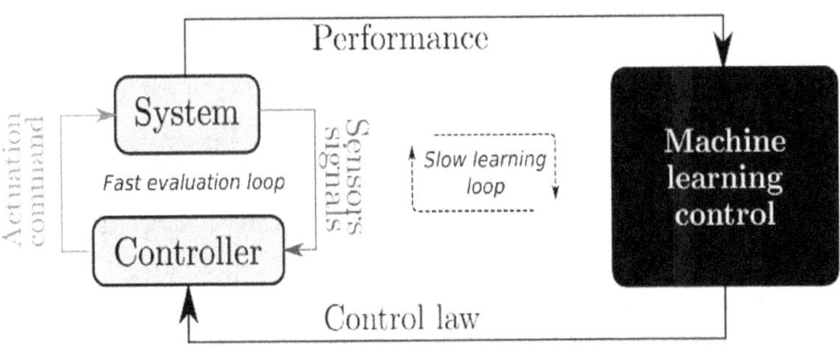

Figure 9. Machine Learning for Control

Machine learning for control refers to the application of ML techniques to design, optimize, and improve control systems for robotic and autonomous systems. Unlike traditional control methods, which rely on explicit mathematical models of the system dynamics, ML-based control approaches learn control policies directly from data, enabling adaptive and robust control in complex and dynamic environments. Machine learning for control encompasses a wide range of techniques, including supervised learning, reinforcement learning, and imitation learning, each offering unique advantages and capabilities for addressing different control tasks.

Applications of Machine Learning for Control

Machine learning techniques have found applications in various control domains within robotics and automation, including motion control, trajectory planning, manipulation, navigation, and autonomous decision-making. In motion control, machine learning algorithms can learn control policies for achieving precise and smooth motion trajectories, minimizing tracking errors, and optimizing energy consumption. In manipulation tasks, machine learning enables robots to learn grasp strategies, object manipulation skills, and adaptive control behaviors for interacting with objects of varying shapes, sizes, and properties. In navigation and autonomous systems, machine learning facilitates the development of control policies for path planning, obstacle avoidance, localization, and mapping, enabling robots to navigate complex and dynamic environments with autonomy and efficiency.

Supervised Learning for Control

Supervised learning techniques involve training a model to map input-output pairs by learning from labeled data. In the context of control, supervised learning can be applied to learn control policies for tracking desired trajectories, regulating system states, or achieving specific control objectives. For example, in trajectory tracking tasks, supervised learning algorithms can learn mappings between sensory inputs (e.g., camera images, sensor readings) and control commands (e.g., motor torques, actuator commands), enabling robots to learn to follow desired trajectories accurately and robustly.

Reinforcement Learning for Control

Reinforcement learning (RL) is a powerful paradigm for learning control policies through interaction with an environment to maximize cumulative rewards. In RL-based control, an agent learns to make decisions by trial and error, receiving feedback in the form of rewards or penalties based on its actions. RL algorithms, such as Q-learning, policy gradients, and deep reinforcement learning, have been successfully applied to a wide range of control tasks in robotics, including robot navigation, manipulation, and autonomous decision-making. RL-based control offers the flexibility to learn complex control policies in high-dimensional state and action spaces, making it well-suited for robotic applications with non-linear dynamics and uncertain environments.

Imitation Learning and Learning from Demonstration

Imitation learning, also known as learning from demonstration, involves learning control policies by observing and imitating expert demonstrations. In imitation learning, an agent learns to mimic the behavior of a human or an expert controller by learning mappings from observed states to corresponding actions. Imitation learning techniques, such as behavioral cloning and inverse reinforcement learning, have been applied to various control tasks in robotics, including autonomous driving, robot manipulation, and humanoid robot locomotion. By leveraging expert demonstrations, imitation learning enables robots to acquire complex control behaviors and skills from human expertise, reducing the need for manual engineering and tuning of control algorithms.

Challenges and Considerations

Despite the promise of machine learning for control, several challenges and considerations must be addressed to realize its full potential in robotics and automation. These challenges include the need for large-scale and diverse training data, the generalization of learned control policies to new environments, the robustness of learned policies to noise and uncertainties, and the safety and reliability of autonomous systems in real-world deployment. Additionally, ethical considerations surrounding the use of machine learning in safety-critical applications, such as autonomous vehicles and medical robotics, require careful attention to ensure the responsible and ethical development and deployment of ML-based control systems.

Future Directions and Emerging Trends

The future of machine learning for control in robotics holds promising avenues for innovation and advancement. Emerging trends and research directions include the development of hybrid control approaches that combine the strengths of traditional control methods with machine learning techniques, the exploration of meta-learning and lifelong learning techniques for continual adaptation and improvement of control policies, and the integration of human expertise and preferences into learned control behaviors through human-in-the-loop learning and interactive learning paradigms. Additionally, advancements in explainable AI and interpretable machine learning are expected to enhance the transparency and trustworthiness of ML-based control systems, enabling better understanding and validation of learned control policies by human users and stakeholders.

Machine learning for control represents a transformative paradigm shift in robotics and automation, enabling robots and autonomous systems to learn adaptive and intelligent control behaviors from data and experience. By leveraging the capabilities of machine learning, robots can achieve higher levels of autonomy, flexibility, and robustness in complex and dynamic environments, paving the way for new applications and advancements in various domains, including manufacturing, healthcare, transportation, and exploration. As research and development in machine learning for control continue to progress, it is essential to address the challenges and considerations surrounding its deployment and ensure that ML-based control systems meet safety, reliability, and ethical standards in real-world applications.

Applications of Machine Learning in Robotics

Machine learning (ML) has emerged as a transformative technology with a wide range of applications in robotics, enabling robots to perceive, learn, and adapt to complex environments with unprecedented efficiency and autonomy. In this section, we explore the diverse applications of machine learning in robotics, spanning perception, control, navigation, human-robot interaction, and more.

Perception

One of the primary applications of machine learning in robotics is in enhancing perception capabilities. Machine learning algorithms enable robots to interpret sensor data, recognize objects, and understand the surrounding environment with remarkable accuracy and efficiency. In the field of computer vision, convolutional neural networks (CNNs) have revolutionized object recognition, enabling robots to identify and classify objects in real-time. Image segmentation techniques based on deep learning architectures allow robots to segment and understand complex scenes, facilitating tasks such as object detection, tracking, and scene understanding. These advancements in perception have profound implications for a wide range of robotics applications, including autonomous vehicles, surveillance systems, and industrial automation.

Control and Manipulation

Machine learning techniques play a crucial role in enhancing the control and manipulation capabilities of robots. Reinforcement learning algorithms enable robots to learn optimal control policies through trial and error, allowing them to perform complex manipulation tasks with precision and efficiency. In the field of robot manipulation, deep reinforcement learning has been used to train robots to grasp and manipulate objects in cluttered and dynamic environments, enabling applications such as robotic assembly, pick-and-place tasks, and warehouse automation. Machine learning-based control strategies also enable robots to adapt to changes in their environment, learn from human demonstrations, and optimize their behavior over time, leading to more flexible and adaptable robotic systems.

Navigation and Path Planning

Machine learning algorithms have revolutionized navigation and path planning for autonomous robots. In the domain of mobile robotics, reinforcement learning-based approaches enable robots to learn optimal navigation policies in complex and dynamic environments, allowing them to avoid obstacles, plan efficient paths, and navigate autonomously with minimal human intervention. Machine learning techniques such as deep learning and probabilistic inference have been applied to simultaneous localization and mapping (SLAM) tasks, enabling robots to build accurate maps of their surroundings and localize themselves within these maps in real-time. These advancements in navigation and path planning have paved the way for applications such as autonomous vehicles, delivery drones, and robotic exploration missions in hazardous or inaccessible environments.

Human-Robot Interaction

Machine learning plays a crucial role in facilitating natural and intuitive interactions between humans and robots. In the field of human-robot interaction (HRI), machine learning techniques enable robots to understand and respond to human gestures, speech, and expressions, enhancing communication and collaboration between humans and robots. Natural language processing algorithms allow robots to understand and generate human-like speech, enabling applications such as voice-controlled interfaces, virtual assistants, and interactive robots for education and entertainment. Machine learning-based affective computing techniques enable robots to recognize and respond to human emotions, enhancing their ability to empathize and engage with users in socially and emotionally meaningful ways. These advancements in HRI have the potential to revolutionize various domains, including healthcare, education, and assistive technology.

Healthcare and Assistive Robotics

Machine learning holds promise for revolutionizing healthcare and assistive robotics, enabling robots to assist with a wide range of tasks, from medical diagnosis and treatment to rehabilitation and eldercare. In medical imaging, deep learning algorithms have shown remarkable performance in tasks such as image classification, segmentation, and disease detection, enabling applications such as computer-aided diagnosis and personalized treatment planning. Machine learning-based predictive modeling techniques enable robots to anticipate and respond to the needs of patients, providing personalized care and support. Assistive robots equipped with machine learning capabilities can assist individuals with disabilities or age-related impairments with tasks such as mobility assistance, medication management, and daily living activities, enhancing their independence and quality of life.

Industrial Automation

In the field of industrial automation, machine learning plays a crucial role in optimizing manufacturing processes, improving productivity, and reducing costs. Machine learning algorithms enable robots to learn from sensor data and optimize their performance in tasks such as robotic assembly, welding, and quality inspection. Predictive maintenance techniques based on machine learning enable early detection of equipment failures and optimization of maintenance schedules, minimizing downtime and maximizing efficiency. Machine learning-based optimization algorithms enable robots to adapt to changing production requirements and optimize resource allocation in real-time, leading to more flexible and responsive manufacturing systems. These advancements in industrial automation have the potential to revolutionize manufacturing industries, making them more competitive and sustainable in the global marketplace.

Ethical and Societal Implications

While machine learning holds immense promise for revolutionizing robotics, it also raises significant ethical and societal implications that must be carefully considered. Concerns such as algorithmic bias, privacy infringement, and job displacement require thoughtful attention to ensure that machine learning technologies are developed and deployed responsibly and ethically. Addressing these challenges requires interdisciplinary collaboration between researchers, policymakers, and stakeholders to develop frameworks for responsible AI and robotics that prioritize transparency, fairness, and accountability.

Machine learning plays a crucial role in advancing robotics, enabling robots to perceive, learn, and adapt to complex environments with unprecedented autonomy and efficiency. By harnessing the power of machine learning techniques, robots can revolutionize a wide range of applications, from perception and control to navigation and human-robot interaction, with profound implications for industries, healthcare, and society at large. However, realizing the full potential of machine learning in robotics requires careful consideration of ethical, societal, and regulatory challenges, ensuring that these technologies are developed and deployed in a responsible and inclusive manner.

Challenges and Limitations of ML in Robotics

Machine learning (ML) has emerged as a powerful tool for enhancing the capabilities of robotic systems, enabling them to perceive, reason, and act autonomously in complex and dynamic environments. However, despite its promise, ML in robotics is not without its challenges and limitations. In this section, we explore some of the key challenges and limitations of applying ML to robotics, ranging from data scarcity and quality to safety and ethical considerations.

Data Scarcity and Quality

One of the primary challenges in applying ML to robotics is the scarcity and quality of training data. Unlike traditional ML domains such as image classification or natural language processing, where large labeled datasets are readily available, robotics often involves tasks that require specialized or domain-specific data. Collecting high-quality training data for robotics applications can be costly, time-consuming, and challenging, especially in real-world scenarios with complex and dynamic environments. Furthermore, the quality of training data can significantly impact the performance and generalization ability of ML models, necessitating careful attention to data collection, preprocessing, and augmentation techniques.

Robustness to Real-World Variability and Uncertainty

Robotic systems operate in dynamic and uncertain environments, where conditions such as lighting, weather, and object appearance can vary unpredictably. ML models trained on static or controlled datasets may struggle to generalize to real-world scenarios with inherent variability and uncertainty. Robustness to environmental variability and uncertainty is crucial for ensuring the reliability and effectiveness of ML-based robotic systems. Techniques such as domain adaptation, transfer learning, and data augmentation can help improve the robustness of ML models to variations in the environment, but addressing this challenge remains an ongoing area of research in ML for robotics.

Safety and Reliability

Safety is a paramount concern in robotics, particularly in applications involving human-robot interaction or autonomous navigation in shared spaces. ML-based robotic systems must exhibit safe and reliable behavior under various operating conditions to mitigate the risk of accidents or harm to humans and the environment. However, ensuring the safety and reliability of ML-based systems presents unique challenges, as the underlying decision-making processes of ML models can be complex and opaque. Interpreting and explaining the decisions of ML models, particularly deep neural networks, is an ongoing challenge in robotics, as it requires mechanisms for providing transparency, accountability, and trustworthiness in autonomous systems.

Ethical and Societal Implications

The integration of ML into robotics raises profound ethical and societal implications that warrant careful consideration. Autonomous systems powered by ML algorithms may make decisions that impact individuals and communities in significant ways, raising questions about accountability, fairness, and transparency. Bias in training data or algorithmic decision-making can lead to unjust outcomes or discrimination, exacerbating existing societal inequalities. Moreover, concerns about data privacy, consent, and autonomy in human-robot interaction must be addressed to ensure the ethical development and deployment of ML-based robotic systems. Balancing the benefits of ML-driven automation with ethical considerations and societal values is essential for fostering trust and acceptance of robotic technologies.

Computational Complexity and Resource Constraints

ML algorithms, particularly deep learning models, can be computationally intensive and resource-intensive, requiring significant computational power and memory resources for training and inference. In resource-constrained robotic systems, such as mobile robots or embedded devices, meeting these computational demands can be challenging. Optimizing ML algorithms for efficiency, scalability, and real-time performance is essential for deploying ML-based robotic systems in practical applications. Techniques such as model compression, quantization, and hardware acceleration can help mitigate the computational complexity of ML algorithms, but trade-offs between performance and resource constraints must be carefully considered.

Adaptability and Continual Learning

Robotic systems operate in dynamic and evolving environments where conditions may change over time. ML models trained on static datasets may struggle to adapt to changes in the environment or learn from new experiences. Continual learning, or the ability of ML models to learn incrementally from sequential data streams, is essential for enabling adaptive and self-improving robotic systems. However, achieving continual learning in robotics poses technical challenges such as catastrophic forgetting, where learning new information erases previously learned knowledge. Developing algorithms and architectures that support continual learning and lifelong adaptation is an active area of research in ML for robotics.

While machine learning holds great promise for enhancing the capabilities of robotic systems, it is not without its challenges and limitations. Addressing these challenges requires interdisciplinary collaboration, innovative research, and a commitment to ethical and responsible development practices. By addressing issues such as data scarcity and quality, robustness to real-world variability, safety and reliability, ethical considerations, computational complexity, and adaptability, we can unlock the full potential of machine learning in robotics and pave the way for the development of intelligent, autonomous, and socially responsible robotic systems.

ML Model Deployment in Robotics

The deployment of machine learning (ML) models in robotics represents a critical stage in the development and deployment of intelligent robotic systems. As robotic applications become increasingly complex and autonomous, the integration of ML models enables robots to perceive, learn, and adapt to their environments with greater flexibility and efficiency. In this section, we explore the various aspects of ML model deployment in robotics, encompassing model selection, training, validation, optimization, deployment strategies, and real-world considerations.

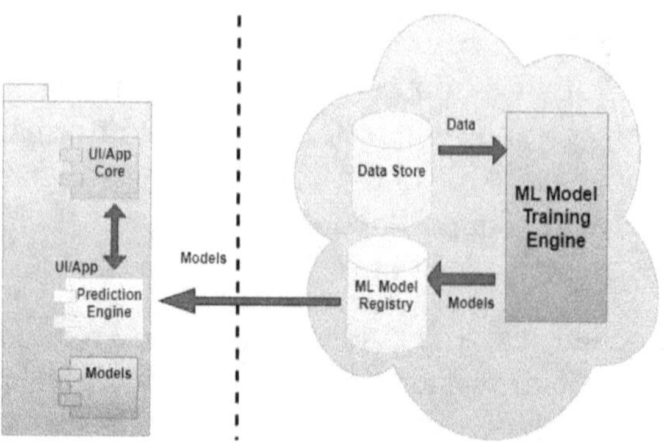

Figure 10. Model Deployment

Importance of Model Deployment

The model deployment marks the transition from the development and training phase to the operational deployment of ML models in real-world robotic systems. The effectiveness and performance of ML models depend not only on their accuracy and generalization capabilities but also on their seamless integration into the target robotic platform. Successful deployment ensures that ML-powered robotic systems can reliably perform their intended tasks in diverse environments and conditions, ranging from industrial settings to healthcare facilities and outdoor environments.

Model Selection and Training

The process of model deployment begins with the selection and training of appropriate ML models tailored to the specific requirements and constraints of the robotic application. Model selection involves choosing the most suitable algorithm and architecture based on factors such as the nature of the task, available data, computational resources, and performance metrics. Once selected, the chosen model is trained using labeled or unlabeled data, leveraging techniques such as supervised, unsupervised, or reinforcement learning to optimize model parameters and improve predictive performance.

Validation and Evaluation

Before deployment, ML models undergo rigorous validation and evaluation to assess their performance and generalization capabilities across different scenarios and datasets. Validation involves testing the trained models on independent datasets or through cross-validation techniques to ensure that they generalize well to unseen data and mitigate the risk of overfitting. Evaluation metrics such as accuracy, precision, recall, and F1 score are used to quantify the performance of ML models and identify areas for improvement.

Optimization and Fine-Tuning

Optimization plays a crucial role in enhancing the efficiency and effectiveness of ML models for deployment in robotic systems. Model optimization techniques aim to reduce computational complexity, memory footprint, and inference latency while maintaining or improving performance metrics. Techniques such as pruning, quantization, and model distillation are employed to optimize ML models for deployment on resource-constrained robotic platforms, such as embedded systems and mobile robots. Fine-tuning involves adjusting model hyperparameters and architecture to improve performance on specific tasks or domains, further enhancing the adaptability and robustness of ML-powered robotic systems.

Deployment Strategies

Deploying ML models in robotic systems requires careful consideration of deployment strategies to ensure seamless integration and operation in real-world environments. One common approach is on-device deployment, where ML models are deployed directly on the robotic hardware, enabling real-time inference and autonomous decision-making. Cloud-based deployment involves offloading computation to remote servers leveraging cloud resources for training, inference, and data storage. Hybrid deployment strategies combine on-device and cloud-based approaches, optimizing resource utilization and scalability while minimizing latency and communication overhead.

Real-World Considerations

Deploying ML models in robotics entails addressing various real-world considerations, including safety, reliability, interpretability, and ethical implications. Safety-critical robotic applications, such as autonomous vehicles and surgical robots, require stringent validation and testing procedures to ensure safe and reliable operation in dynamic and uncertain environments. Interpretability and explainability of ML models are essential for building trust and understanding their decisions, particularly in applications involving human-robot interaction or critical decision-making tasks.

Case Studies and Applications

Real-world case studies and applications demonstrate the practical implications and benefits of deploying ML models in robotics across various domains and industries. Examples include autonomous vehicles equipped with computer vision and reinforcement learning algorithms for navigation and decision-making, industrial robots using deep learning for defect detection and quality control in manufacturing, and assistive robots employing natural language processing for human-robot communication and task coordination.

Future Directions and Challenges

Looking ahead, the deployment of ML models in robotics presents exciting opportunities for innovation and advancement, as well as significant challenges to overcome. Future directions include research into decentralized and distributed learning approaches for collaborative robotic systems, advancements in edge computing and federated learning for on-device model deployment, and efforts to address ethical and regulatory considerations surrounding autonomous systems and AI-powered robotics.

The deployment of ML models in robotics represents a pivotal step toward realizing the full potential of intelligent and autonomous robotic systems. By leveraging the principles and techniques of machine learning, robotic applications can achieve greater adaptability, efficiency, and autonomy, transforming industries, enhancing human-robot interaction, and addressing societal challenges in a wide range of domains.

ML Ethics and Bias in Robotics

As machine learning (ML) becomes increasingly integrated into robotics systems, ethical considerations and concerns surrounding bias have come to the forefront. The intersection of ML and robotics raises complex ethical questions about the impact of autonomous systems on society, as well as the potential for bias and discrimination in decision-making processes. In this section, we explore the ethical challenges posed by ML in robotics, the implications of bias in robotic systems, and strategies for addressing these issues to ensure responsible and ethical deployment of autonomous technologies.

Ethical Considerations in ML for Robotics

Ethical considerations play a crucial role in the development and deployment of ML-based robotics systems. As autonomous systems gain autonomy and decision-making capabilities, questions arise about accountability, transparency, and fairness in their actions. Ethical principles such as beneficence, non-maleficence, autonomy, and justice guide the design and implementation of robotic systems to ensure that they align with societal values and norms. Additionally, ethical frameworks such as the IEEE Global Initiative for Ethical Considerations in Artificial Intelligence and Autonomous Systems provide guidelines for ethical decision-making and responsible innovation in robotics.

Bias in ML Algorithms

Bias in ML algorithms refers to the systematic errors or inaccuracies in decision-making processes that result from the data used to train the algorithms. Bias can arise from various sources, including biased training data, algorithmic biases, and societal biases embedded in the data collection process. In robotics, biased algorithms can lead to discriminatory outcomes, exacerbate existing inequalities, and undermine trust in autonomous systems. Common types of bias in ML algorithms include racial bias, gender bias, and socioeconomic bias, which can manifest in various aspects of robotic decision-making, such as object recognition, language processing, and risk assessment.

Implications of Bias in Robotics

The implications of bias in robotics extend beyond technical issues to ethical, social, and legal concerns. Biased robotic systems can perpetuate and amplify existing societal inequalities, leading to discriminatory outcomes and unjust treatment of individuals from marginalized groups. In domains such as healthcare, criminal justice, and employment, biased algorithms can have far-reaching consequences, affecting access to healthcare services, fair treatment under the law, and employment opportunities. Additionally, biased robotic systems can erode trust in autonomous technologies, hinder adoption, and exacerbate public skepticism and resistance to innovation.

Addressing Bias in Robotics

Addressing bias in robotics requires a multifaceted approach that involves stakeholders from diverse disciplines, including robotics researchers, ethicists, policymakers, and community members. Strategies for mitigating bias in robotic systems include:

Diverse and representative datasets: Ensuring that training data are diverse, inclusive, and representative of the population to minimize biases inherent in the data.

Algorithmic transparency: Making ML algorithms and decision-making processes transparent and interpretable to enable scrutiny and accountability.

Bias detection and mitigation techniques: Employing techniques such as bias auditing, fairness-aware learning, and debiasing algorithms to identify and mitigate biases in ML models.

Ethical by design: Integrating ethical considerations into the design and development of robotic systems from the outset to proactively address potential biases and ethical dilemmas.

Regulatory and Policy Implications

Regulatory frameworks and policies play a crucial role in governing the ethical and responsible use of ML in robotics. Governments and regulatory bodies are increasingly recognizing the need for regulations and guidelines to address ethical concerns and mitigate risks associated with biased autonomous systems. Initiatives such as the European Union's General Data Protection Regulation (GDPR) and the Algorithmic Accountability Act in the United States aim to enhance transparency, accountability, and fairness in algorithmic decision-making processes. Additionally, industry standards and codes of conduct provide guidelines for ethical behavior and responsible innovation in robotics and AI.

Ethical Decision-Making in Robotics

Ethical decision-making in robotics requires a collaborative and interdisciplinary approach that considers the perspectives and values of diverse stakeholders. Ethical frameworks such as the Principles for the Ethical Design and Implementation of Robotics and AI developed by the IEEE Robotics and Automation Society provide guiding principles for ethical decision-making in robotics. These principles emphasize the importance of human oversight, accountability, transparency, and societal impact assessment in the design, deployment, and use of robotic systems. By integrating ethical considerations into the design and development process, roboticists can ensure that autonomous systems uphold ethical standards and contribute to the well-being of individuals and communities.

In ML, ethics and bias in robotics are critical issues that require careful consideration and proactive measures to address. By recognizing the ethical implications of ML in robotics, acknowledging the existence of bias, and implementing strategies to mitigate biases and promote fairness, roboticists can ensure the responsible and ethical deployment of autonomous technologies. By fostering collaboration, transparency, and accountability, we can harness the power of ML and robotics to create a future where autonomous systems contribute to societal well-being and advance human values.

Future Trends in ML for Robotics

Machine learning (ML) has emerged as a transformative technology in robotics, enabling robots to perceive, reason, and act autonomously in complex and dynamic environments. As ML continues to evolve, new trends and advancements are shaping the future of robotics, unlocking unprecedented capabilities and possibilities for intelligent and adaptive robotic systems. In this section, we explore some of the key future trends in ML for robotics, encompassing advancements in algorithms, techniques, applications, and ethical considerations.

Continual Learning and Lifelong Adaptation

One of the most promising trends in ML for robotics is the advancement of continual learning techniques, enabling robots to acquire new knowledge and skills over time through interaction with their environment. Traditional ML approaches often rely on static datasets and offline training, limiting their ability to adapt to changing conditions and learn from new experiences. Continual learning algorithms address this limitation by allowing robots to incrementally update their models and adapt their behavior in real-time, enabling lifelong adaptation to new tasks, environments, and challenges.

Interpretable and Explainable AI

As robotic systems become increasingly autonomous and intelligent, the need for interpretable and explainable AI (XAI) becomes paramount. Interpretable AI techniques aim to provide insights into the decision-making process of ML models, allowing humans to understand and trust the behavior of robotic systems. Explainable AI methods enable robots to provide transparent explanations for their actions and decisions, enhancing transparency, accountability, and safety in human-robot interaction. Future advancements in interpretable and explainable AI will be critical for building trust and acceptance of autonomous robotic systems in society.

Human-Centered Machine Learning

Human-centered machine learning approaches focus on designing robotic systems that seamlessly integrate with human users, complementing and augmenting human capabilities. By considering human preferences, preferences, and cognitive processes, robots can adapt their behavior to better meet the needs and expectations of their human counterparts. Human-centered machine learning techniques enable robots to learn from human demonstrations, interpret natural language commands, and anticipate user intentions, fostering intuitive and collaborative human-robot interaction. Future advancements in human-centered machine learning will enable robots to serve as trusted and valuable partners in various domains, including healthcare, education, and entertainment.

Adaptive and Self-Improving Systems

Adaptive and self-improving systems represent a paradigm shift in robotics, where robots continuously monitor their performance, identify areas for improvement, and autonomously update their behavior and capabilities. These systems leverage advanced ML algorithms, such as reinforcement learning and meta-learning, to optimize their performance in real-time and adapt to changing conditions and requirements. Adaptive and self-improving robots can autonomously learn from their successes and failures, refine their strategies, and evolve their skills over time, leading to more resilient, efficient, and adaptive robotic systems.

Ethical Considerations and Responsible AI

As robotic systems become increasingly integrated into society, ethical considerations surrounding the use of ML in robotics become more prominent. Responsible AI frameworks and guidelines are essential for ensuring the ethical design, deployment, and use of robotic systems. Ethical considerations in ML for robotics include issues such as fairness, transparency, privacy, accountability, and bias mitigation. Future advancements in ML for robotics must prioritize ethical principles and values, fostering trust, inclusivity, and social acceptance of autonomous robotic systems.

The future of ML for robotics holds immense promise, with advancements in continual learning, interpretable AI, human-centered machine learning, adaptive systems, and ethical considerations shaping the evolution of robotic systems. By embracing these future trends and addressing associated challenges, we can unlock the full potential of ML-powered robotics to revolutionize various industries, enhance human productivity and quality of life, and address global challenges in areas such as healthcare, transportation, and environmental sustainability.

Chapter 5

Robot Manipulation and Grasping

Robotic Arm Kinematics and Dynamics

Robotic arms serve as the workhorses of many industrial and research applications, performing a wide range of tasks with precision and efficiency. Understanding the kinematics and dynamics of robotic arms is essential for designing, controlling, and optimizing their performance in various applications. In this section, we delve into the principles of robotic arm kinematics and dynamics, exploring their mathematical formulations, key concepts, and practical implications.

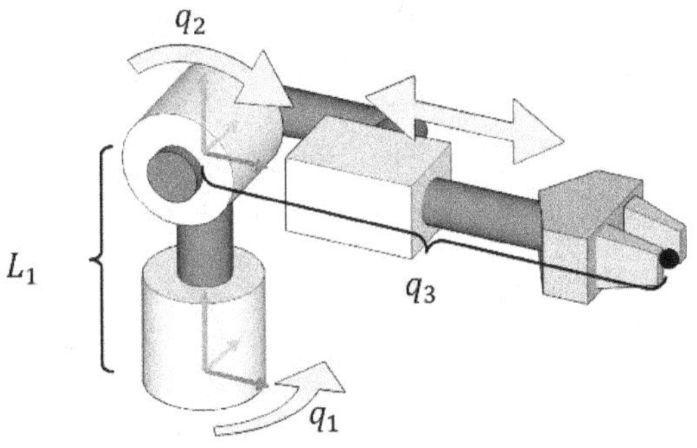

Figure 1. Robotic Arms

Kinematics of Robotic Arms

Kinematics deals with the study of motion without considering the forces that cause it. In the context of robotic arms, kinematics focuses on describing the relationship between the joint angles or positions and the position and orientation of the end-effector—the tool or payload attached to the arm. The kinematic analysis of robotic arms involves several key concepts:

Forward Kinematics: Forward kinematics refers to the process of determining the position and orientation of the end-effector based on the joint angles or positions. This involves propagating the transformations from the base to the end-effector through the robot's kinematic chain using the Denavit-Hartenberg parameters or transformation matrices.

Inverse Kinematics: Inverse kinematics involves solving the inverse relationship and determining the joint angles or positions required to achieve a desired end-effector pose. This is often a more challenging problem due to the nonlinearity and redundancy of robotic arm configurations.

Workspace Analysis: Workspace analysis involves determining the reachable space or volume that the end-effector can occupy within its operational range. This is crucial for assessing the capabilities and limitations of robotic arms in performing specific tasks.

Dynamics of Robotic Arms

Dynamics deals with the study of motion, considering the forces and torques that cause it. In the context of robotic arms, dynamics focuses on understanding the relationships between joint torques or forces and the resulting motion of the arm. The dynamic analysis of robotic arms involves several key concepts:

Newton-Euler Equations: Newton-Euler equations describe the relationships between the applied forces, torques, and resulting accelerations in a robotic arm. These equations are derived based on Newton's laws of motion and Euler's rotational equations.

Lagrange-Euler Equations: Lagrange-Euler equations provide an alternative formulation of robotic arm dynamics using the principle of virtual work. These equations are derived from Lagrange's equations of motion and Euler-Lagrange's equations, offering a concise and elegant representation of robotic arm dynamics.

Dynamic Modeling: Dynamic modeling involves deriving mathematical models that describe the behavior of robotic arms under the influence of external forces and torques. These models are essential for simulating and predicting the motion of robotic arms, as well as designing control algorithms to regulate their behavior.

Practical Implications

Understanding the kinematics and dynamics of robotic arms has significant practical implications for various applications:

Motion Planning: Kinematic and dynamic models are essential for motion planning algorithms that generate collision-free trajectories for robotic arms while optimizing performance metrics such as time, energy, and smoothness.

Control Design: Kinematic and dynamic models serve as the basis for designing control algorithms that regulate the motion of robotic arms to achieve desired end-effector trajectories while ensuring stability, accuracy, and robustness.

Task Execution: Kinematic and dynamic analysis enables the accurate execution of tasks such as pick-and-place operations, assembly tasks, and manipulation of objects in industrial automation, manufacturing, and research settings.

Optimization and Simulation: Kinematic and dynamic models facilitate optimization and simulation techniques to improve the performance and efficiency of robotic arm systems, enabling designers to explore different configurations, control strategies, and task scenarios.

Challenges and Future Directions

While significant progress has been made in the kinematic and dynamic analysis of robotic arms, several challenges and opportunities remain for future research:

Redundancy Resolution: Dealing with redundancy in robotic arm configurations remains a challenging problem in inverse kinematics, requiring advanced optimization and redundancy resolution techniques.

Dynamic Interaction: Modeling the dynamic interaction between robotic arms and their environment, including contact forces, friction, and compliance, presents opportunities for improving manipulation capabilities and adaptability.

Human-Robot Collaboration: Integrating robotic arms into collaborative environments with humans requires developing control strategies that ensure safety, efficiency, and intuitive interaction while considering human factors and preferences.

Soft Robotics and Compliant Manipulation: Exploring soft robotics and compliant manipulation techniques offers new possibilities for robotic arm design and control, enabling safer, more adaptable, and more human-friendly robotic systems.

The study of kinematics and dynamics plays a central role in understanding and optimizing the behavior of robotic arms for various applications. By leveraging mathematical models and computational techniques, researchers and engineers can design, control, and deploy robotic arms that exhibit precision, efficiency, and adaptability in performing complex manipulation tasks in diverse environments.

End Effector Design and Grippers

The end effector, also known as the robot's hand, is a crucial component of robotic systems responsible for interacting with the environment. End effectors come in various forms and designs, each tailored to specific tasks and applications. Grippers, a subset of end effectors, are particularly essential for manipulation tasks involving grasping, holding, and manipulating objects. In this section, we explore the principles, design considerations, types, and applications of end effectors and grippers in robotics.

Principles of End Effector Design

End effector design is driven by the task requirements, environmental constraints, and performance criteria of robotic systems. The primary function of an end effector is to securely grasp and manipulate objects while exerting minimal force and maintaining stability. Key design considerations include:

Figure 2. End Effector Design and Grippers

Mechanical Structure: End effectors must be structurally robust to withstand external forces and torques encountered during manipulation tasks.

Actuation Mechanisms: End effectors may be actuated using various mechanisms, such as pneumatic, hydraulic, electric, or a combination thereof, depending on the desired performance and application requirements.

Sensing Capabilities: Incorporating sensors, such as force/torque sensors and tactile sensors, enhances the end effector's ability to perceive and adapt to the environment, enabling more precise and reliable manipulation.

Adaptability: End effectors should be adaptable to a wide range of objects, shapes, and sizes, facilitating versatile manipulation capabilities across different tasks and environments.

Types of End Effectors and Grippers

End effectors and grippers come in a diverse range of designs, each suited to specific manipulation tasks and object characteristics. Common types of end effectors and grippers include:

Parallel-Jaw Grippers: Parallel-jaw grippers consist of two opposing jaws that move parallel to each other to grasp objects. They are versatile and widely used in various applications due to their simplicity and adaptability to different object shapes and sizes.

Finger Grippers: Finger grippers feature multiple fingers or digits that can articulate independently to conform to the shape of the object being grasped. They offer enhanced dexterity and flexibility, making them suitable for handling irregularly shaped objects and delicate items.

Suction Cups: Suction cups utilize vacuum pressure to adhere to smooth surfaces and lift objects. They are commonly used in applications involving flat, non-porous objects, such as glass panels, tiles, and electronic components.

Compliant Grippers: Compliant grippers incorporate compliant materials or mechanisms to adapt to the shape of the object and maintain a secure grasp without exerting excessive force. They are suitable for handling fragile objects or objects with irregular shapes.

Specialized Grippers: Specialized grippers are designed for specific applications, such as robotic surgery, food handling, and industrial automation. Examples include needle grippers for manipulating soft tissues, magnetic grippers for ferrous objects, and pneumatic grippers for high-speed assembly tasks.

Design Considerations for Grippers

When designing grippers, several factors must be taken into account to ensure optimal performance and efficiency:

Gripping Force: Grippers should exert sufficient force to securely hold the object without damaging it. The gripping force depends on factors such as the weight, shape, and surface properties of the object.

Friction and Surface Interaction: Optimizing the contact surface and friction properties of the gripper jaws enhances grip stability and prevents slippage during manipulation tasks.

Adaptability: Grippers should be capable of adjusting their grip configuration to accommodate objects of varying sizes, shapes, and orientations, maximizing versatility and efficiency in handling tasks.

Sensing and Feedback: Integrating sensors into the gripper enables real-time feedback on grip force, object position, and contact pressure, facilitating precise and adaptive manipulation.

Applications of End Effectors and Grippers

End effectors and grippers find applications across a wide range of industries and domains, including:

Manufacturing and Automation: End effectors are used in manufacturing and automation processes for tasks such as pick-and-place, assembly, packaging, and material handling.

Logistics and Warehousing: Grippers facilitate the sorting, palletizing, and transportation of goods in logistics and warehousing facilities, improving efficiency and throughput.

Healthcare and Biomedical: Specialized grippers are employed in surgical robotics for tasks such as tissue manipulation, suture placement, and instrument manipulation during minimally invasive procedures.

Agriculture and Food Processing: Grippers are utilized in agricultural robotics for tasks such as fruit harvesting, crop inspection, and sorting in food processing plants.

Challenges and Future Directions

Despite advancements in end effector and gripper design, several challenges remain to be addressed:

Versatility and Adaptability: Enhancing the adaptability of grippers to handle a wider range of object shapes, sizes, and materials remains a challenge, particularly in unstructured environments.

Sensing and Perception: Integrating advanced sensing and perception capabilities into grippers to provide real-time feedback and adaptive control poses technical and computational challenges.

Human-Robot Interaction: Designing grippers that can interact safely and intuitively with humans in collaborative settings requires advancements in safety mechanisms and human-centered design principles.

Ethical and Social Implications: Addressing ethical considerations surrounding the use of robotic grippers, such as privacy, safety, and job displacement, is essential to fostering trust and acceptance of robotic technologies in society.

End effectors and grippers play a crucial role in enabling robotic manipulation tasks across various industries and applications. By understanding the principles, design considerations, and challenges associated with end-effector and gripper design, robotics researchers and engineers can continue to innovate and develop solutions that enhance the versatility, efficiency, and safety of robotic manipulation systems.

Grasping Strategies and Algorithms

Grasping is a fundamental capability for robotic manipulation, enabling robots to interact with objects in their environment for various tasks such as picking, placing, and assembly. Grasping strategies and algorithms play a crucial role in determining how robots approach and manipulate objects to achieve successful grasps. In this section, we explore the principles, techniques, and advancements in grasping strategies and algorithms in robotics.

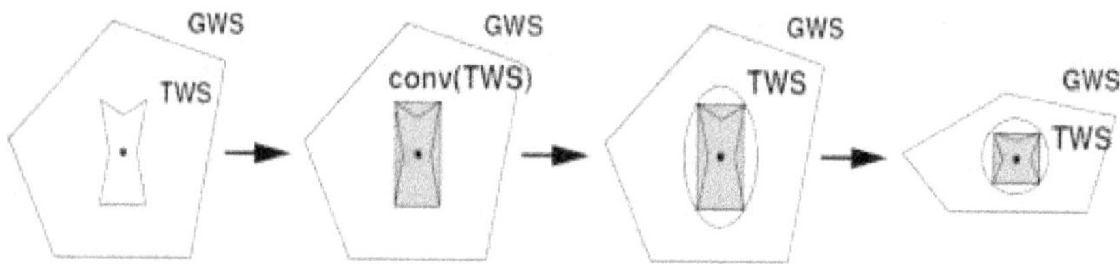

Figure 3. Grasping Strategies

Importance of Grasping Strategies

Grasping is a complex task that involves coordinating the motion of robotic manipulators to securely hold objects of different shapes, sizes, and properties. Effective grasping strategies are essential for enabling robots to manipulate objects with precision, reliability, and efficiency. By understanding the principles of grasping and developing robust algorithms, robots can perform a wide range of manipulation tasks in diverse environments, from industrial settings to household applications.

Types of Grasping Strategies

Grasping strategies can be categorized based on the approach used to interact with objects and achieve stable grasps. Some common types of grasping strategies include:

Power Grasping: In power grasping, the robot applies sufficient force to firmly grasp the object, ensuring stability and security. Power grasps are suitable for lifting heavy objects or handling objects with irregular shapes or uneven surfaces.

Precision Grasping: Precision grasping involves using precise movements to grasp small or delicate objects with finesse and accuracy. Precision grasps are commonly used in tasks requiring dexterity and manipulation of objects with intricate features or precise positioning requirements.

Pinch Grasping: Pinch grasping involves using two or more fingers or grippers to pinch and lift objects. Pinch grasps provide versatility and adaptability for grasping objects of various shapes and sizes, allowing robots to manipulate objects with different geometries and orientations.

Grasping Algorithms

Grasping algorithms determine the optimal approach for the robot to grasp objects based on factors such as object geometry, surface properties, and task requirements. These algorithms leverage mathematical models, sensor data, and machine learning techniques to analyze the object's characteristics and plan a grasp that maximizes stability and manipulability. Some common grasping algorithms include:

Analytical Grasp Synthesis: Analytical grasp synthesis algorithms use geometric and kinematic models of the robot and the object to compute stable grasp configurations. These algorithms analyze the object's shape, size, and surface features to identify suitable grasp points and finger positions for achieving a secure grasp.

Empirical Grasp Planning: Empirical grasp planning algorithms rely on pre-defined grasp templates or heuristics to generate grasps based on the object's properties and task requirements. These algorithms leverage experience and domain knowledge to select grasps that are likely to be successful in various scenarios.

Learning-Based Grasp Synthesis: Learning-based grasp synthesis techniques use machine learning algorithms, such as deep neural networks, to learn grasp patterns from data and experience. These algorithms analyze large datasets of grasp examples and learn to predict grasp configurations that are likely to succeed based on the object's visual appearance, geometry, and context.

Challenges and Considerations

Despite advancements in grasping strategies and algorithms, several challenges remain to be addressed to enable robots to grasp objects reliably in real-world scenarios. These challenges include:

Object Variability: Objects in the real world exhibit diverse shapes, sizes, and properties, making it challenging to develop grasping algorithms that generalize across different object categories.

Uncertainty and Occlusions: Uncertainty in object pose estimation and occlusions from cluttered environments can hinder the robot's ability to plan and execute successful grasps.

Real-Time Execution: Grasping algorithms must be efficient and capable of real-time execution to enable robots to react quickly to changes in the environment and grasp objects in dynamic settings.

Future Directions

Future research directions in grasping strategies and algorithms aim to address these challenges and further enhance the capabilities of robotic manipulation. Some potential areas for advancement include:

Soft Robotics: Soft robotic grippers and manipulators offer the potential for adaptive and compliant grasping, allowing robots to grasp objects of varying shapes and sizes with greater flexibility and adaptability.

Multi-Modal Sensing: Integration of multiple sensing modalities, such as vision, tactile, and force sensing, can provide robots with richer perceptual information for grasp planning and execution in complex and uncertain environments.

Learning from Demonstration: Learning from demonstration techniques enables robots to acquire grasping skills through imitation and interaction with human operators, facilitating faster adaptation to new tasks and environments.

Grasping strategies and algorithms are essential components of robotic manipulation, enabling robots to interact with objects in their environment effectively. By leveraging principles from robotics, mathematics, and machine learning, researchers continue to develop innovative approaches for grasping that enhance the capabilities and versatility of robotic systems. As we navigate the future of grasping in robotics, addressing challenges and embracing emerging technologies will be crucial for unlocking the full potential of robotic manipulation in diverse real-world applications.

Force and Tactile Sensing for Manipulation

In the realm of robotics, the ability to sense and interpret forces and tactile information is paramount for enabling robots to interact with their environment and manipulate objects with precision and dexterity. Force and tactile sensing technologies provide robots with the necessary feedback to grasp objects securely, monitor contact forces, detect slip events, and adapt their manipulation strategies in response to changes in the environment. In this section, we explore the principles, technologies, applications, and advancements in force and tactile sensing for manipulation tasks in robotics.

Principles of Force Sensing

Force sensing involves the measurement and interpretation of forces acting on a robotic manipulator during interaction with objects and surfaces. These forces can include contact forces exerted by the robot on the environment, reaction forces exerted by the environment on the robot, and external forces applied to the robot. Force sensing enables robots to detect object properties, assess grasp stability, regulate interaction forces, and ensure safe and effective manipulation. Key principles of force sensing include the use of force transducers, such as load cells and force/torque sensors, to measure forces and torques along different axes of the robotic manipulator.

Technologies for Force Sensing

Various technologies are employed for force sensing in robotics, each offering unique advantages and capabilities. Load cells are commonly used for measuring forces and torques in robotic manipulators, utilizing strain gauges or piezoelectric materials to convert mechanical deformation into electrical signals. Force/torque sensors, consisting of multiple load cells arranged in a specific configuration, provide multi-axis force and torque measurements for comprehensive force feedback. Other technologies, such as piezoresistive sensors, capacitive sensors, and optical sensors, offer alternatives for force sensing applications requiring high sensitivity, resolution, and bandwidth.

Applications of Force Sensing

Force sensing finds applications across a wide range of manipulation tasks in robotics, from industrial automation to healthcare and assistive technology. In industrial settings, force sensing enables robots to perform tasks such as assembly, machining, and material handling with precision and reliability. Force feedback in surgical robotics allows surgeons to perform delicate procedures with enhanced dexterity and tactile feedback, improving patient outcomes and reducing procedure times. In collaborative robotics, force sensing facilitates safe human-robot interaction by detecting and responding to external forces, ensuring the safety and well-being of human operators.

Principles of Tactile Sensing

Tactile sensing involves the measurement and interpretation of contact pressures and surface properties during interaction with objects and surfaces. Tactile sensors provide robots with tactile feedback akin to the sense of touch in humans, enabling them to perceive surface texture, shape, hardness, and temperature. Tactile sensing plays a crucial role in grasping and manipulation tasks by enabling robots to adapt their grip force, detect object slippage, and discriminate between different objects based on their tactile properties.

Technologies for Tactile Sensing

A variety of tactile sensing technologies are utilized in robotics, each offering unique advantages for specific applications. Resistive tactile sensors consist of a flexible material embedded with conductive elements, whose resistance changes in response to applied pressure, allowing for the measurement of contact pressures and distributed forces. Capacitive tactile sensors measure changes in capacitance caused by deformation of the sensor surface, providing high-resolution tactile feedback for object manipulation and surface characterization. Other tactile sensing technologies include piezoelectric sensors, piezoresistive sensors, and optical sensors, offering alternatives for applications requiring high sensitivity, spatial resolution, and durability.

Applications of Tactile Sensing

Tactile sensing enables robots to perform a variety of manipulation tasks with precision and adaptability. In grasping and manipulation, tactile sensors provide robots with feedback on grasp stability, object properties, and contact conditions, allowing for the adjustment of grip force and manipulation strategy to ensure successful task completion. In object recognition and characterization, tactile sensors enable robots to discriminate between objects based on their surface properties, such as texture, shape, and hardness, facilitating tasks such as object classification and sorting. In interactive tasks, such as human-robot collaboration and haptic interaction, tactile sensing enhances the robot's ability to perceive and respond to human touch, enabling natural and intuitive interaction in various domains.

Advancements and Future Directions

Advancements in force and tactile sensing technologies continue to drive innovation in robotics, enabling robots to perform increasingly complex manipulation tasks with precision and efficiency. Future directions in force and tactile sensing for manipulation include the development of integrated sensing solutions that combine force and tactile sensing modalities to provide comprehensive feedback for manipulation tasks. Additionally, advancements in materials science, sensor fabrication, and signal processing hold promise for enhancing the sensitivity, resolution, and robustness of force and tactile sensors, further expanding their applications in robotics. As robots continue to evolve and become increasingly integrated into our daily lives, force and tactile sensing will play a crucial role in enabling safe, efficient, and intuitive interaction between robots and the world around them.

Dexterous Manipulation Techniques

Dexterous manipulation refers to the ability of robotic systems to perform intricate and precise manipulation tasks that require fine motor skills, adaptability, and versatility. Unlike conventional manipulation, which often involves simple pick-and-place operations, dexterous manipulation techniques enable robots to manipulate objects with multiple degrees of freedom, apply varying levels of force and torque, and adapt their grasp to the shape, size, and properties of the object. In this section, we explore the principles, methods, challenges, and applications of dexterous manipulation techniques in robotics.

Principles of Dexterous Manipulation

At the core of dexterous manipulation lies the concept of multi-fingered manipulation, where robotic hands equipped with multiple fingers and joints mimic the capabilities of the human hand. Dexterous manipulation techniques leverage the dexterity and flexibility of robotic hands to achieve complex manipulation tasks, such as grasping, rotating, flipping, and reorienting objects in three-dimensional space. By controlling the motion and coordination of individual fingers and joints, robots can achieve a wide range of manipulation behaviors, from delicate object handling to robust grasping and manipulation in cluttered environments.

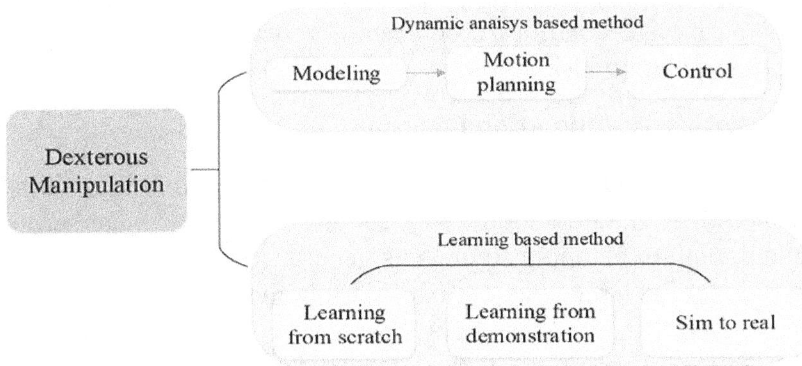

Figure 4. Dexterous Manipulation

Multi-Fingered Robotic Hands

The design of multi-fingered robotic hands plays a crucial role in enabling dexterous manipulation. Unlike traditional grippers with simple pincer-like structures, multi-fingered robotic hands feature multiple fingers with articulated joints, tactile sensors, and compliance mechanisms, allowing for greater flexibility, adaptability, and dexterity in grasping and manipulation. Key design considerations for multi-fingered robotic hands include finger morphology, actuation mechanisms, sensor integration, and control strategies. By mimicking the structure and function of the human hand, multi-fingered robotic hands enable robots to perform a wide range of manipulation tasks with precision and efficiency.

Grasping Strategies

Dexterous manipulation techniques encompass a variety of grasping strategies tailored to different object geometries, sizes, and properties. Power grasps involve gripping an object with maximum force to ensure stability and security, suitable for heavy or irregularly shaped objects. Precision grasps utilize precise fingertip control to grasp small or delicate objects with minimal force, ensuring gentle handling and manipulation. Pinch grasps involve gripping an object between two fingers or finger and thumb, providing a balance between stability and precision. Adaptive grasping techniques allow robots to adjust their grasp in real-time based on object shape, weight distribution, and environmental conditions, enhancing versatility and robustness in manipulation tasks.

Dexterous Manipulation Planning

Planning and control algorithms play a critical role in enabling dexterous manipulation in robotic systems. Dexterous manipulation planning algorithms generate optimal grasping and manipulation strategies by considering factors such as object geometry, finger kinematics, contact constraints, and task objectives. These algorithms leverage techniques from motion planning, optimization, and machine learning to generate trajectories for finger motion, optimize finger contact points, and ensure stable grasping and manipulation. Real-time adaptation and re-planning capabilities enable robots to respond to changes in the environment and adapt their manipulation strategies accordingly, enhancing flexibility and adaptability in dexterous manipulation tasks.

Sensing and Perception

Sensing and perception technologies are essential for enabling dexterous manipulation in robotic systems. Tactile sensors embedded in robotic hands provide feedback on contact forces, pressure distribution, and object properties, enabling robots to adjust their grasp and manipulation behavior in response to tactile feedback. Visual and depth sensors provide information about object pose, shape, and orientation, facilitating object detection, recognition, and pose estimation for grasping. By integrating sensing and perception with dexterous manipulation planning and control, robots can achieve robust and adaptive manipulation capabilities in complex and dynamic environments.

Challenges and Considerations

Despite the advancements in dexterous manipulation techniques, several challenges remain to be addressed to unlock the full potential of robotic systems in this domain. Challenges include the complexity of multi-fingered manipulation planning and control, the integration of sensing and perception for robust manipulation in cluttered environments, the development of scalable and affordable multi-fingered robotic hands, and the generalization of dexterous manipulation techniques to diverse objects and tasks. Addressing these challenges requires interdisciplinary collaboration, innovative research, and advances in areas such as robotics, artificial intelligence, materials science, and biomechanics.

Applications of Dexterous Manipulation

Dexterous manipulation techniques find applications across various industries and domains, including manufacturing, healthcare, agriculture, and space exploration. In manufacturing, robots equipped with dexterous manipulation capabilities can perform tasks such as assembly, quality inspection, and small parts handling with precision and efficiency. In healthcare, dexterous manipulation robots assist surgeons in minimally invasive procedures, enabling precise manipulation of surgical instruments and enhancing patient outcomes. In agriculture, robots equipped with dexterous manipulation capabilities can harvest crops, prune plants, and perform delicate tasks in greenhouse environments, improving efficiency and productivity in farming practices. In space exploration, dexterous manipulation robots enable the assembly, maintenance, and repair of space structures and equipment in microgravity environments, supporting long-duration space missions and exploration efforts.

Future Directions

The future of dexterous manipulation holds exciting possibilities for advancing the capabilities of robotic systems and enabling new applications and domains. Future directions in dexterous manipulation research include the development of more sophisticated multi-fingered robotic hands with enhanced dexterity, adaptability, and robustness. Advancements in sensing and perception technologies will enable robots to perceive and interact with the environment more effectively, enhancing manipulation capabilities in cluttered and unstructured environments. Machine learning and AI techniques will play a crucial role in enabling robots to learn from experience, adapt their manipulation strategies, and generalize to new tasks and objects. Ethical considerations surrounding the use of dexterous manipulation robots, such as safety, privacy, and accountability, will also be important areas of focus in future research and development efforts.

Dexterous manipulation techniques represent a significant advancement in robotics, enabling robots to perform intricate manipulation tasks with precision, adaptability, and versatility. By leveraging multi-fingered robotic hands, advanced planning and control algorithms, sensing and perception technologies, and interdisciplinary research approaches, we can unlock the full potential of dexterous manipulation in robotics and enable robots to tackle a wide range of real-world challenges and applications.

Motion Planning for Manipulation

Motion planning is a fundamental aspect of robotics, enabling robots to autonomously navigate and manipulate objects in complex and dynamic environments. In the context of manipulation, motion planning refers to the process of generating collision-free trajectories for the robot's end-effector to achieve desired manipulation tasks such as grasping, picking, placing, and assembly. This section explores the principles, techniques, challenges, and applications of motion planning for manipulation in robotics.

Fundamentals of Motion Planning

Motion planning for manipulation involves several key components, including perception, kinematics, dynamics, and task specifications. The first step in motion planning is perception, where the robot perceives the environment through sensors such as cameras, LIDAR, and depth sensors to identify objects and their positions. Kinematic models describe the relationship between the robot's joint angles and the position and orientation of its end-effector, while dynamic models account for the robot's physical constraints and dynamics. Task specifications define the desired manipulation tasks, such as grasping an object or moving it to a specific location.

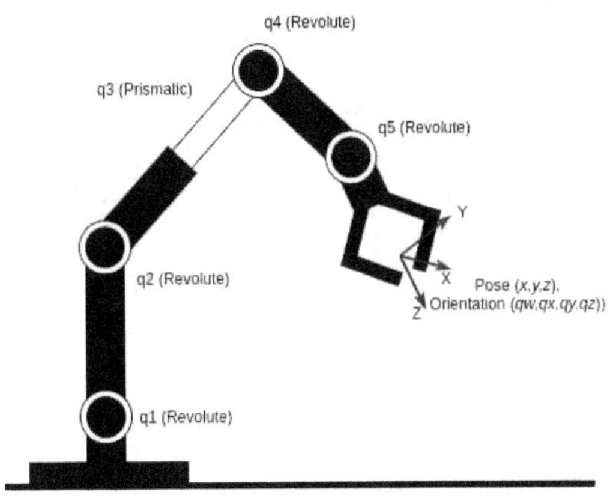

Figure 5. Motion Planning

Configuration Space and Collision Avoidance

One of the fundamental concepts in motion planning is configuration space (C-space), which represents all possible configurations of the robot's joints. In manipulation tasks, the C-space also includes the configuration of the manipulated objects. Motion planning algorithms operate in the C-space to generate collision-free trajectories for the robot's end-effector. Collision avoidance is a critical consideration in motion planning, as it ensures the safety of the robot and its surroundings. Techniques such as obstacle avoidance algorithms, potential fields, and probabilistic roadmap methods are used to navigate the robot through cluttered environments while avoiding collisions with obstacles.

Grasp and Manipulation Planning

Grasp and manipulation planning involves determining the optimal grasps and manipulation strategies to achieve a given manipulation task. Grasp planning algorithms generate candidate grasps for objects based on their geometry and physical properties, considering factors such as stability, reachability, and clearance. Manipulation planning algorithms generate motion trajectories that enable the robot to manipulate objects from their initial to desired configurations while avoiding collisions and optimizing performance metrics such as efficiency and stability. These algorithms often integrate perception, kinematics, and dynamics to generate robust and efficient manipulation plans.

Sampling-Based Motion Planning

Sampling-based motion planning algorithms are widely used in manipulation tasks due to their scalability, versatility, and effectiveness in high-dimensional configuration spaces. These algorithms, such as Rapidly-exploring Random Trees (RRT) and Probabilistic Roadmap Methods (PRMs), randomly sample the C-space and construct a graph representing the connectivity of the sampled configurations. They then search this graph to find feasible paths from the robot's initial to goal configurations, often employing heuristics to guide the search process efficiently. Sampling-based algorithms are well-suited for manipulation tasks with complex environments and high-dimensional state spaces.

Optimization-Based Motion Planning

Optimization-based motion planning approaches formulate manipulation planning as an optimization problem, where the goal is to find the trajectory that minimizes a cost function while satisfying constraints such as collision avoidance and task specifications. These algorithms use numerical optimization techniques such as gradient descent, nonlinear programming, or convex optimization to find the optimal trajectory that balances competing objectives such as path length, smoothness, and manipulation stability. Optimization-based approaches offer the advantage of explicitly modeling task constraints and objectives, allowing for more precise control over the generated trajectories.

Learning-Based Motion Planning

Learning-based motion planning methods leverage machine learning techniques to learn motion policies directly from data or experience. These methods include imitation learning, reinforcement learning, and learning from demonstration, where the robot learns to mimic human or expert demonstrations to perform manipulation tasks. Learning-based approaches offer the advantage of adaptability and generalization to diverse environments and tasks, but they require large amounts of training data and may suffer from issues such as overfitting and generalization errors.

Challenges and Future Directions

Despite significant advancements, motion planning for manipulation still faces several challenges that limit its effectiveness and applicability in real-world scenarios. Challenges include scalability to high-dimensional state spaces, robustness to uncertainty and dynamic environments, real-time computation and execution, and integration with learning-based approaches. Future directions in motion planning for manipulation include the development of hybrid approaches that combine sampling-based, optimization-based, and learning-based methods to leverage their respective strengths and mitigate their limitations. Additionally, advancements in sensor technology, computational algorithms, and artificial intelligence are expected to drive further progress in motion planning for manipulation, enabling robots to perform increasingly complex and versatile manipulation tasks in diverse real-world environments.

Applications and Case Studies

Motion planning for manipulation finds applications across various industries and domains, including manufacturing, logistics, healthcare, and service robotics. In manufacturing, motion planning enables robots to assemble products, handle materials, and perform intricate manipulation tasks with precision and efficiency. In logistics, robots use motion planning to navigate warehouses, pick and pack items, and load/unload cargo. In healthcare, surgical robots use motion planning to assist surgeons in minimally invasive procedures, while rehabilitation robots help patients regain motor skills through guided manipulation exercises. Case studies highlight the practical applications and successes of motion planning algorithms in real-world manipulation tasks, demonstrating their impact on enhancing productivity, safety, and quality of life.

Motion planning for manipulation is a critical component of robotic systems, enabling robots to navigate and interact with their environment autonomously. By leveraging principles from perception, kinematics, dynamics, and optimization, motion planning algorithms generate collision-free trajectories that enable robots to perform complex manipulation tasks with precision and efficiency. As robotics continues to advance, motion planning algorithms will play an increasingly important role in enabling robots to adapt and operate effectively in diverse real-world environments, unlocking new possibilities for automation, efficiency, and innovation.

Object Recognition for Grasping

Object recognition plays a critical role in robotic manipulation, enabling robots to identify and understand the objects in their environment and plan appropriate grasping strategies. In this section, we explore the importance of object recognition for grasping, the challenges involved, and the various techniques and algorithms employed in this task.

Importance of Object Recognition

Object recognition is essential for robotic manipulation tasks, as it allows robots to perceive and understand the objects they encounter in their environment. By accurately recognizing objects, robots can determine their properties, such as shape, size, orientation, and material composition, which are crucial for planning effective grasping strategies. Object recognition enables robots to distinguish between different objects, classify them into categories, and identify specific instances, facilitating tasks such as picking, placing, sorting, and assembly in diverse settings.

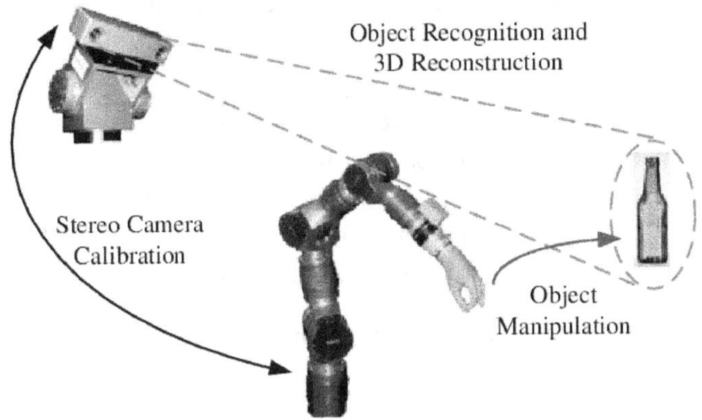

Figure 6. Object Recognition for Grasping

Challenges in Object Recognition

Despite the advancements in computer vision and machine learning, object recognition for grasping remains a challenging task due to several factors. One of the primary challenges is the variability and complexity of real-world objects, which exhibit diverse shapes, sizes, textures, and appearances. Objects may also undergo occlusions, partial visibility, and variations in lighting conditions, further complicating the recognition process. Additionally, the need for real-time performance and robustness to noise and uncertainties imposes additional constraints on object recognition algorithms.

Techniques for Object Recognition

A variety of techniques and algorithms have been developed for object recognition in robotic manipulation, ranging from traditional computer vision methods to advanced deep learning approaches. Classical computer vision techniques often rely on handcrafted features such as edges, corners, and textures, combined with methods such as template matching, feature extraction, and geometric matching. These methods are effective for simple objects and structured environments but may struggle with variability and complexity.

Deep learning has emerged as a powerful approach to object recognition, leveraging the representational power of neural networks to learn complex patterns and features directly from raw data. Convolutional Neural Networks (CNNs) have been particularly successful in image recognition tasks, enabling robots to learn discriminative features from large datasets and achieve state-of-the-art performance in object recognition. Transfer learning techniques allow models trained on large datasets such as ImageNet to be adapted to specific robotic manipulation tasks with limited labeled data.

Integration with Grasping Planning

Object recognition is closely integrated with grasping planning algorithms, as the ability to accurately perceive objects directly influences the choice of grasping strategies. Once objects are recognized, robots can generate grasp poses based on their geometric properties, such as surface normals, curvature, and grasp affordances. Grasping planning algorithms take into account factors such as object pose, robot kinematics, gripper capabilities, and task constraints to compute optimal grasp poses that maximize stability, manipulability, and success rates.

Sensor Modalities for Object Recognition

Object recognition can be performed using various sensor modalities, including cameras, depth sensors, and tactile sensors. Cameras are commonly used for visual object recognition, capturing images or videos of the scene, and extracting visual features for classification. Depth sensors, such as LiDAR or depth cameras, provide additional depth information, enabling robots to perceive object shapes and distances more accurately. Tactile sensors offer the ability to sense object properties such as texture, hardness, and compliance, complementing visual information for robust object recognition and grasping.

Applications and Case Studies

Object recognition for grasping finds applications in a wide range of domains, including industrial automation, logistics, healthcare, and service robotics. In industrial settings, robots use object recognition to identify and manipulate parts in assembly lines, improving efficiency and productivity. In logistics and warehouse automation, robots recognize and sort packages for order fulfillment and inventory management. In healthcare robotics, object recognition facilitates tasks such as surgical assistance, medication delivery, and patient monitoring. Real-world case studies demonstrate the effectiveness of object recognition techniques in enabling robotic manipulation tasks in diverse environments and scenarios.

Future Directions and Challenges

Despite the progress made in object recognition for grasping, several challenges remain to be addressed to further improve the performance and robustness of robotic manipulation systems. Future research directions include developing algorithms that are more robust to variations in object appearance and environmental conditions, enhancing the scalability and generalization capabilities of deep learning models, and integrating multi-modal sensor data for more comprehensive object perception. Additionally, addressing ethical considerations such as privacy, consent, and bias in object recognition algorithms is essential for ensuring the responsible and ethical deployment of robotic manipulation systems in real-world settings.

Object recognition is a fundamental task in robotic manipulation, enabling robots to perceive and understand the objects in their environment and plan appropriate grasping strategies. By accurately recognizing objects, robots can perform a wide range of manipulation tasks with precision and efficiency, contributing to advancements in various domains such as manufacturing, logistics, healthcare, and service robotics. Despite the challenges involved, ongoing research and innovation in object recognition techniques promise to further enhance the capabilities of robotic manipulation systems, enabling them to operate effectively in diverse and complex real-world environments.

Human-Robot Collaboration in Manipulation

The integration of robots into human environments has sparked significant interest in enabling seamless collaboration between humans and robots, particularly in manipulation tasks. Human-robot collaboration (HRC) in manipulation involves the joint efforts of humans and robots to perform tasks that leverage their complementary strengths, skills, and abilities. In this section, we explore the principles, challenges, techniques, and applications of human-robot collaboration in manipulation, highlighting the potential benefits and opportunities for advancing the field of robotics.

Principles of Human-Robot Collaboration

Human-robot collaboration in manipulation is grounded in the principles of shared autonomy, mutual understanding, and effective communication between humans and robots. Shared autonomy refers to the division of labor and decision-making responsibilities between humans and robots based on their respective capabilities and expertise. Mutual understanding involves the ability of humans and robots to interpret and anticipate each other's intentions, preferences, and actions, enabling smooth coordination and cooperation. Effective communication encompasses verbal and non-verbal interactions, such as gestures, gaze cues, and haptic feedback, to facilitate collaboration and convey information between humans and robots.

Collaboration Models

Several collaboration models have been proposed to characterize the interactions between humans and robots in manipulation tasks. These models range from hierarchical control architectures, where humans provide high-level instructions and supervisory control while robots execute low-level tasks autonomously, to peer-to-peer collaboration models, where humans and robots share decision-making authority and work together as equals. Hybrid collaboration models combine elements of both hierarchical and peer-to-peer collaboration, allowing for flexible adaptation to task requirements and human preferences.

Cooperative Manipulation Strategies

Cooperative manipulation strategies aim to leverage the unique capabilities of humans and robots to achieve shared goals efficiently and effectively. In cooperative manipulation, humans provide cognitive and perceptual capabilities, such as planning, decision-making, and task understanding, while robots contribute physical capabilities, such as strength, precision, and endurance. Task allocation and task sequencing algorithms are used to assign subtasks to humans and robots based on their expertise and availability, optimizing task performance and minimizing overall completion time.

Shared Autonomy and Assistance

Shared autonomy techniques enable humans and robots to collaborate in manipulation tasks by dynamically adjusting the level of autonomy and assistance provided by the robot based on the human's needs and preferences. Shared autonomy algorithms monitor the human's actions and intentions using sensors and perception systems, providing assistance, guidance, and feedback to support the human's actions and enhance task performance. Shared autonomy can range from passive assistance, where the robot observes and provides suggestions to the human, to active intervention, where the robot actively assists and intervenes to ensure task completion.

Human-Centered Design and Interaction

Human-centered design principles are essential for designing intuitive and user-friendly interfaces and interaction modalities that facilitate effective collaboration between humans and robots in manipulation tasks. User studies and iterative design processes are used to elicit user preferences, preferences, and feedback, informing the design of interfaces and interaction paradigms that accommodate diverse user needs and preferences. Interaction modalities such as gesture recognition, speech recognition, and augmented reality interfaces enable natural and intuitive communication between humans and robots, enhancing collaboration and user satisfaction.

Challenges and Considerations

Despite the potential benefits of human-robot collaboration in manipulation, several challenges and considerations must be addressed to realize its full potential. These challenges include ensuring safety and reliability in collaborative environments, addressing trust and acceptance issues among human users, adapting to diverse user preferences and skill levels, and integrating human and robot capabilities seamlessly. Ethical considerations surrounding privacy, autonomy, and accountability also need to be carefully considered to ensure that human-robot collaboration in manipulation respects human rights and values.

Applications and Case Studies

Human-robot collaboration in manipulation finds applications across various domains and industries, including manufacturing, healthcare, logistics, and entertainment. In manufacturing, collaborative robots (cobots) work alongside human workers to assemble, inspect, and package products, improving efficiency, flexibility, and ergonomics in production processes. In healthcare, robots assist healthcare professionals with tasks such as patient lifting, rehabilitation, and surgical assistance, enhancing patient care and reducing the risk of injury for healthcare workers. In logistics, collaborative robots automate order fulfillment, inventory management, and warehouse operations, enabling faster and more accurate processing of orders and shipments.

Future Directions

The future of human-robot collaboration in manipulation holds promise for advancing the capabilities and impact of robotic systems in various domains. Future directions in HRC in manipulation include the development of adaptive and context-aware collaboration algorithms, the integration of multi-modal interaction modalities for intuitive communication, and the exploration of novel collaboration paradigms such as human-swarm interaction and human-robot symbiosis. By addressing key challenges and embracing emerging technologies, human-robot collaboration in manipulation has the potential to revolutionize the way humans and robots work together, leading to safer, more efficient, and more productive collaborative environments.

Human-robot collaboration in manipulation represents a transformative approach to harnessing the strengths of humans and robots to accomplish complex tasks collaboratively. By embracing principles of shared autonomy, effective communication, and human-centered design, we can create collaborative robotic systems that enhance productivity, safety, and user satisfaction in various domains. As we continue to advance the field of human-robot collaboration in manipulation, it is essential to prioritize ethical considerations, user-centered design principles, and interdisciplinary collaboration, ensuring that collaborative robotic systems serve as trusted and valuable partners in human endeavors.

Industrial Applications of Robot Manipulation

Robot manipulation plays a pivotal role in revolutionizing industrial processes across various sectors, offering enhanced precision, efficiency, and flexibility in manufacturing and assembly tasks. In this section, we explore the diverse range of industrial applications of robot manipulation, highlighting its transformative impact on production processes, quality assurance, and overall operational efficiency.

Assembly Automation

Assembly automation is one of the primary applications of robot manipulation in the industrial sector. Robots equipped with specialized grippers and end-effectors are capable of assembling intricate components with precision and consistency, reducing the need for manual labor and minimizing production costs. From automotive assembly lines to electronics manufacturing facilities, robot manipulators play a crucial role in streamlining assembly processes, improving product quality, and accelerating time-to-market for new products.

Pick-and-Place Operations

Pick-and-place operations involve the repetitive task of picking objects from one location and placing them in another. Robot manipulators excel in performing pick-and-place tasks with speed and accuracy, making them indispensable in warehouse logistics, packaging, and material handling operations. By automating pick-and-place operations, industrial facilities can increase throughput, reduce labor costs, and optimize inventory management, thereby enhancing overall operational efficiency and customer satisfaction.

Material Handling and Logistics

Material handling and logistics represent another key area where robot manipulation finds widespread application in industrial settings. Robots equipped with advanced grippers and vision systems can efficiently handle a wide variety of materials, including raw materials, work-in-progress components, and finished products. Automated material handling systems enable seamless integration with conveyor belts, storage racks, and other infrastructure, facilitating smooth and efficient material flow throughout the production facility.

Quality Inspection and Testing

Robot manipulation is also instrumental in quality inspection and testing processes, where precise manipulation capabilities are essential for assessing product quality and detecting defects. Robots equipped with sensors and vision systems can perform detailed inspections of manufactured components, identifying defects such as surface imperfections, dimensional variations, and assembly errors. Automated quality inspection systems not only enhance product quality but also reduce the likelihood of defects reaching the end customer, thereby improving customer satisfaction and brand reputation.

Welding and Fabrication

In the field of metalworking and fabrication, robot manipulation plays a crucial role in performing welding, cutting, and other fabrication tasks with precision and repeatability. Industrial robots equipped with welding torches and specialized end-effectors can execute complex welding operations on metal components, achieving high-quality welds with minimal human intervention. Automated welding systems offer advantages such as improved weld consistency, reduced material waste, and enhanced worker safety in hazardous environments.

Collaborative Robotics

Collaborative robotics, or cobots, represent a growing trend in industrial automation, where robots work alongside human operators to perform tasks collaboratively. Robot manipulators equipped with advanced sensing and safety features can operate safely in close proximity to humans, enabling collaborative assembly, inspection, and material handling tasks. Cobots offer benefits such as increased flexibility, adaptability, and productivity while also addressing labor shortages and ergonomic concerns in industrial environments.

Customization and Flexibility

One of the key advantages of robot manipulation in industrial applications is its ability to adapt to changing production requirements and accommodate customization demands. Modern industrial robots are designed with flexibility and versatility in mind, allowing for quick reprogramming and reconfiguration to handle different tasks and product variants. This flexibility enables manufacturers to respond rapidly to market trends, customer preferences, and production fluctuations, thereby maintaining a competitive edge in today's dynamic business environment.

Integration with Industry 4.0 Technologies

Robot manipulation is increasingly integrated with Industry 4.0 technologies such as the Internet of Things (IoT), artificial intelligence (AI), and cloud computing to create interconnected and intelligent manufacturing systems. Robots equipped with sensors and IoT devices can collect real-time data on production metrics, quality parameters, and equipment health, enabling predictive maintenance and proactive decision-making. AI-powered algorithms analyze this data to optimize production processes, minimize downtime, and maximize overall equipment effectiveness (OEE).

The industrial applications of robot manipulation are vast and diverse, spanning various sectors such as automotive, aerospace, electronics, and consumer goods manufacturing. From assembly automation and pick-and-place operations to quality inspection and collaborative robotics, robot manipulators play a crucial role in enhancing productivity, quality, and efficiency in industrial processes. As technology continues to advance and new innovations emerge, the future of robot manipulation in industrial applications holds even greater potential for transforming manufacturing operations and driving economic growth and competitiveness on a global scale.

Challenges in Robot Manipulation

Robot manipulation, encompassing tasks such as grasping, picking, placing, and assembly, presents a multitude of challenges that must be overcome to achieve reliable and effective performance in real-world environments. Despite significant advancements in robotics technology, several key challenges persist, spanning areas such as perception, planning, control, and hardware design. In this section, we explore some of the most pressing challenges in robot manipulation and discuss potential strategies for addressing them.

Object Variability and Uncertainty

One of the primary challenges in robot manipulation is dealing with the inherent variability and uncertainty present in real-world objects and environments. Objects come in diverse shapes, sizes, and materials, making it challenging for robots to develop generalizable grasping and manipulation strategies. Furthermore, uncertainty in object pose, occlusions, and sensor noise further complicates the manipulation process, requiring robots to adapt and generalize their actions to novel scenarios. Overcoming these challenges requires robust perception algorithms capable of accurately detecting and estimating object properties, as well as planning and control strategies that can handle uncertainty and variability in object shape and pose.

Grasping Under Uncertainty

Grasping objects with precision and reliability remains a significant challenge in robot manipulation, particularly in unstructured and dynamic environments. Robots must determine optimal grasping points and configurations while accounting for factors such as object geometry, friction, and stability. Uncertainty in object pose and sensor measurements further complicates the grasping process, leading to failures and inefficiencies. Developing robust grasping algorithms that can adapt to uncertainty and variability in object properties is essential for enabling robots to manipulate objects effectively in real-world scenarios.

Perception-Action Integration

Effective robot manipulation relies on seamless integration between perception and action, enabling robots to perceive their environment and adapt their actions accordingly. However, achieving tight coupling between perception and action remains a significant challenge due to factors such as sensor noise, latency, and limited field of view. Furthermore, the complexity of perception algorithms and the computational burden of real-time processing pose additional challenges for integration with action planning and execution. Addressing these challenges requires developing efficient and scalable perception-action pipelines that can handle diverse sensory inputs and rapidly generate appropriate responses for manipulation tasks.

Dexterous Manipulation and Fine Motor Skills

Achieving dexterous manipulation and fine motor skills remains an elusive goal in robotics, with many manipulation tasks requiring delicate and precise interactions with objects. Traditional robotic grippers and end-effectors are often limited in their ability to grasp and manipulate objects with complex shapes or fragile structures. Furthermore, the lack of tactile feedback and the difficulty of modeling and controlling the dynamics of fine manipulation further complicate the task. Advancing the state-of-the-art in dexterous manipulation requires developing novel gripper designs, integrating tactile and force sensing capabilities, and leveraging advanced control algorithms to achieve precise and agile manipulation of objects.

Robustness to Environmental Variability

Robot manipulation tasks often take place in unstructured and dynamic environments, where robots must contend with factors such as clutter, obstacles, and changing conditions. Ensuring robustness to environmental variability is crucial for enabling robots to operate effectively in such environments. However, traditional manipulation algorithms may struggle to generalize across diverse scenarios or adapt to unexpected changes in the environment. Developing robust manipulation strategies that can handle environmental variability and uncertainty is essential for enabling robots to perform manipulation tasks reliably in real-world settings.

Human-Robot Collaboration

As robots increasingly interact with humans in shared environments, enabling seamless collaboration between humans and robots becomes a critical challenge. Human-robot collaboration requires robots to understand human intentions, preferences, and actions and to adapt their behavior accordingly. However, achieving effective collaboration between humans and robots involves addressing technical challenges such as motion planning, safety, and communication, as well as social and psychological factors such as trust, acceptance, and transparency. Developing collaborative manipulation techniques that prioritize safety, efficiency, and user experience is essential for fostering productive and harmonious interactions between humans and robots.

Ethical and Societal Implications

Robot manipulation raises significant ethical and societal implications that must be carefully considered. As robots increasingly take on roles traditionally performed by humans, concerns arise about job displacement, economic inequality, and the ethical implications of autonomous decision-making. Furthermore, issues such as privacy, security, and liability become more pronounced as robots interact more closely with humans in various domains. Addressing these ethical and societal challenges requires interdisciplinary collaboration and a holistic approach that considers the broader implications of robot manipulation on individuals, communities, and society as a whole.

Robot manipulation presents a diverse array of challenges spanning perception, planning, control, hardware design, and ethical considerations. Addressing these challenges requires interdisciplinary collaboration, innovative research, and a commitment to developing robust and adaptive manipulation techniques that can enable robots to operate effectively and responsibly in real-world environments. By tackling these challenges head-on, we can unlock the full potential of robot manipulation to revolutionize industries, enhance human productivity, and improve quality of life.

Soft Robotics for Manipulation

Soft robotics represents a transformative paradigm in robotics, offering novel solutions for manipulation tasks in diverse environments and applications. Unlike traditional rigid robots, soft robots are characterized by their compliance, adaptability, and deformability, allowing them to interact with objects and environments in ways that are more flexible and robust. In this section, we explore the principles, technologies, applications, and future prospects of soft robotics for manipulation tasks.

Principles of Soft Robotics

At the core of soft robotics lies the concept of compliance, which refers to the ability of robots to deform and conform to their surroundings. Unlike rigid robots, which rely on precise mechanical structures and actuators, soft robots employ soft materials such as elastomers, polymers, and gels to achieve flexibility and deformability. This compliance enables soft robots to interact with objects and environments with greater resilience, adaptability, and safety, making them well-suited for manipulation tasks in unstructured and dynamic environments.

Soft Actuation and Sensing Technologies

Soft robots rely on innovative actuation and sensing technologies to achieve their flexible and adaptive behavior. Pneumatic and hydraulic actuators, such as soft pneumatic actuators (SPAs) and fluidic elastomer actuators (FEAs), enable soft robots to generate motion and manipulate objects through the controlled inflation and deflation of flexible chambers. These actuators offer advantages such as lightweight, low-cost, and high compliance, making them ideal for applications requiring delicate manipulation and interaction with humans.

In addition to soft actuation, soft robots employ advanced sensing technologies to perceive and respond to their environment. Flexible sensors, such as capacitive, resistive, and optical sensors embedded within soft materials, enable soft robots to detect forces, deformations, and environmental cues. Tactile sensors provide feedback on contact forces and surface properties, allowing soft robots to grasp and manipulate objects with precision and dexterity. These sensing technologies enable soft robots to adapt their behavior in real-time, enhancing their autonomy and versatility in manipulation tasks.

Soft Gripping and Manipulation Strategies

Soft robots employ unique gripping and manipulation strategies enabled by their compliant and deformable nature. Unlike traditional rigid grippers, which rely on precise mechanisms and control algorithms, soft grippers conform to the shape of objects through passive or active deformation, enabling them to grasp objects of varying shapes, sizes, and materials. Examples of soft gripping mechanisms include suction cups, jamming-based grippers, and robotic tentacles, which exploit principles such as vacuum suction, granular jamming, and continuum bending to achieve versatile and robust grasping.

Soft robots also leverage innovative manipulation strategies, such as enveloping, rolling, and wrapping, to interact with objects and perform manipulation tasks. Enveloping involves wrapping around an object to secure it, while rolling enables the robot to move objects by deforming its body. Wrapping involves encircling an object with flexible appendages, such as tentacles or arms, to manipulate it with precision and control. These manipulation strategies enable soft robots to perform tasks such as object repositioning, packaging, and handling delicate objects with care.

Applications of Soft Robotics for Manipulation

Soft robotics finds applications across a wide range of domains, including manufacturing, healthcare, agriculture, and search and rescue. In manufacturing, soft robots are used for tasks such as picking, packing, and assembly in unstructured environments where traditional rigid robots struggle to operate. In healthcare, soft robots assist with tasks such as surgical manipulation, rehabilitation, and patient care, offering safe and gentle interaction with humans. In agriculture, soft robots are employed for tasks such as fruit harvesting, crop inspection, and handling fragile produce, improving efficiency and reducing damage.

Challenges and Future Directions

Despite the significant advancements in soft robotics for manipulation, several challenges remain to be addressed to unlock its full potential. These challenges include the development of robust and reliable soft actuators and sensors, the integration of soft robots with traditional rigid systems, and the scalability of soft robotic technologies for large-scale applications. Future directions in soft robotics for manipulation include the exploration of novel materials and fabrication techniques, the development of bio-inspired designs and control strategies, and the integration of soft robots with autonomous systems for collaborative manipulation tasks.

Soft robotics represents a promising avenue for advancing manipulation capabilities in robotics, offering flexibility, adaptability, and safety in interacting with objects and environments. By leveraging principles of compliance, innovative actuation and sensing technologies, and unique gripping and manipulation strategies, soft robots have the potential to revolutionize various industries and domains. As we continue to explore the possibilities of soft robotics for manipulation, it is essential to address challenges and foster interdisciplinary collaboration to realize the full potential of this transformative technology.

Bio-Inspired Manipulation Techniques

Nature has long been a source of inspiration for robotics, offering elegant solutions to complex problems through millions of years of evolution. Bio-inspired manipulation techniques draw upon principles observed in biological systems, such as animals and plants, to design robotic manipulators capable of performing tasks with efficiency, adaptability, and dexterity. In this section, we explore the principles, techniques, applications, and future directions of bio-inspired manipulation in robotics, highlighting the interdisciplinary synergy between biology, engineering, and computer science.

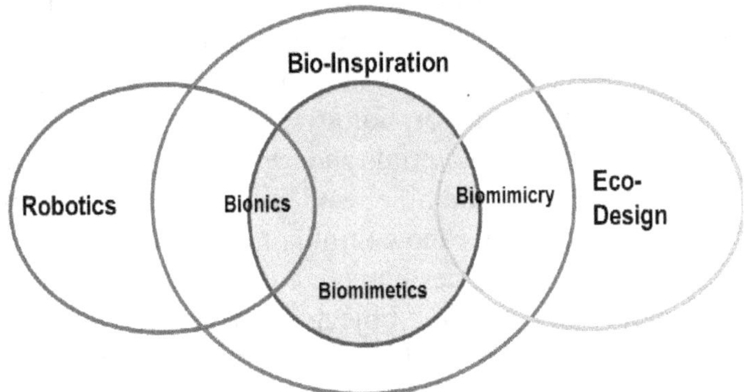

Figure 7. Bio-Inspired Manipulation

Principles of Biomimicry

Biomimicry is the practice of emulating biological systems to solve engineering challenges, and it serves as the foundation for bio-inspired manipulation techniques. Key principles of biomimicry include observing, understanding, and abstracting biological mechanisms and structures, such as locomotion, sensing, and manipulation, and applying these principles to the design and control of robotic systems. By mimicking the efficiency, versatility, and robustness of biological systems, bio-inspired robots can navigate diverse environments, interact with objects, and adapt to changing conditions with agility and grace.

Biomimetic Grippers and Hands

One of the most prominent areas of bio-inspired manipulation is the design of grippers and hands inspired by the dexterity and versatility of biological appendages. Biomimetic grippers draw inspiration from the diverse range of gripping mechanisms found in nature, such as the adhesive properties of gecko feet, the suction capabilities of octopus tentacles, and the compliant structures of human fingers. These grippers leverage innovative materials, actuation mechanisms, and control strategies to achieve robust and adaptive grasping of objects with various shapes, sizes, and surface properties.

Soft Robotics and Morphological Adaptation

Soft robotics represents a paradigm shift in robotic manipulation, drawing inspiration from the flexibility, compliance, and deformability of biological tissues. Soft robotic manipulators mimic the morphology and mechanics of biological organisms, employing materials such as silicone, elastomers, and hydrogels to create flexible and adaptable structures. By leveraging soft materials and compliant actuators, soft robots can conform to complex shapes, navigate constrained environments, and interact with delicate objects without causing damage. Furthermore, soft robots exhibit inherent safety and resilience, making them suitable for applications in human-robot interaction and healthcare.

Biologically Inspired Control Strategies

In addition to mimicking the physical characteristics of biological systems, bio-inspired manipulation techniques also draw inspiration from the control strategies employed by living organisms. Biological systems exhibit remarkable capabilities in sensing, feedback control, and adaptive behavior, which serve as models for designing robust and adaptive control algorithms for robotic manipulation. Inspired by the sensory-motor loops observed in animals, bio-inspired control strategies leverage sensor feedback to adaptively adjust manipulator motion and grasp force in response to changes in the environment, enabling robots to handle uncertainties and disturbances with agility and precision.

Applications and Case Studies

Bio-inspired manipulation techniques find applications across various domains, including industrial automation, healthcare, search and rescue, and exploration. In industrial automation, biomimetic grippers and hands enable robots to handle objects with irregular shapes and delicate surfaces, improving efficiency and flexibility in manufacturing processes. In healthcare, soft robotic manipulators offer safe and gentle interaction with patients, facilitating tasks such as rehabilitation therapy and surgical assistance. In search and rescue missions, bio-inspired robots equipped with compliant actuators and adaptive control strategies can navigate complex terrains and manipulate debris to locate and rescue survivors in disaster scenarios.

Challenges and Future Directions

While bio-inspired manipulation techniques hold great promise for advancing the capabilities of robotic systems, several challenges remain to be addressed to unlock their full potential. Challenges include the development of robust and scalable fabrication techniques for biomimetic structures, the integration of sensory feedback for adaptive control, and the understanding of complex biological systems to extract relevant design principles. Future directions in bio-inspired manipulation include the exploration of hybrid robotic systems combining bio-inspired and traditional robotic components, the development of bio-hybrid systems integrating living organisms with robotic platforms, and the advancement of autonomous adaptation and learning in bio-inspired robots.

Bio-inspired manipulation techniques offer a compelling approach to designing robotic systems with enhanced capabilities for interacting with the world. By drawing inspiration from nature's solutions to manipulation challenges, bio-inspired robots can achieve dexterity, adaptability, and versatility comparable to their biological counterparts. As we continue to explore the principles and possibilities of bio-inspired manipulation, we pave the way for a new era of robotics that transcends the boundaries between biology and technology, unlocking unprecedented opportunities for innovation and discovery.

Manipulation in Unstructured Environments

Robotic manipulation in unstructured environments presents a significant challenge, as robots must navigate and interact with dynamic and unpredictable surroundings. Unlike controlled industrial settings, unstructured environments such as homes, disaster sites, and outdoor spaces pose unique challenges for manipulation tasks due to variability in object shapes, sizes, and positions, as well as the presence of obstacles and occlusions. In this section, we explore the complexities of manipulation in unstructured environments, along with strategies, technologies, and advancements aimed at addressing these challenges.

Understanding Unstructured Environments

Unstructured environments lack the predictability and structure found in controlled settings, presenting robots with a myriad of uncertainties and obstacles. Homes, for example, contain a diverse array of objects, furniture, and clutter, making manipulation tasks challenging due to occlusions, varying lighting conditions, and complex spatial arrangements. Disaster sites, on the other hand, may be characterized by debris, rubble, and uneven terrain, requiring robots to navigate through hazardous environments while performing manipulation tasks such as debris clearing or search and rescue operations. Outdoor environments present additional challenges, such as varying weather conditions, natural obstacles, and dynamic terrain.

Challenges in Manipulation

Manipulation in unstructured environments poses several challenges that must be overcome to achieve successful task execution. One of the primary challenges is perception, as robots must accurately perceive and localize objects amidst clutter and occlusions. Object detection and pose estimation algorithms must be robust to variations in lighting, background clutter, and object appearance. Grasping presents another challenge, as robots must select appropriate grasps and adapt their grasping strategies to accommodate object variability and uncertainty. Planning and control algorithms must account for uncertainties in object pose, friction, and contact dynamics, ensuring stable and reliable manipulation in dynamic environments.

Strategies for Manipulation

Several strategies have been proposed to address the challenges of manipulation in unstructured environments. Perception-driven manipulation techniques leverage advanced sensing modalities, such as 3D cameras, depth sensors, and LIDAR, to capture detailed information about the environment and objects. Object recognition and pose estimation algorithms use this sensory data to identify objects and estimate their poses relative to the robot. Grasping strategies incorporate uncertainty-aware planning and adaptive grasping techniques to handle object variability and uncertainty. Reactive manipulation approaches enable robots to react dynamically to changes in the environment and adapt their manipulation strategies in real-time.

Technologies and Tools

Advancements in sensing, planning, and control technologies have enabled robots to perform manipulation tasks in unstructured environments with increasing autonomy and reliability. Robotic platforms equipped with multi-modal sensors, such as RGB-D cameras, tactile sensors, and force/torque sensors, provide rich sensory feedback for perception and manipulation tasks. Planning algorithms, such as probabilistic motion planning and trajectory optimization, enable robots to generate collision-free paths and trajectories in complex environments. Learning-based approaches, including deep reinforcement learning and imitation learning, allow robots to acquire manipulation skills through interaction with the environment and human demonstrations.

Applications and Case Studies

Manipulation in unstructured environments has numerous applications across various domains, including disaster response, environmental monitoring, construction, and agriculture. Robots equipped with manipulation capabilities can assist in disaster recovery efforts by clearing debris, locating survivors, and delivering supplies in hazardous environments. In agriculture, robots can perform tasks such as fruit harvesting, weed removal, and soil sampling, enhancing efficiency and reducing labor costs.

Construction robots equipped with manipulation capabilities can aid in tasks such as bricklaying, welding, and material handling, improving productivity and safety on construction sites.

Future Directions and Challenges

Despite advancements in manipulation technology, several challenges remain to be addressed to realize the full potential of manipulation in unstructured environments. Robust perception algorithms capable of handling occlusions, clutter, and object variability are needed to improve object detection and pose estimation in complex environments. Grasping and manipulation techniques must be further developed to handle uncertainty and adapt to dynamic changes in the environment. Integration of learning-based approaches with traditional planning and control methods holds promise for enabling robots to acquire manipulation skills autonomously through experience and interaction with the environment.

Manipulation in unstructured environments presents a complex and challenging problem for robotics, requiring robots to perceive, reason, and act autonomously in dynamic and unpredictable surroundings. By leveraging advancements in sensing, planning, and control technologies, robots can perform manipulation tasks in diverse environments with increasing autonomy and reliability. Future research directions in manipulation aim to address remaining challenges in perception, grasping, and adaptation, paving the way for robots to operate effectively in real-world scenarios and contribute to a wide range of applications in unstructured environments.

Manipulation Planning and Execution

Manipulation planning and execution are essential components of robotic systems, enabling robots to perform complex manipulation tasks with precision and efficiency. In this section, we delve into the intricacies of manipulation planning and execution, exploring the underlying principles, algorithms, challenges, and applications in the realm of robotics.

Manipulation planning encompasses the process of generating sequences of actions to achieve desired manipulation tasks, such as picking, placing, and assembling objects. It involves determining optimal trajectories for the robot's end-effector, taking into account factors such as obstacle avoidance, kinematic constraints, and task objectives. Manipulation planning plays a critical role in enabling robots to navigate complex environments, interact with objects, and execute tasks autonomously.

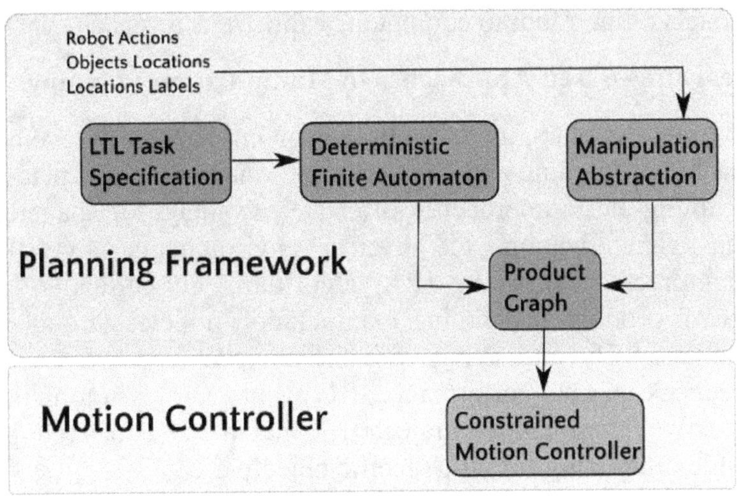

Figure 8. Manipulation Planning

Fundamentals of Manipulation Planning

At the core of manipulation planning lies the representation of the robot's configuration space and the task-specific constraints. Configuration space representation captures the feasible configurations of the robot's joints and end-effector, while task constraints specify the desired goals and constraints of the manipulation task, such as object poses, obstacle positions, and end-effector orientation. Manipulation planning algorithms leverage this representation to generate feasible trajectories that satisfy task requirements while optimizing criteria such as time, energy, and safety.

Planning Algorithms for Manipulation

Several planning algorithms have been developed to address manipulation planning challenges, ranging from classical approaches to modern techniques. Classical planning algorithms, such as motion planning algorithms like Rapidly-exploring Random Trees (RRT) and Probabilistic Roadmaps (PRM), focus on generating collision-free paths for the robot's end-effector in configuration space. These algorithms typically rely on geometric representations of the environment and kinematic models of the robot to compute feasible trajectories.

Learning-Based Approaches to Manipulation Planning

In recent years, there has been growing interest in leveraging machine learning techniques for manipulation planning. Learning-based approaches offer the advantage of adaptability and generalization to diverse environments and tasks. Reinforcement learning (RL) algorithms, in particular, have shown promise in learning manipulation policies through trial and error. By interacting with the environment and receiving feedback on task performance, RL agents can learn to generate effective manipulation trajectories that achieve desired goals while optimizing for task-specific objectives.

Integration of Perception and Planning

Perception plays a crucial role in manipulation planning, as robots must accurately perceive the environment and objects to plan effective manipulation strategies. Integration of perception and planning involves leveraging sensor data, such as camera images and depth information, to estimate object poses, identify obstacles, and localize the robot's end-effector relative to the objects of interest. Perception-aware planning algorithms utilize this information to generate manipulation trajectories that account for uncertainties in object poses and environmental conditions.

Challenges in Manipulation Planning and Execution

Despite advancements in manipulation planning algorithms, several challenges remain to be addressed. One of the primary challenges is the complexity of manipulation tasks in real-world environments, which often involve uncertainty, variability, and dynamic changes. Manipulation planning algorithms must be robust to uncertainties in perception, sensor noise, and environmental dynamics while also accounting for constraints such as kinematic limits and collision avoidance. Additionally, real-time computation and execution of manipulation trajectories pose challenges, particularly in dynamic and unstructured environments.

Applications of Manipulation Planning and Execution

Manipulation planning and execution find applications across various industries and domains, including manufacturing, logistics, healthcare, and service robotics. In manufacturing, robots are used for tasks such as assembly, welding, and machining, where manipulation planning is crucial for optimizing production processes and ensuring product quality. In logistics, robots are employed for order fulfillment, package sorting, and warehouse automation, relying on manipulation planning to handle diverse objects and navigate complex environments. In healthcare, surgical robots assist surgeons in performing minimally invasive procedures, where manipulation planning is essential for precise and safe manipulation of surgical instruments.

Future Directions in Manipulation Planning

Future advancements in manipulation planning are poised to address current challenges and unlock new capabilities for robotic systems. Research directions include the development of more robust and efficient planning algorithms that can handle uncertainties and dynamic environments effectively. Additionally, advancements in learning-based approaches, such as deep reinforcement learning and imitation learning, hold promise for enabling robots to acquire manipulation skills from demonstration and experience. Furthermore, the integration of manipulation planning with high-level reasoning and decision-making capabilities will enable robots to perform complex manipulation tasks in diverse and dynamic real-world environments.

Manipulation planning and execution are integral components of robotic systems, enabling robots to perform a wide range of manipulation tasks autonomously and effectively. By leveraging advanced planning algorithms, learning-based approaches, and integration with perception, robots can navigate complex environments, interact with objects, and execute tasks with precision and efficiency. As robotics continues to evolve, manipulation planning will play a central role in advancing the capabilities of robotic systems and enabling them to address real-world challenges across various industries and domains.

Future Trends in Robot Manipulation

Robot manipulation, encompassing grasping, picking, placing, and assembly tasks, is a fundamental capability that enables robots to interact with the physical world autonomously. As robotics continues to advance, new trends and innovations are shaping the future of robot manipulation, unlocking new possibilities for efficiency, adaptability, and autonomy. In this section, we explore some of the key future trends in robot manipulation, including advancements in technology, algorithms, applications, and ethical considerations.

Dexterous Manipulation and Fine Motor Skills

One of the most significant trends in robot manipulation is the pursuit of dexterous manipulation capabilities that enable robots to perform intricate tasks with precision and agility. Traditional robot grippers often rely on rigid mechanisms and simple grasping strategies, limiting their ability to handle delicate objects or perform fine-grained manipulation. Future advancements in dexterous manipulation will involve the development of soft, compliant, and multi-fingered grippers inspired by human hands, allowing robots to manipulate objects with greater dexterity and sensitivity. These capabilities will enable robots to perform tasks such as handling fragile objects, tying knots, or assembling intricate components with ease and precision.

Soft Robotics and Compliant Manipulation

Soft robotics represents a paradigm shift in robot manipulation, moving away from rigid structures and towards flexible, compliant materials that mimic the properties of natural organisms. Soft robotic manipulators offer several advantages, including enhanced safety, adaptability to unstructured environments, and the ability to interact with humans and delicate objects without causing harm. Future trends in soft robotics will focus on the development of novel materials, actuators, and control strategies that enable robots to deform, conform, and manipulate objects with soft and compliant surfaces. These advances will pave the way for applications such as surgical robotics, assistive technology, and human-robot collaboration in diverse settings.

Collaborative Manipulation in Human-Robot Teams

As robots increasingly coexist and collaborate with humans in shared workspaces, collaborative manipulation becomes essential for enabling effective teamwork and coordination between humans and robots. Collaborative manipulation involves the seamless integration of human and robot actions to achieve common goals, leveraging the complementary strengths of humans and robots in manipulation tasks. Future trends in collaborative manipulation will focus on developing intuitive interfaces and interaction modalities that facilitate seamless communication and coordination between human operators and robotic systems. These advancements will enable robots to assist humans in tasks such as manufacturing, healthcare, and disaster response, improving efficiency, safety, and overall productivity.

Learning-Based Approaches to Manipulation

Machine learning techniques have revolutionized robot manipulation by enabling robots to learn from data and experience rather than relying solely on pre-defined algorithms or models. Future trends in robot manipulation will involve the continued integration of learning-based approaches, including deep learning, reinforcement learning, and imitation learning, to enhance robot manipulation capabilities. Learning-based approaches enable robots to adapt to new environments, generalize across different tasks, and improve performance through iterative trial and error. These advancements will enable robots to acquire complex manipulation skills autonomously, leading to more versatile and adaptable robotic systems.

Multi-Modal Sensing and Perception

Effective manipulation requires robots to perceive and understand their environment through multi-modal sensing, encompassing visual, tactile, auditory, and proprioceptive feedback. Future trends in robot manipulation will involve the integration of advanced sensor technologies and perception algorithms to enable robots to acquire rich and contextual information about objects and their surroundings. Multi-modal sensing enables robots to grasp objects with varying shapes, sizes, and textures, detect surface properties, and adapt their manipulation strategies accordingly. These advancements will enhance the robustness, versatility, and adaptability of robot manipulation in diverse environments and applications.

Ethical Considerations and Human-Centric Design

As robotic manipulation becomes more prevalent in society, ethical considerations surrounding the design, deployment, and use of robotic systems become increasingly important. Future trends in robot manipulation will prioritize human-centric design principles, ensuring that robotic systems are designed to prioritize human safety, well-being, and autonomy. Ethical considerations in robot manipulation include issues such as transparency, accountability, privacy, and fairness in decision-making. These considerations will shape the development of robotic systems that enhance human capabilities, foster trust, and promote equitable access to technology for all individuals.

The future of robot manipulation holds immense promise, with advancements in dexterous manipulation, soft robotics, collaborative manipulation, learning-based approaches, multi-modal sensing, and ethical considerations shaping the evolution of robotic systems. By embracing these future trends and addressing associated challenges, we can unlock the full potential of robot manipulation to revolutionize various industries, enhance human productivity and quality of life, and address global challenges in areas such as healthcare, manufacturing, and environmental sustainability. As we navigate the future of robot manipulation, it is essential to prioritize ethical principles, human values, and societal well-being, ensuring that robotic systems serve as trusted and beneficial partners in the human quest for progress and innovation.

Chapter 6

Robot Learning and Adaptation

Learning from Demonstration (LfD)

Learning from Demonstration (LfD) is a prominent paradigm in robotics that enables robots to acquire new skills and behaviours by observing and imitating human demonstrations. By leveraging human expertise and experience, LfD allows robots to learn complex tasks without the need for explicit programming or manual intervention. In this section, we delve into the principles, techniques, applications, and challenges of Learning from Demonstration in robotics.

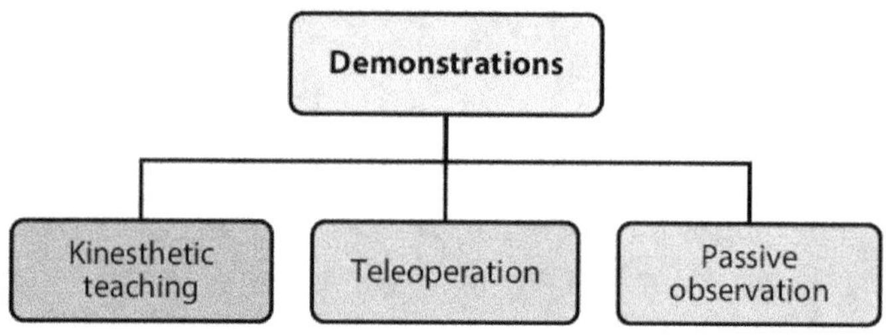

Figure 1. Learning from Demonstration

Principles of Learning from Demonstration

At its core, Learning from Demonstration is based on the idea of transferring knowledge from a human demonstrator to a robotic agent through observation and imitation. The key principles underlying LfD include:

Observation: The robot observes demonstrations performed by a human expert, capturing sensory information such as visual, auditory, and proprioceptive cues.

Imitation: The robot learns to mimic the demonstrated behavior by mapping observed sensory inputs to appropriate motor actions, such as joint trajectories or end-effector movements.

Generalization: The robot generalizes the learned behavior to new situations or variations of the task, enabling it to adapt to different environments or contexts.

Techniques for Learning from Demonstration

Learning from Demonstration encompasses a variety of techniques and algorithms, ranging from simple behavioral cloning to more sophisticated approaches such as Inverse Reinforcement Learning (IRL) and Apprenticeship Learning. Some commonly used techniques include:

Behavioral Cloning: In behavioral cloning, the robot learns a mapping from observed states to corresponding actions using supervised learning techniques. This approach directly imitates the demonstrated behavior without explicitly modeling the underlying dynamics of the task.

Inverse Reinforcement Learning (IRL): In IRL, the robot infers the underlying reward function or cost function from observed demonstrations, allowing it to learn the underlying principles or objectives of the task. By learning from the preferences demonstrated by the expert, the robot can generalize to new situations and make decisions autonomously.

Apprenticeship Learning: Apprenticeship Learning combines elements of both behavioral cloning and IRL, allowing the robot to learn from a mixture of expert demonstrations and environmental feedback. This approach enables the robot to adapt to changes in the task or environment while still benefiting from expert guidance.

Applications of Learning from Demonstration

Learning from Demonstration has been applied to a wide range of robotics tasks and domains, including:

Robot Manipulation: LfD is used to teach robots to perform manipulation tasks such as grasping, picking, placing, and assembly. By observing human demonstrations, robots can learn complex manipulation skills and adapt them to different objects and environments.

Autonomous Driving: In autonomous driving, LfD is employed to teach vehicles to navigate safely and efficiently in complex traffic scenarios. By observing human drivers, autonomous vehicles can learn to recognize and respond to various traffic situations, including lane following, merging, and obstacle avoidance.

Assistive Robotics: LfD is utilized in assistive robotics to help individuals with disabilities perform daily tasks more independently. By observing human movements, assistive robots can learn to assist with activities such as dressing, eating, and grooming, tailored to the specific needs of the user.

Human-Robot Collaboration: LfD facilitates collaboration between humans and robots in shared workspaces, enabling robots to learn from human expertise and adapt to collaborative tasks. By observing human workers, robots can learn to coordinate actions, anticipate intentions, and assist with tasks such as assembly, manufacturing, and logistics.

Challenges and Considerations

Despite its potential benefits, Learning from Demonstration presents several challenges and considerations:

Data Quality and Quantity: The quality and quantity of demonstration data can significantly impact the effectiveness of learning. Noisy or incomplete demonstrations may lead to poor performance or incorrect generalization by the robot.

Generalization and Adaptation: Ensuring that learned behaviors generalize to new situations or variations of the task is a non-trivial challenge. Robots must be able to adapt their learned behaviors to changes in the environment, object properties, or task requirements.

Safety and Reliability: Guaranteeing the safety and reliability of learned behaviors is essential, particularly in applications where robots interact closely with humans or operate in dynamic environments. Robustness to uncertainties and unforeseen circumstances is crucial for safe deployment.

Ethical Considerations: Ethical considerations such as privacy, consent, and fairness must be taken into account when deploying Learning from Demonstration systems, particularly in contexts where human data is involved. Ensuring transparency and accountability in robot decision-making is essential for building trust and acceptance.

Future Directions

The future of Learning from Demonstration in robotics holds several promising avenues for exploration and advancement:

Interactive Learning: Interactive learning approaches that enable bidirectional communication between the robot and the human demonstrator can enhance the efficiency and effectiveness of learning. Real-time feedback and correction mechanisms can improve the quality of learned behaviors and facilitate faster skill acquisition.

Multi-Modal Learning: Integrating multiple modalities of demonstration, such as visual, auditory, and haptic information, can enrich the learning process and improve the robot's understanding of the demonstrated task. Multi-modal learning enables robots to capture subtle cues and nuances in human demonstrations, leading to more robust and versatile learned behaviors.

Hierarchical Learning: Hierarchical learning frameworks that decompose complex tasks into simpler sub-tasks or primitives can facilitate learning and adaptation in multi-step manipulation tasks. By learning hierarchical representations of tasks, robots can acquire more structured and reusable knowledge, enabling efficient transfer to new tasks and environments.

Ethical and Responsible Learning: Ensuring that learning algorithms are ethically and responsibly deployed is paramount. Future research should focus on developing robust and transparent learning frameworks that prioritize safety, fairness, and accountability in robotic decision-making. Building trust and acceptance in Learning from Demonstration systems is essential for their widespread adoption and integration into society.

Learning from Demonstration is a powerful paradigm that enables robots to acquire new skills and behaviors through observation and imitation of human demonstrations. By leveraging human expertise and experience, robots can learn complex manipulation tasks and adapt them to different environments and contexts. Despite its challenges, Learning from Demonstration holds immense potential for revolutionizing robotics applications in areas such as manipulation, autonomous driving, assistive robotics, and human-robot collaboration. By addressing challenges and advancing research in key areas such as data quality, generalization, safety, and ethics, we can unlock the full potential of Learning from Demonstration to create intelligent, adaptive, and trustworthy robotic systems.

Imitation Learning and Apprenticeship Learning

Imitation learning and apprenticeship learning are two prominent techniques in the field of robot learning, enabling robots to acquire new skills and behaviors by observing and mimicking human demonstrations. These techniques leverage the wealth of knowledge and expertise possessed by human instructors to teach robots complex tasks and behaviors efficiently. In this section, we delve into the concepts, algorithms, applications, and challenges of imitation learning and apprenticeship learning in robotics.

Imitation learning, also known as learning from demonstration (LfD), is a learning paradigm in which robots learn to perform tasks by observing and imitating demonstrations provided by human instructors or expert agents. The goal of imitation learning is to enable robots to acquire new skills and behaviors without the need for explicit programming or task-specific algorithms. Instead, robots learn through trial and error, refining their actions based on feedback from observed demonstrations.

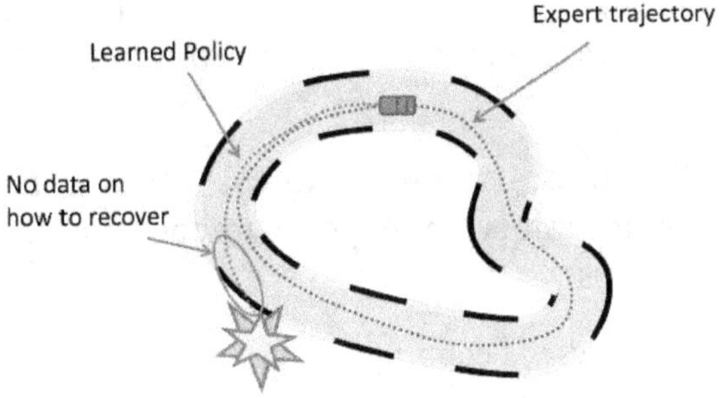

Figure 2. Imitation Learning

Approaches to Imitation Learning

a. Behavioral Cloning

Behavioral cloning is a straightforward approach to imitation learning, where the robot learns a mapping from observed states to corresponding actions by directly mimicking the behavior demonstrated by a human teacher. This approach typically involves training a supervised learning model, such as a neural network, to approximate the mapping between states and actions based on a dataset of observed demonstrations.

b. Inverse Reinforcement Learning (IRL)

Inverse reinforcement learning is an alternative approach to imitation learning that focuses on inferring the underlying reward function or policy that motivates the demonstrated behavior. In IRL, the robot learns to replicate the observed behavior by maximizing a reward signal that aligns with the demonstrated behavior. This approach allows robots to generalize beyond the specific demonstrations provided by learning the underlying principles or objectives of the task.

Applications of Imitation Learning

Imitation learning has a wide range of applications across various domains, including manufacturing, healthcare, service robotics, and autonomous vehicles. Some common applications of imitation learning include:

Industrial Robotics: Teaching robots to perform complex assembly tasks by observing demonstrations from human workers.

Surgical Robotics: Training surgical robots to replicate the movements and techniques of expert surgeons during minimally invasive procedures.

Service Robotics: Teaching service robots to assist with household chores, such as cleaning, cooking, and laundry, by imitating human behaviors.

Autonomous Vehicles: Training self-driving cars to navigate traffic and follow driving rules by observing the behavior of human drivers.

Apprenticeship learning, also known as learning from apprenticeship, extends the principles of imitation learning by allowing robots to learn from a combination of observed demonstrations and environmental feedback. In apprenticeship learning, the robot not only imitates the demonstrated behavior but also adapts its actions based on feedback from the environment, allowing for more flexible and adaptive learning.

Approaches to Apprenticeship Learning

a. Apprenticeship Imitation Learning

Apprenticeship imitation learning combines the principles of imitation learning with reinforcement learning techniques, enabling robots to learn from both observed demonstrations and environmental rewards. In this approach, the robot learns a policy that maximizes the expected cumulative reward, incorporating both the rewards obtained from executing demonstrated actions and the rewards obtained from exploring the environment.

b. Inverse Reinforcement Learning with Environment Interaction

Inverse reinforcement learning with environment interaction extends the principles of inverse reinforcement learning by incorporating feedback from the environment into the learning process. In this approach, the robot learns the underlying reward function by observing both the demonstrated behavior and the rewards obtained from interacting with the environment. This allows the robot to adapt its behavior based on the observed rewards, leading to more robust and adaptive learning.

Applications of Apprenticeship Learning

Apprenticeship learning has applications in domains where tasks involve a combination of demonstrated behavior and environmental feedback. Some common applications of apprenticeship learning include:

Robotics Manipulation: Training robots to manipulate objects in unstructured environments by combining observed demonstrations with feedback from tactile sensors or vision systems.

Human-Robot Collaboration: Teaching robots to collaborate with humans in shared workspaces by learning from human demonstrations and adapting their behavior based on environmental feedback.

Autonomous Systems: Training autonomous systems, such as drones or mobile robots, to navigate dynamic environments by imitating human pilots or drivers and adjusting their behavior based on environmental feedback.

Challenges and Considerations

While imitation learning and apprenticeship learning offer promising approaches to robot learning, they also present several challenges and considerations, including:

Generalization: Ensuring that learned behaviors generalize to new environments and variations of tasks.

Data Efficiency: Efficiently learning from limited or noisy demonstrations to avoid overfitting or poor performance.

Safety and Robustness: Ensuring that learned behaviors are safe and robust to uncertainties and variations in the environment.

Ethical Considerations: Addressing ethical concerns related to the potential biases or unintended consequences of learned behaviors, particularly in applications with human interaction or societal impact.

Imitation learning and apprenticeship learning are powerful techniques for enabling robots to acquire new skills and behaviors by observing and imitating human demonstrations. These techniques have applications across a wide range of domains, from industrial robotics to healthcare and autonomous systems. By addressing the challenges and considerations associated with imitation learning and apprenticeship learning, we can unlock the full potential of robot learning and pave the way for more autonomous, adaptive, and intelligent robotic systems.

Reinforcement Learning for Robotics

Reinforcement learning (RL) has emerged as a powerful paradigm for enabling autonomous decision-making and control in robotic systems. By learning from interaction with the environment, RL algorithms enable robots to adapt their behavior over time to achieve specified goals or maximize cumulative rewards. In this section, we explore the principles, techniques, applications, challenges, and future directions of reinforcement learning for robotics.

Principles of Reinforcement Learning

Reinforcement learning is based on the concept of learning through trial and error, where an agent interacts with an environment and learns to take actions that maximize cumulative rewards over time. The RL framework consists of an agent, which makes decisions, an environment with which the agent interacts, and a reward signal, which provides feedback to the agent based on its actions. The agent learns to map states of the environment to actions through exploration and exploitation strategies, aiming to maximize long-term rewards.

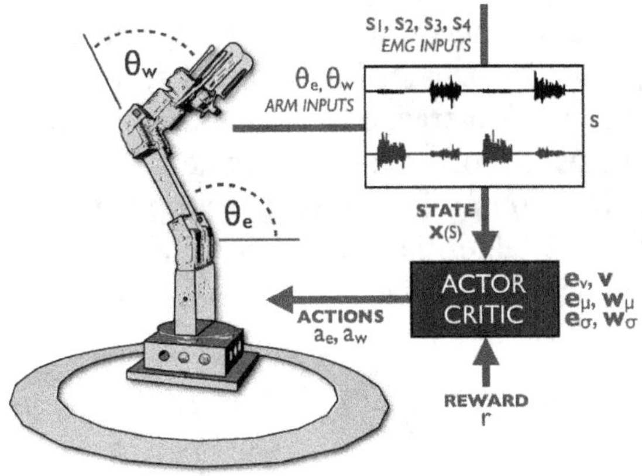

Figure 3. Reinforcement Learning

Markov Decision Processes (MDPs)

At the core of reinforcement learning lies the formalism of Markov decision processes (MDPs), which provide a mathematical framework for modeling sequential decision-making under uncertainty. An MDP consists of states, actions, transition probabilities, and rewards, where the agent's goal is to learn a policy, mapping states to actions, that maximizes the expected cumulative reward. RL algorithms, such as Q-learning, policy gradients, and actor-critic methods, leverage the MDP framework to learn optimal policies through experience.

Applications of Reinforcement Learning in Robotics

Reinforcement learning has found numerous applications in robotics, enabling robots to autonomously learn complex behaviors and tasks. In autonomous navigation, RL algorithms learn to navigate through environments while avoiding obstacles and reaching specified goals. In manipulation tasks, such as grasping and object manipulation, robots learn to adapt their actions to achieve desired outcomes. RL also plays a crucial role in robotic control tasks, such as balancing, trajectory tracking, and robotic arm control.

Challenges in Reinforcement Learning for Robotics

While reinforcement learning offers significant promise for robotics, it also poses several challenges that must be addressed for effective deployment in real-world scenarios. One challenge is the sample inefficiency of RL algorithms, which often require a large number of interactions with the environment to learn optimal policies. In robotic systems, where interactions may be costly or time-consuming, this poses practical challenges. Additionally, RL algorithms must be robust to environmental variability, uncertainty, and sensor noise to generalize well across different conditions.

Transfer Learning and Multi-Task Reinforcement Learning

To address the sample inefficiency of RL and improve generalization across tasks and environments, researchers have explored techniques such as transfer learning and multi-task reinforcement learning. Transfer learning enables robots to leverage knowledge from previously learned tasks or domains to accelerate learning in new tasks or environments. Multi-task reinforcement learning allows robots to learn multiple related tasks simultaneously, sharing knowledge and experiences across tasks to improve overall performance. These techniques enhance the scalability and efficiency of RL algorithms for robotics.

Simulation-Based Reinforcement Learning

Simulation-based reinforcement learning approaches leverage computer simulations of the environment to accelerate learning and exploration. By training RL agents in simulated environments, robots can acquire basic skills and behaviors before transferring them to the real world. Simulation-based RL also enables robots to explore dangerous or inaccessible environments safely. However, ensuring the fidelity and realism of simulations remains a challenge, as discrepancies between simulation and reality may lead to poor transferability of learned policies.

Ethical Considerations and Safety in Reinforcement Learning

As reinforcement learning becomes more prevalent in robotics, ethical considerations surrounding the safety and reliability of RL-based systems become increasingly important.

RL algorithms have the potential to learn suboptimal or unsafe policies, leading to unintended consequences or harm. Ensuring the safety of RL-based robotic systems requires robust validation, testing, and verification procedures, as well as mechanisms for human oversight and intervention. Ethical considerations also include issues such as fairness, accountability, and transparency in decision-making processes.

Future Directions and Trends

The future of reinforcement learning for robotics holds several promising directions for research and development. Advancements in deep reinforcement learning, meta-learning, and hierarchical reinforcement learning are expected to further improve the scalability, efficiency, and generalization capabilities of RL algorithms for robotics. Additionally, integrating RL with other learning paradigms, such as supervised learning and imitation learning, can enhance the versatility and adaptability of robotic systems. Future research will also focus on addressing ethical and safety concerns, as well as deploying RL-based robotic systems in real-world applications.

Reinforcement learning offers a powerful framework for enabling autonomous decision-making and control in robotic systems. By learning from interaction with the environment, RL algorithms enable robots to acquire complex behaviors and skills, adapt to changing conditions, and achieve specified goals. While challenges remain in terms of sample efficiency, robustness, and safety, ongoing research and advancements in reinforcement learning are expected to drive innovation and progress in robotics, paving the way for autonomous and intelligent robotic systems in diverse applications and domains.

Evolutionary Robotics

Evolutionary Robotics (ER) is a fascinating interdisciplinary field that draws inspiration from biological evolution to design and optimize robotic systems. By mimicking the principles of natural selection, ER harnesses the power of evolutionary algorithms to automatically generate and improve robot controllers and morphologies, enabling robots to adapt and evolve in complex and dynamic environments. In this section, we explore the principles, methods, applications, and future directions of Evolutionary Robotics.

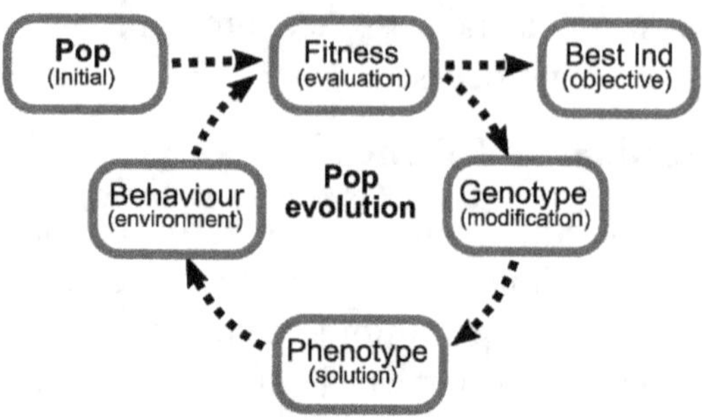

Figure 4. Evolutionary Robotics

Principles of Evolutionary Robotics

Evolutionary Robotics is grounded in the principles of evolutionary biology, particularly the process of natural selection, which acts on the variation present in populations of organisms to drive the emergence of traits that enhance survival and reproduction. In ER, robots are treated as artificial organisms, and their controllers or morphologies are subject to variation, selection, and reproduction through evolutionary algorithms. By simulating the process of evolution in silico, ER enables robots to evolve adaptive behaviors and structures that enable them to perform tasks in challenging and dynamic environments.

Evolutionary Algorithms in Robotics

Evolutionary Robotics employs a variety of evolutionary algorithms to search the space of possible robot controllers or morphologies and optimize them for specific tasks or objectives. Commonly used evolutionary algorithms include Genetic Algorithms (GA), Evolutionary Strategies (ES), Genetic Programming (GP), and Neuroevolution, each with its unique strengths and applications. These algorithms typically operate by maintaining a population of candidate solutions, evaluating their performance through simulation or physical experimentation, and iteratively evolving better solutions over successive generations through mechanisms such as selection, crossover, and mutation.

Methods in Evolutionary Robotics

Evolutionary Robotics encompasses a range of methods and techniques for evolving robot controllers and morphologies. In controller evolution, robots are equipped with artificial neural networks (ANNs) or other computational models that serve as their controllers, and evolutionary algorithms are used to optimize the synaptic weights or parameters of these networks to achieve desired behaviors. In morphology evolution, robots are endowed with physical bodies that can evolve in shape, size, and structure to improve their performance in specific tasks or environments. Hybrid approaches combine controller and morphology evolution to co-evolve both the control policies and physical attributes of robots.

Applications of Evolutionary Robotics

Evolutionary Robotics finds applications across various domains and industries, including but not limited to:

Robotic locomotion: evolving gaits and control strategies for legged or wheeled robots to navigate challenging terrains.

Robotic manipulation: evolving grasping and manipulation behaviors for robotic arms to handle objects of different shapes, sizes, and weights.

Swarm robotics: evolving collective behaviors and coordination strategies for groups of robots to accomplish tasks such as exploration, search and rescue, or construction.

Autonomous vehicles: evolving decision-making and navigation strategies for unmanned aerial vehicles (UAVs), autonomous cars, or underwater robots to navigate safely and efficiently in complex environments.

Challenges and Considerations in Evolutionary Robotics

Despite its promise and potential, Evolutionary Robotics faces several challenges and considerations, including:

Computational complexity: Evolutionary algorithms can be computationally expensive and time-consuming, especially for high-dimensional problems or complex environments.

Robustness and scalability: Evolved solutions may lack robustness or fail to generalize to unseen conditions, requiring additional validation and refinement.

Ethical implications: Evolutionary Robotics raises ethical considerations regarding the autonomy and responsibility of evolved systems, as well as potential societal impacts.

Future Directions in Evolutionary Robotics

The future of Evolutionary Robotics holds exciting possibilities and directions, including:

Multi-objective optimization: Evolving robot controllers or morphologies to optimize multiple conflicting objectives simultaneously, such as performance, energy efficiency, and robustness.

Interactive evolution: Involving human users in the evolutionary process to guide or shape the evolution of robot behaviors or designs according to their preferences or requirements.

Embodied evolution: Integrating physical robots into the evolutionary loop to enable real-time adaptation and learning in physical environments.

Evolutionary Robotics offers a powerful framework for designing and optimizing robotic systems through the principles of evolution. By leveraging evolutionary algorithms and techniques, ER enables robots to adapt and evolve autonomously, leading to the emergence of novel behaviors and structures that enhance their capabilities and versatility. As ER continues to evolve itself, it holds the potential to revolutionize robotics and unlock new frontiers in autonomous and adaptive robotic systems.

Bayesian Learning Methods

Bayesian learning methods form a powerful framework for modeling uncertainty and making probabilistic inferences in machine learning tasks. Originating from Bayesian statistics, these methods provide a principled approach to reasoning under uncertainty, enabling robust and flexible learning in diverse domains, including robotics. In this section, we delve into the principles, algorithms, applications, and advancements in Bayesian learning methods, highlighting their significance in the context of robot learning and adaptation.

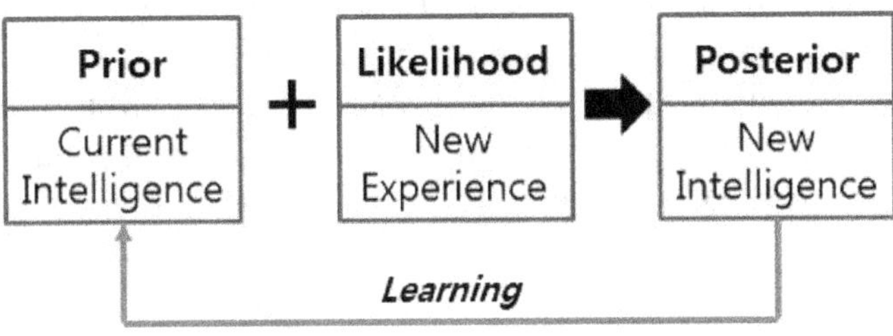

Figure 5. Bayesian Learning

Bayesian learning is rooted in the principles of Bayesian statistics, which views probability as a measure of belief or uncertainty rather than as a frequency of events. At the core of Bayesian learning is Bayes' theorem, which describes how prior beliefs are updated in light of new evidence to form posterior beliefs. In the context of machine learning, Bayesian learning methods provide a formal framework for representing and updating uncertainty about model parameters, enabling robust and principled decision-making in the face of incomplete or noisy data.

Bayesian Inference

Bayesian inference is the process of updating prior beliefs based on observed data to obtain posterior beliefs about model parameters. It involves computing the posterior distribution of parameters given the data and prior beliefs using Bayes' theorem. Unlike frequentist methods, which estimate point estimates of parameters, Bayesian inference provides a complete distribution over parameters, capturing uncertainty in the estimation process. Bayesian inference can be performed analytically for simple models or numerically using techniques such as Markov Chain Monte Carlo (MCMC) or Variational Inference (VI) for complex models.

Bayesian Modeling

Bayesian modeling involves specifying probabilistic models that capture the relationships between observed data and latent variables of interest. These models typically consist of likelihood functions that describe the probability of observing the data given the parameters and prior distributions that encode prior beliefs about the parameters. Bayesian modeling allows for the incorporation of prior knowledge, regularization of model parameters, and propagation of uncertainty throughout the learning process. Common Bayesian models include Bayesian linear regression, Bayesian neural networks, and Bayesian hierarchical models.

Bayesian Decision Theory

Bayesian decision theory extends Bayesian inference to decision-making tasks by integrating uncertainty and utility considerations into the decision-making process. It involves choosing actions that maximize expected utility under the posterior distribution of parameters. Bayesian decision theory provides a principled framework for making decisions under uncertainty, allowing robots to weigh the costs and benefits of different actions and adapt their behavior accordingly. Applications of Bayesian decision theory in robotics include sensor fusion, optimal control, and sequential decision-making in autonomous systems.

Bayesian Learning Algorithms

Bayesian learning algorithms encompass a variety of techniques for parameter estimation, model selection, and decision-making within the Bayesian framework. These algorithms include Bayesian linear regression, Bayesian logistic regression, Gaussian processes, Bayesian neural networks, and probabilistic graphical models such as Bayesian networks and Markov random fields. Bayesian learning algorithms offer several advantages, including principled handling of uncertainty, regularization of model complexity, and incorporation of prior knowledge. They are particularly well-suited for tasks with limited data or noisy observations.

Advancements in Bayesian Learning

Advancements in Bayesian learning methods have been driven by developments in probabilistic modeling, computational techniques, and applications in diverse domains. Recent trends include the development of scalable algorithms for Bayesian inference, such as variational inference and Monte Carlo methods, which enable efficient estimation of complex probabilistic models. Additionally, advancements in deep learning and probabilistic programming languages have facilitated the integration of Bayesian methods with deep neural networks, enabling uncertainty-aware deep learning models for tasks such as classification, regression, and reinforcement learning.

Applications in Robotics

Bayesian learning methods find numerous applications in robotics, where uncertainty and variability are inherent in perception, decision-making, and control tasks. In robot perception, Bayesian methods are used for sensor fusion, object recognition, and simultaneous localization and mapping (SLAM), enabling robots to robustly estimate their state and environment despite noisy sensor measurements. In robot control and decision-making, Bayesian reinforcement learning algorithms enable robots to learn optimal policies for navigation, manipulation, and task execution in uncertain and dynamic environments. Additionally, Bayesian decision-making frameworks enable robots to reason about uncertainty in human intentions, enabling safe and effective human-robot interaction.

Challenges and Future Directions

Despite their advantages, Bayesian learning methods face several challenges in practical applications, including computational scalability, model complexity, and the specification of appropriate prior distributions. Future research directions in Bayesian learning for robotics include the development of scalable algorithms for Bayesian inference, the integration of Bayesian methods with deep learning and reinforcement learning, and the exploration of uncertainty-aware decision-making strategies for autonomous systems. Additionally, addressing ethical and societal implications, such as fairness, transparency, and accountability, will be crucial for the responsible deployment of Bayesian learning-enabled robotic systems in real-world settings.

Bayesian learning methods provide a principled framework for modeling uncertainty and making probabilistic inferences in machine learning tasks. In robotics, Bayesian learning enables robots to reason under uncertainty, adapt to changing environments, and make informed decisions in complex and dynamic settings. By embracing Bayesian principles and algorithms, researchers and practitioners can develop more robust, adaptive, and intelligent robotic systems that enhance human productivity, safety, and quality of life.

Cognitive Robotics and Learning

Cognitive robotics represents an interdisciplinary field that merges principles from robotics, artificial intelligence, cognitive science, and neuroscience to create robots with advanced cognitive capabilities, such as perception, reasoning, learning, and adaptation. In this section, we delve into the intersection of cognitive robotics and learning, exploring how robots can acquire, process, and apply knowledge to perform complex tasks autonomously.

Understanding Cognitive Robotics

Cognitive robotics aims to imbue robots with cognitive abilities that enable them to perceive, reason, and act in a manner similar to humans. Unlike traditional robots that rely on predefined algorithms and instructions, cognitive robots leverage learning mechanisms to acquire knowledge from their environment and adapt their behavior based on new information. These robots employ sensorimotor processing, representation, reasoning, and learning to interact intelligently with their surroundings, making decisions in uncertain and dynamic environments.

Learning Paradigms in Cognitive Robotics

Learning plays a central role in cognitive robotics, enabling robots to acquire knowledge and skills through experience and interaction. Cognitive robots utilize various learning paradigms, including supervised learning, unsupervised learning, reinforcement learning, and learning from demonstration. Supervised learning involves training robots with labeled data to perform specific tasks, while unsupervised learning enables robots to discover patterns and structures in unlabeled data. Reinforcement learning allows robots to learn optimal behaviors through trial and error while learning from demonstration enables robots to imitate and generalize from human demonstrations.

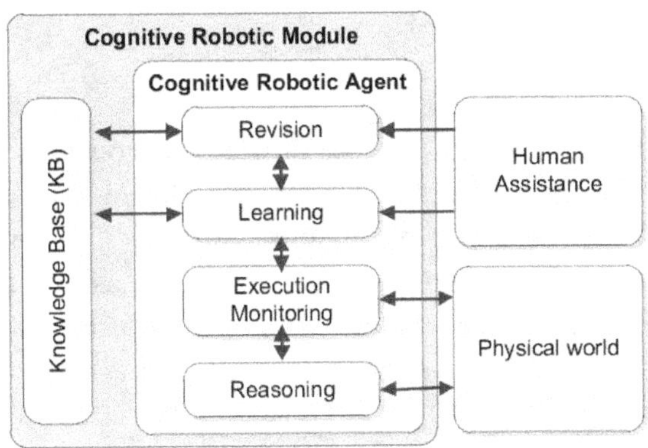

Figure 6. Cognitive Robotics

Perception and Sensing in Cognitive Robotics

Perception is a critical aspect of cognitive robotics, enabling robots to perceive and interpret their environment through sensor data. Cognitive robots employ advanced sensing technologies, such as cameras, LIDAR, radar, and tactile sensors, to capture information about objects, surfaces, and interactions. Machine learning techniques are then used to process and analyze this sensory data, enabling robots to recognize objects, infer their properties, and understand spatial relationships. Perception in cognitive robotics involves not only low-level sensory processing but also high-level cognitive reasoning and interpretation.

Reasoning and Decision-Making

Reasoning and decision-making are fundamental cognitive abilities that enable robots to make sense of their perceptions and take appropriate actions. Cognitive robots employ various reasoning mechanisms, including deductive reasoning, inductive reasoning, probabilistic reasoning, and symbolic reasoning, to infer knowledge, make predictions, and plan actions. Machine learning algorithms, such as Bayesian inference, probabilistic graphical models, and deep learning, are integrated into robotic systems to facilitate intelligent decision-making under uncertainty. These reasoning and decision-making capabilities enable cognitive robots to plan and execute complex tasks autonomously.

Learning and Adaptation

Learning and adaptation are continuous processes in cognitive robotics, allowing robots to acquire new knowledge, refine their skills, and adapt to changing environments. Cognitive robots employ lifelong learning techniques, such as online learning, transfer learning, and meta-learning, to incrementally update their models and behaviors over time. Reinforcement learning enables robots to learn from experience and optimize their actions based on feedback from the environment. Learning from demonstration allows robots to acquire new skills by observing and imitating human behavior. These learning and adaptation mechanisms enable cognitive robots to remain flexible, robust, and adaptive in dynamic and uncertain environments.

Cognitive Architectures

Cognitive architectures provide a framework for organizing and integrating the various cognitive capabilities of robots, including perception, reasoning, learning, and action. These architectures model the cognitive processes of the human brain and provide a hierarchical structure for representing and processing information. Common cognitive architectures used in cognitive robotics include Soar, ACT-R, CLARION, and OpenCog. These architectures enable robots to exhibit intelligent behavior by simulating human-like cognitive processes, such as perception-action loops, attentional control, memory retrieval, and decision-making.

Applications of Cognitive Robotics and Learning

Cognitive robotics and learning have diverse applications across various domains, including healthcare, manufacturing, agriculture, transportation, and service robotics. In healthcare, cognitive robots assist with tasks such as patient monitoring, rehabilitation, and assistance for the elderly. In manufacturing, cognitive robots optimize production processes, perform quality inspection, and adapt to changing production environments. In agriculture, cognitive robots aid in crop monitoring, pest control, and harvesting operations. In transportation, cognitive robots enable autonomous vehicles to navigate safely and efficiently in complex urban environments. In service robotics, cognitive robots provide assistance in tasks such as household chores, customer service, and entertainment.

Challenges and Future Directions

Despite the advancements in cognitive robotics and learning, several challenges remain to be addressed to realize the full potential of cognitive robots. These challenges include the scalability of cognitive architectures, robustness of perception and reasoning algorithms, interpretability of learned models, integration of multi-modal sensing, and ethical considerations surrounding autonomous and intelligent systems. Future directions in cognitive robotics and learning involve the development of more efficient and scalable cognitive architectures, the integration of symbolic and subsymbolic reasoning, the enhancement of human-robot interaction capabilities, and the exploration of ethical and societal implications of cognitive robotics.

Cognitive robotics and learning represent a convergence of robotics, artificial intelligence, and cognitive science, enabling robots to exhibit intelligent behavior through perception, reasoning, learning, and adaptation. By leveraging machine learning techniques and cognitive architectures, cognitive robots acquire knowledge, make decisions, and interact with their environment in a manner that resembles human cognition. The future of cognitive robotics holds immense promise for revolutionizing various industries, enhancing human-robot collaboration, and addressing global challenges. As we continue to advance the field of cognitive robotics and learning, it is essential to prioritize ethical principles, transparency, and human values to ensure the responsible and beneficial deployment of cognitive robotic systems.

Online Learning in Robotics

Online learning, also known as incremental learning or lifelong learning, is a dynamic learning paradigm that enables robots to continuously update their knowledge and adapt their behavior based on new data and experiences. In the context of robotics, online learning plays a crucial role in enabling robots to operate effectively in dynamic and uncertain environments where the conditions may change over time. In this section, we explore the concept of online learning in robotics, including its principles, techniques, applications, challenges, and future directions.

Principles of Online Learning

At its core, online learning involves the incremental acquisition of knowledge and skills by a robot through exposure to new data and feedback. Unlike batch learning, where models are trained offline on static datasets, online learning algorithms update models continuously as new data becomes available. This real-time adaptation enables robots to respond dynamically to changes in their environment, refine their behavior based on feedback, and improve their performance over time. Key principles of online learning in robotics include adaptability, efficiency, and scalability, enabling robots to learn and evolve in real-world settings.

Techniques for Online Learning

Online learning encompasses a variety of techniques and algorithms that enable robots to update their models and adapt their behavior in response to new data. One common approach is online batch learning, where models are periodically updated using batches of new data collected over time. Another approach is online incremental learning, where models are updated continuously as new data arrives, allowing robots to adapt rapidly to changes in their environment. Techniques such as stochastic gradient descent, recursive least squares, and ensemble methods are commonly used in online learning to update models efficiently and incrementally.

Applications of Online Learning in Robotics

Online learning has a wide range of applications in robotics, enabling robots to adapt and improve their performance across various tasks and domains. In autonomous navigation, online learning algorithms enable robots to continuously update their maps and navigation policies based on new sensor data, allowing them to navigate effectively in dynamic environments. In manipulation tasks, online learning techniques enable robots to refine their grasping and manipulation strategies based on feedback from tactile sensors or human demonstrations, improving their dexterity and reliability over time. Other applications of online learning in robotics include object recognition, task planning, and human-robot interaction.

Challenges in Online Learning for Robotics

While online learning offers numerous benefits for robotic systems, it also poses several challenges and considerations that must be addressed to enable effective deployment in real-world settings. One challenge is the trade-off between exploration and exploitation, where robots must balance the need to explore new behaviors with the desire to exploit known strategies that have proven successful in the past. Another challenge is the management of memory and computational resources, as robots must efficiently store and update models while operating in resource-constrained environments. Additionally, safety and ethical considerations must be taken into account when deploying online learning algorithms in robotic systems to ensure that robots behave responsibly and ethically as they learn and adapt.

Future Directions in Online Learning for Robotics

Looking ahead, several promising directions and research areas are emerging in the field of online learning for robotics. One direction is the development of more efficient and scalable online learning algorithms that can handle large-scale, high-dimensional data streams in real-time. Another direction is the integration of online learning with other learning paradigms, such as reinforcement learning and imitation learning, to enable robots to acquire complex skills and behaviors autonomously. Additionally, advances in sensor technology, such as the proliferation of Internet-of-Things (IoT) devices and wearable sensors, are creating new opportunities for online learning in robotics by providing robots with access to rich and diverse sources of data about their environment and interactions.

Online learning holds great promise for advancing the capabilities of robotic systems, enabling them to adapt and learn in real-time as they interact with their environment. By continuously updating their models and behaviors based on new data and experiences, robots can improve their performance, reliability, and autonomy across a wide range of tasks and domains. While challenges remain, ongoing research and development efforts in online learning for robotics are paving the way for a future where robots are truly adaptive, intelligent, and capable partners in human endeavors.

Active Learning for Robots

Active learning is a subfield of machine learning that focuses on the efficient selection of informative data points for labeling or annotation. By actively querying the most relevant instances for labeling, active learning algorithms aim to minimize the amount of labeled data required to achieve a satisfactory model performance. In the context of robotics, active learning plays a crucial role in enabling robots to learn effectively from limited human feedback and adapt their behavior autonomously in dynamic and uncertain environments. In this section, we explore the principles, methods, applications, and challenges of active learning for robots.

Principles of Active Learning

At the core of active learning lies the principle of uncertainty sampling, which involves selecting data points for labeling based on their uncertainty or informativeness. Common uncertainty measures include entropy, margin, and uncertainty estimates from probabilistic models. By prioritizing uncertain or ambiguous instances for labeling, active learning algorithms aim to reduce the model's uncertainty and improve its performance with minimal human intervention. Other principles of active learning include query synthesis, query by committee, and expected model change, each offering unique strategies for selecting informative data points.

Methods and Techniques

Various active learning strategies have been developed to facilitate efficient data selection for robotic learning tasks. Uncertainty-based methods, such as uncertainty sampling and query by committee, prioritize data points with high uncertainty or disagreement among model predictions. Diversity-based methods aim to select instances that cover a diverse range of feature space or represent different clusters within the data distribution. Expected error reduction methods estimate the potential reduction in model error by labeling specific instances, guiding the selection process towards regions of high prediction error. Hybrid methods combine multiple criteria to balance exploration and exploitation, leveraging the strengths of different active learning strategies in diverse learning scenarios.

Applications in Robotics

Active learning finds applications in various robotic domains, including perception, control, manipulation, and navigation. In perception tasks, such as object recognition and semantic segmentation, active learning enables robots to select informative images or regions for annotation, improving model performance with minimal human labeling effort. In control and manipulation tasks, active learning facilitates the acquisition of task-specific knowledge and adaptation to changing environments, enabling robots to refine their policies and strategies through interactive learning. In navigation and exploration tasks, active learning guides robots to explore unknown regions or select informative trajectories for mapping and localization, optimizing resource allocation and exploration efficiency.

Challenges and Considerations

Despite its potential benefits, active learning for robots faces several challenges and considerations. One key challenge is the design of informative query strategies that balance exploration and exploitation, effectively selecting data points that contribute to both model improvement and task performance. Another challenge is the integration of active learning with real-time robotic systems, where computational efficiency and scalability are critical for practical deployment in dynamic environments. Ethical considerations also arise in active learning for robotics, particularly concerning human oversight, accountability, and transparency in the decision-making process. Addressing these challenges requires interdisciplinary collaboration between robotics, machine learning, and ethics, ensuring that active learning algorithms are robust, reliable, and aligned with societal values and norms.

Future Directions and Opportunities

Future research directions in active learning for robots span a wide range of topics, including algorithmic advancements, application-specific developments, and ethical considerations. Algorithmic advancements may focus on developing more efficient and scalable active learning strategies that can handle large-scale, high-dimensional data and real-time robotic systems. Application-specific developments may explore the integration of active learning with specific robotic tasks and domains, such as human-robot interaction, collaborative manipulation, and lifelong learning. Ethical considerations may guide the development of responsible and accountable active learning algorithms that prioritize human values, fairness, and transparency in robotic decision-making. By embracing these future directions and opportunities, active learning for robots can continue to advance the capabilities and autonomy of robotic systems, enabling them to learn and adapt effectively in diverse and dynamic environments.

Active learning offers a powerful framework for enabling robots to learn effectively from limited human feedback and adapt autonomously to changing environments. By leveraging principles of uncertainty, diversity, and expected error reduction, active learning algorithms enable robots to select informative data points for labeling, improving model performance with minimal human intervention. Despite its challenges, active learning holds great promise for advancing the capabilities and autonomy of robotic systems in various domains, from perception and manipulation to navigation and exploration. By addressing key challenges and embracing future opportunities, active learning for robots can pave the way for more intelligent, adaptive, and trustworthy robotic systems that can seamlessly integrate into our daily lives and contribute to solving real-world challenges.

Lifelong Learning in Robotics

Lifelong learning, also known as continual learning or lifelong adaptation, refers to the ability of robotic systems to acquire and retain knowledge over an extended period, continually improving their performance and adapting to changing conditions and requirements. In the context of robotics, lifelong learning enables robots to autonomously learn new tasks, environments, and skills over time without the need for manual reprogramming or retraining by human operators. This section explores the principles, techniques, challenges, and applications of lifelong learning in robotics, highlighting its importance in enabling autonomous and adaptive robotic systems.

Principles of Lifelong Learning

At the core of lifelong learning in robotics are principles derived from cognitive science and machine learning aimed at enabling robots to learn, adapt, and improve their performance over time. Key principles of lifelong learning include:

Incremental learning: Robots incrementally update their models and knowledge base with new data and experiences, allowing them to continuously improve their performance without requiring retraining from scratch.

Transfer learning: Robots transfer knowledge and skills learned in one task or domain to new tasks or domains, leveraging existing knowledge to accelerate learning and adaptation in new contexts.

Memory retention: Robots retain important information and experiences learned over time, allowing them to build upon past knowledge and avoid forgetting previously learned skills or concepts.

Generalization: Robots generalize from past experiences to new situations, enabling them to apply learned knowledge and skills to unseen scenarios and adapt to novel challenges.

Techniques for Lifelong Learning

Lifelong learning in robotics relies on a variety of techniques and algorithms that enable robots to acquire, retain, and adapt knowledge over time. These techniques include:

Incremental model updating: Robots update their models and algorithms continuously with new data, allowing them to adapt to changes in the environment or task requirements.

Memory-based learning: Robots store past experiences and observations in memory and use them to inform future decisions and actions, enabling them to learn from past mistakes and successes.

Transfer learning: Robots transfer knowledge and representations learned in one task or domain to new tasks or domains, facilitating rapid adaptation to new situations.

Meta-learning: Robots learn to learn by acquiring meta-knowledge about the learning process itself, enabling them to adapt their learning strategies to different tasks and environments.

Challenges in Lifelong Learning

Despite its potential benefits, lifelong learning in robotics poses several challenges that must be addressed to enable effective and robust lifelong adaptation. These challenges include:

Catastrophic forgetting: Robots may forget previously learned knowledge or skills when learning new tasks or domains, leading to performance degradation over time.

Task interference: Learning new tasks may interfere with or disrupt previously learned knowledge or representations, hindering the robot's ability to generalize across tasks.

Sample efficiency: Lifelong learning algorithms must be sample-efficient, meaning they should require minimal data to learn new tasks or adapt to new environments.

Robustness to non-stationarity: Lifelong learning algorithms must be robust to changes in the environment, task requirements, or data distribution over time, ensuring that the robot's performance remains consistent in dynamic settings.

Applications of Lifelong Learning in Robotics

Lifelong learning has numerous applications across various domains of robotics, enabling robots to adapt to diverse tasks, environments, and user preferences. Some examples of lifelong learning applications in robotics include:

Autonomous navigation: Robots learn to navigate in complex and dynamic environments, continuously updating their maps and navigation policies based on new sensory input and experiences.

Manipulation and grasping: Robots learn to manipulate objects of varying shapes, sizes, and textures, adapting their grasping strategies and manipulation techniques to different objects and environments.

Human-robot interaction: Robots learn to interpret and respond to human commands and gestures, adapting their behavior and communication strategies based on user feedback and preferences.

Industrial automation: Robots learn to perform complex manufacturing tasks, such as assembly, packaging, and quality inspection, adapting their processes and workflows to changing production requirements.

Future Directions in Lifelong Learning

As robotics continues to evolve, several future directions and research directions in lifelong learning are emerging, including:

Continual learning algorithms: Development of novel lifelong learning algorithms that address challenges such as catastrophic forgetting, task interference, and sample efficiency, enabling robots to learn and adapt more effectively over time.

Meta-learning and self-improving systems: Exploration of meta-learning techniques that enable robots to acquire meta-knowledge about the learning process itself, enabling them to adapt their learning strategies and algorithms to different tasks and environments.

Ethical considerations: Consideration of ethical implications and considerations surrounding lifelong learning in robotics, including issues such as data privacy, fairness, transparency, and accountability in autonomous learning systems.

Lifelong learning holds great promise for robotics, enabling robots to acquire, retain, and adapt knowledge and skills over time, without the need for manual intervention or reprogramming by human operators. By embracing principles, techniques, and challenges of lifelong learning, robotic systems can become more autonomous, adaptive, and versatile, enabling them to operate effectively in dynamic and uncertain environments and serve as valuable partners in various domains and applications.

Transfer Learning in Robotics

Transfer learning has emerged as a powerful technique in machine learning and robotics, enabling robots to leverage knowledge acquired from one task or domain to improve performance in a different but related task or domain. Transfer learning addresses the challenge of data scarcity and the need for efficiency in learning new tasks by reusing knowledge learned from previous experiences. In this section, we explore the principles, methods, applications, challenges, and future directions of transfer learning in robotics.

Transfer learning is based on the idea that knowledge gained from solving one task can be transferred to improve performance on another task. In robotics, transfer learning allows robots to generalize across different environments, tasks, or robot platforms, thus reducing the need for extensive retraining and accelerating the learning process. By leveraging transfer learning, robots can adapt more quickly to new situations, improve robustness, and achieve higher performance with limited data.

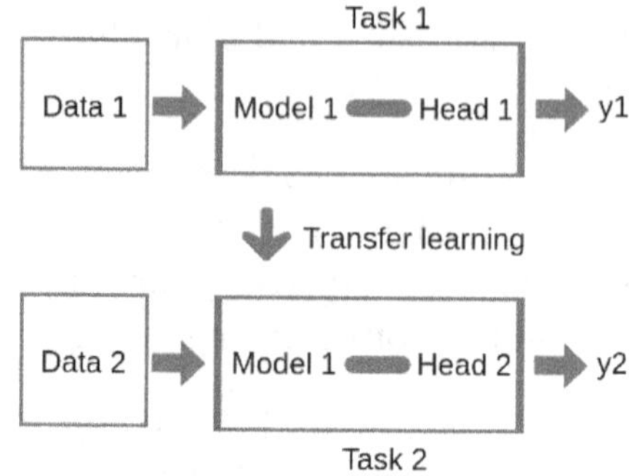

Figure 7. Transfer Learning

Principles of Transfer Learning

Transfer learning relies on the assumption that certain aspects of knowledge are transferable between tasks or domains. The key principles of transfer learning include:

Task similarity: Transfer learning is most effective when the source and target tasks share similarities in terms of input space, output space, or underlying structure.

Feature representation: Learning transferable feature representations that capture relevant information across tasks or domains is crucial for successful transfer learning.

Transferability: The transferability of knowledge depends on factors such as the amount of shared information between tasks, the domain gap between source and target domains, and the complexity of the tasks.

Methods of Transfer Learning

Several methods of transfer learning have been developed to facilitate knowledge transfer in robotics:

Instance-based transfer: Reusing specific instances or experiences from the source task to bootstrap learning in the target task.

Feature-based transfer: Learning transferable feature representations that capture common patterns across tasks or domains.

Model-based transfer: Transferring entire models or parts of models trained on the source task to the target task, with or without fine-tuning.

Relation-based transfer: Leveraging relationships between tasks or domains to guide transfer learning, such as through domain adaptation or meta-learning.

Applications of Transfer Learning in Robotics

Transfer learning finds applications across various domains and tasks in robotics:

Navigation and mapping: Transferring knowledge from simulated environments to real-world scenarios to improve robot localization and mapping.

Manipulation and grasping: Transferring grasping strategies learned on one object to improve performance on similar objects with varying shapes, sizes, or textures.

Object recognition and classification: Transferring knowledge from large-scale datasets to improve the accuracy of object recognition in specific domains or environments.

Autonomous driving: Transferring knowledge learned from driving in one city to improve performance in a new city with different traffic conditions.

Challenges and Considerations

Despite its benefits, transfer learning in robotics presents several challenges and considerations:

Domain shift: Differences between the source and target domains may lead to a domain shift, affecting the transferability of knowledge.

Catastrophic forgetting: Transfer learning may inadvertently overwrite important knowledge from the target task when adapting from the source task, leading to catastrophic forgetting.

Ethical considerations: Transfer learning raises ethical considerations related to data privacy, fairness, and bias when transferring knowledge between different contexts or populations.

Future Directions

Future directions in transfer learning for robotics include:

Adversarial transfer learning: Developing techniques to mitigate the effects of domain shift through adversarial training or domain adaptation methods.

Meta-transfer learning: Investigating methods for learning transferable knowledge across a diverse range of tasks and environments through meta-learning approaches.

Human-guided transfer learning: Exploring ways to incorporate human guidance and feedback to improve the effectiveness of transfer learning in robotics.

Transfer learning holds great promise for enabling robots to adapt more quickly and effectively to new tasks, environments, and challenges. By leveraging knowledge transfer across tasks and domains, robots can achieve higher performance, improve robustness, and accelerate the learning process. As transfer learning techniques continue to advance, they will play an increasingly important role in enabling autonomous and adaptive robotic systems to navigate complex and dynamic real-world environments.

Learning Control Policies

In robotics, control policies dictate the actions taken by robots to achieve desired objectives in various tasks, such as navigation, manipulation, and interaction with the environment. Traditional control policies are typically designed based on predefined rules or mathematical models, which may not fully capture the complexity and variability of real-world scenarios. Learning control policies, on the other hand, leverage machine learning techniques to enable robots to adapt and improve their behavior through experience and interaction with the environment. In this section, we explore the concept of learning control policies, their significance in robotics, and the methods used to develop and deploy them effectively.

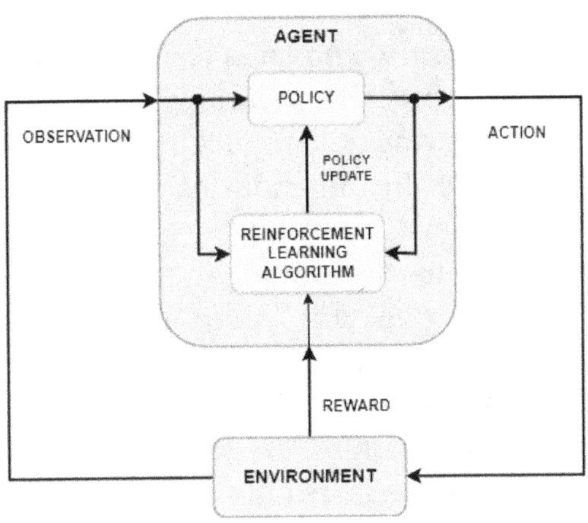

Figure 8. Learning Control Policies

Learning control policies represent a paradigm shift in robotics, enabling robots to acquire and refine their control strategies autonomously without the need for explicit programming or human intervention. By learning from data and feedback collected during task execution, robots can adapt their behavior to changing conditions, optimize performance, and improve efficiency over time. Learning control policies offer several advantages over traditional approaches, including flexibility, adaptability, and scalability, making them well-suited for dynamic and uncertain environments.

Reinforcement Learning for Control Policies

Reinforcement learning (RL) is a powerful framework for learning control policies, where robots learn to make decisions by interacting with their environment and receiving feedback in the form of rewards or penalties. In RL, the robot's objective is to maximize cumulative reward over time by selecting actions that lead to desirable outcomes. RL algorithms, such as Q-learning, policy gradients, and deep reinforcement learning, enable robots to learn complex control policies for tasks such as navigation, manipulation, and decision-making. RL-based control policies can adapt to novel environments, generalize across different tasks, and improve performance through iterative learning.

Imitation Learning and Learning from Demonstration

Imitation learning, also known as learning from demonstration (LfD), is another approach to learning control policies, where robots learn by observing and mimicking human demonstrations of desired behaviors. In imitation learning, the robot learns a mapping from sensory observations to actions by leveraging expert demonstrations as training data. Techniques such as behavioral cloning, inverse reinforcement learning, and apprenticeship learning enable robots to acquire complex control policies from human demonstrations and generalize them to new situations. Imitation learning is particularly useful for tasks where human expertise is readily available and can provide valuable guidance to the learning process.

Model-Based Learning Approaches

Model-based learning approaches combine data-driven learning with explicit modeling of the robot's dynamics and environment to learn control policies. By leveraging predictive models of the environment, robots can simulate the consequences of different actions and select the most promising ones to achieve their objectives. Model-based reinforcement learning, probabilistic models, and system identification techniques enable robots to learn accurate and efficient control policies for various tasks. Model-based learning approaches offer advantages such as sample efficiency, robustness to uncertainty, and interpretability of learned policies.

Multi-Modal Learning and Sensor Fusion

Multi-modal learning techniques integrate information from multiple sensors and modalities to learn robust and adaptive control policies. By fusing data from visual, tactile, auditory, and proprioceptive sensors, robots can perceive and understand their environment more effectively, leading to better-informed decision-making and action selection. Multi-modal learning enables robots to handle complex and dynamic environments, adapt to sensory uncertainty, and generalize across different conditions. Techniques such as sensor fusion, feature fusion, and attention mechanisms enable robots to leverage the complementary strengths of different sensor modalities for learning control policies.

Challenges and Considerations

Despite the promises of learning control policies, several challenges and considerations need to be addressed to ensure their effectiveness and reliability in real-world applications. Challenges include the need for large and diverse training datasets, the generalization of learned policies to new environments, the robustness of learned policies to sensory noise and uncertainty, and the safety and ethical implications of autonomous learning systems. Addressing these challenges requires advancements in algorithmic techniques, sensor technologies, and validation methodologies to ensure the safe and responsible deployment of learning control policies in robotics.

Applications and Case Studies

Learning control policies find applications across various domains and industries, including autonomous vehicles, industrial automation, healthcare robotics, and service robotics. In autonomous vehicles, learning control policies enable vehicles to navigate complex traffic scenarios, make real-time decisions, and adapt to changing road conditions. In industrial automation, robots learn control policies for tasks such as assembly, pick-and-place, and quality inspection, improving efficiency and productivity in manufacturing processes. In healthcare robotics, robots learn control policies for surgical assistance, rehabilitation, and assistive tasks, enhancing patient care and treatment outcomes.

Future Directions and Trends

Future trends in learning control policies will focus on addressing current challenges and advancing the state-of-the-art in robotics. Emerging trends include the development of more efficient and sample-efficient learning algorithms, the integration of uncertainty-aware learning techniques, the exploration of lifelong learning and continual adaptation, and the incorporation of ethical considerations and human oversight in autonomous learning systems. By embracing these future directions, we can unlock the full potential of learning control policies to revolutionize robotics and enable robots to operate effectively and safely in diverse and complex environments.

Learning control policies represent a transformative approach to robotics, enabling robots to acquire, refine, and adapt their control strategies autonomously through experience and interaction with the environment. By leveraging machine learning techniques such as reinforcement learning, imitation learning, and model-based learning, robots can learn complex control policies for a wide range of tasks and applications. As robotics continues to advance, learning control policies will play an increasingly important role in enabling robots to operate effectively and autonomously in dynamic and uncertain environments, paving the way for new applications and opportunities in robotics and automation.

Robot Skill Acquisition

Robot skill acquisition refers to the process by which robots learn and develop the capabilities necessary to perform specific tasks effectively and autonomously. In recent years, there has been significant interest and research in enabling robots to acquire skills through learning mechanisms, akin to how humans acquire skills through practice and experience. In this section, we explore the various aspects of robot skill acquisition, including learning from demonstration, reinforcement learning, transfer learning, and lifelong learning, along with their applications, challenges, and future directions.

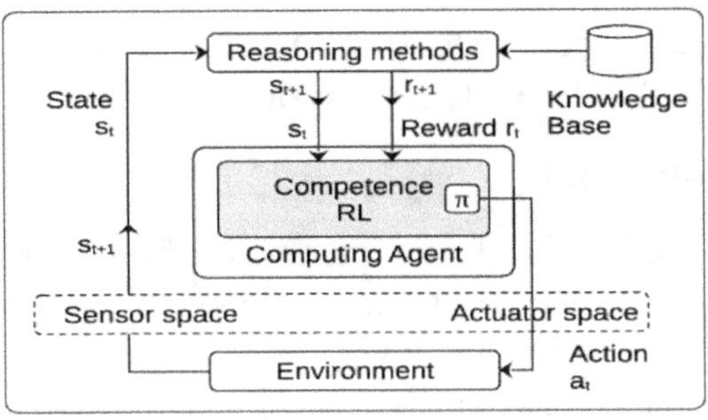

Figure 9. Robot Skill Acquisition

Learning from Demonstration (LfD)

Learning from demonstration (LfD) is a popular approach to robot skill acquisition, where robots learn by observing and imitating human demonstrations of a task. LfD techniques range from simple behavioral cloning to more sophisticated methods such as inverse reinforcement learning and apprenticeship learning. By leveraging human expertise and demonstrations, robots can quickly acquire complex skills and behaviors, enabling them to perform tasks ranging from manipulation and grasping to navigation and interaction with humans. LfD has applications in various domains, including manufacturing, healthcare, and service robotics, where robots can learn from human experts and adapt their behavior to specific tasks and environments.

Reinforcement Learning (RL)

Reinforcement learning (RL) is another powerful paradigm for robot skill acquisition, where robots learn through trial and error by interacting with their environment and receiving feedback in the form of rewards or penalties. RL algorithms enable robots to discover optimal policies for achieving desired goals, such as navigating to a target location, manipulating objects, or performing complex maneuvers. RL has been successfully applied to a wide range of robotic tasks, including autonomous navigation, robotic manipulation, and robotic control. However, RL presents challenges such as sample efficiency, exploration-exploitation trade-offs, and safety considerations, which need to be addressed for real-world deployment of RL-based robotic systems.

Transfer Learning

Transfer learning is a technique that enables robots to transfer knowledge and skills learned in one task or domain to another related task or domain. By leveraging transfer learning, robots can generalize their learning across different tasks, adapt to new environments, and accelerate the learning process for new tasks. Transfer learning has applications in robotic manipulation, where robots can transfer grasping skills learned with one set of objects to a new set of objects with similar characteristics. Transfer learning also enables robots to adapt to changes in their environment or task requirements without the need for extensive retraining, improving the adaptability and efficiency of robotic systems.

Lifelong Learning

Lifelong learning is a concept inspired by the human ability to continuously acquire new knowledge and skills throughout life. In the context of robotics, lifelong learning refers to the ability of robots to incrementally learn and adapt to new tasks, environments, and challenges over time. Lifelong learning algorithms enable robots to retain and build upon previously acquired knowledge, incorporate new experiences into their learning process, and continually improve their performance without forgetting previous skills. Lifelong learning is essential for autonomous robots operating in dynamic and uncertain environments, where the ability to adapt and learn from experience is critical for long-term success.

Challenges and Considerations

While robot skill acquisition holds great promise for advancing the capabilities of robotic systems, several challenges and considerations need to be addressed. These challenges include the need for robust and scalable learning algorithms that can handle complex tasks and environments, the requirement for large and diverse datasets for effective learning, the integration of sensory feedback and perception for accurate skill acquisition, and the ethical considerations surrounding autonomous learning and decision-making in robotic systems. Addressing these challenges will be essential for realizing the full potential of robot skill acquisition in real-world applications.

Applications and Case Studies

Robot skill acquisition has a wide range of applications across various domains, including manufacturing, healthcare, service robotics, and autonomous vehicles. In manufacturing, robots can acquire skills for assembly, welding, and quality inspection, improving efficiency and productivity in production processes. In healthcare, robots can learn to assist with surgical procedures, rehabilitation exercises, and patient care tasks, enhancing the capabilities of healthcare providers and improving patient outcomes. In service robotics, robots can acquire skills for tasks such as household chores, delivery services, and customer assistance, enhancing convenience and quality of life for users.

Future Directions and Trends

The future of robot skill acquisition lies in advancing learning algorithms, incorporating multi-modal sensing and perception, enabling lifelong adaptation, and addressing ethical and safety considerations. Future trends in robot skill acquisition include the development of more efficient and scalable learning algorithms, the integration of learning with reasoning and planning, the enhancement of robot autonomy and adaptability, and the exploration of collaborative and cooperative learning strategies in multi-robot systems. By embracing these future directions and trends, we can unlock the full potential of robot skill acquisition to revolutionize various industries and domains, enhance human-robot collaboration, and address global challenges.

Robot skill acquisition represents a critical aspect of advancing robotic capabilities and enabling robots to perform complex tasks autonomously. By leveraging learning mechanisms such as learning from demonstration, reinforcement learning, transfer learning, and lifelong learning, robots can acquire skills and adapt to new tasks and environments effectively. While there are challenges and considerations to address, the future of robot skill acquisition holds great promise for revolutionizing various industries and domains, improving human-robot interaction, and contributing to the advancement of robotics as a field.

Learning-based Navigation

Navigation is a fundamental capability for autonomous robots, enabling them to move safely and efficiently in complex and dynamic environments. Traditional navigation methods often rely on predefined maps, geometric algorithms, and sensor fusion techniques to plan and execute robot trajectories. However, these approaches may struggle in environments with limited prior knowledge, dynamic obstacles, or changing conditions. Learning-based navigation techniques leverage machine learning algorithms to enable robots to learn navigation policies from data, experience, and interactions with the environment. In this section, we explore the principles, techniques, applications, challenges, and future directions of learning-based navigation for autonomous robots.

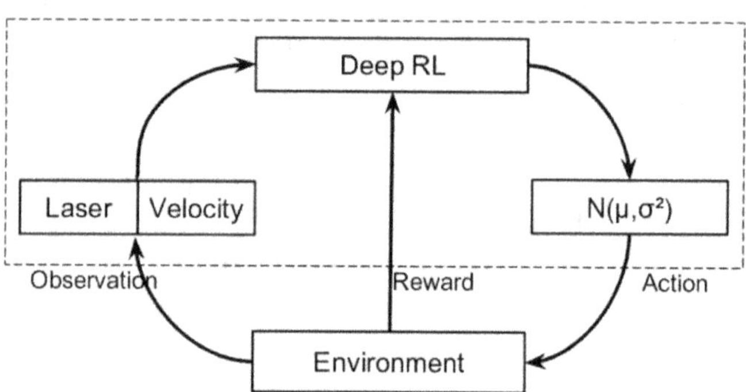

Figure 10. Learning-based Navigation

Learning-based navigation refers to the use of machine learning algorithms to enable robots to navigate autonomously in complex environments. Unlike traditional navigation methods that rely on handcrafted rules and models, learning-based navigation allows robots to learn navigation policies directly from data, bypassing the need for explicit knowledge of the environment. By leveraging data-driven approaches, learning-based navigation enables robots to adapt to diverse environments, handle uncertainties, and learn from their interactions with the world.

Fundamentals of Learning-based Navigation

At the core of learning-based navigation are machine learning algorithms that enable robots to learn navigation policies from sensory inputs and environmental feedback. Supervised learning, reinforcement learning, and imitation learning are common paradigms used in learning-based navigation. Supervised learning techniques train navigation models using labeled data, such as sensor measurements and corresponding actions. Reinforcement learning enables robots to learn navigation policies through trial and error, receiving rewards or penalties based on their actions' outcomes. Imitation learning allows robots to learn navigation behaviors by observing and imitating human or expert demonstrations.

Learning Perception and Mapping

Learning-based navigation often relies on perception and mapping techniques to interpret sensory inputs and generate environment representations. Deep learning algorithms, such as convolutional neural networks (CNNs) and recurrent neural networks (RNNs), are commonly used for perception tasks, such as object detection, scene segmentation, and depth estimation. Mapping algorithms, such as occupancy grids and probabilistic graphical models, enable robots to build and update maps of their surroundings based on sensor data. By integrating learning-based perception and mapping, robots can generate accurate and up-to-date representations of the environment to support navigation.

Trajectory Planning and Control

Learning-based navigation involves generating feasible trajectories and executing them to achieve desired navigation goals. Trajectory planning algorithms use learned navigation policies, environmental information, and robot dynamics to generate collision-free paths from the robot's current position to its goal. Reinforcement learning techniques can be used to train navigation policies that directly map sensory inputs to control commands, enabling robots to navigate in real-time without relying on predefined trajectories. Learning-based control strategies adapt robot motion based on feedback from the environment, enabling robots to handle uncertainties, obstacles, and dynamic changes in the environment.

Applications of Learning-based Navigation

Learning-based navigation finds applications across various domains, including autonomous vehicles, mobile robots, drones, and robotic manipulators. In autonomous vehicles, learning-based navigation enables vehicles to navigate safely and efficiently on roads, handle complex traffic scenarios, and adapt to diverse driving conditions. Mobile robots use learning-based navigation to navigate indoor environments, deliver goods in warehouses, and assist with tasks such as cleaning and surveillance. Drones leverage learning-based navigation to fly autonomously, perform aerial inspections, and deliver packages in urban and rural areas. Robotic manipulators use learning-based navigation to plan and execute manipulation tasks, such as pick-and-place operations, assembly, and object manipulation.

Challenges and Considerations

Despite the advancements in learning-based navigation, several challenges remain to be addressed to enable robust and reliable navigation in real-world environments. Challenges include data scarcity and quality, generalization to unseen environments, robustness to sensor noise and perception errors, safety and ethical considerations, and scalability to large-scale environments. Addressing these challenges requires interdisciplinary research efforts that combine expertise in machine learning, robotics, computer vision, and control theory. Additionally, ethical considerations, such as privacy, fairness, and transparency, must be carefully considered in the design and deployment of learning-based navigation systems.

Future Directions and Trends

Future trends in learning-based navigation are likely to focus on addressing the aforementioned challenges and advancing the state-of-the-art in autonomous navigation. Key directions include the development of more robust and efficient learning algorithms, the integration of multi-modal sensor data for perception and mapping, the exploration of lifelong learning and continual adaptation techniques, and the investigation of collaborative navigation strategies for human-robot interaction. Additionally, research efforts will continue to focus on ethical considerations, ensuring that learning-based navigation systems are designed and deployed in a responsible and socially acceptable manner.

Learning-based navigation represents a promising approach for enabling autonomous robots to navigate safely and effectively in complex and dynamic environments. By leveraging machine learning algorithms, robots can learn navigation policies directly from data and adapt to diverse environmental conditions. While challenges remain to be addressed, ongoing research efforts are paving the way for the development of robust and reliable learning-based navigation systems that have the potential to revolutionize various industries and enhance human-robot interaction.

Learning-based Perception

Perception is a critical component of robotic systems, enabling robots to interpret and understand the world around them through sensory information. Traditional approaches to perception often rely on handcrafted algorithms and heuristics, which may struggle to generalize across diverse environments and tasks. In recent years, there has been a paradigm shift towards learning-based approaches to perception, leveraging the power of machine learning and artificial intelligence to enable robots to learn from data and adapt to changing conditions. In this section, we explore the principles, techniques, applications, and future trends of learning-based perception in robotics.

Principles of Learning-based Perception

Learning-based perception involves training robotic systems to extract meaningful information from sensory data through machine learning algorithms. At its core, learning-based perception aims to mimic human perception by enabling robots to recognize objects, understand scenes, and make informed decisions based on sensory inputs. By learning patterns and relationships from large datasets, robots can generalize across different environments and tasks, enhancing their robustness and adaptability in real-world scenarios.

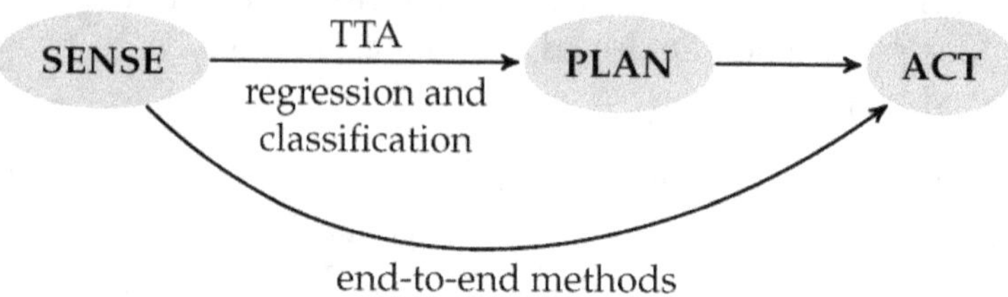

Figure 11. Learning-based Perception

Techniques for Learning-based Perception

There are several techniques for learning-based perception in robotics, including supervised learning, unsupervised learning, and reinforcement learning. Supervised learning involves training models on labeled datasets, where each input is associated with a corresponding output. Convolutional Neural Networks (CNNs) are commonly used in supervised learning for tasks such as object recognition and semantic segmentation. Unsupervised learning, on the other hand, involves training models on unlabeled data to discover hidden patterns and structures. Techniques such as clustering and autoencoders are used in unsupervised learning for tasks such as feature learning and dimensionality reduction. Reinforcement learning enables robots to learn from interaction with the environment, receiving feedback in the form of rewards or penalties based on their actions. Reinforcement learning is particularly useful for tasks such as active perception and sensorimotor control.

Applications of Learning-based Perception

Learning-based perception has a wide range of applications in robotics, spanning various domains such as autonomous vehicles, industrial automation, healthcare robotics, and assistive technology. In autonomous vehicles, learning-based perception enables vehicles to recognize traffic signs, pedestrians, and other vehicles, facilitating safe navigation in complex traffic environments. In industrial automation, robots equipped with learning-based perception can identify and manipulate objects on assembly lines, improving efficiency and productivity. In healthcare robotics, learning-based perception enables robots to interpret medical images, assist in surgical procedures, and provide personalized care to patients.

Challenges and Considerations

Despite the promise of learning-based perception, several challenges and considerations must be addressed to realize its full potential in robotics. One challenge is the need for large and diverse datasets to train perception models effectively. Collecting and annotating such datasets can be time-consuming and expensive, particularly for tasks involving fine-grained recognition or semantic understanding. Another challenge is the robustness and generalization of perception models across different environments and conditions. Perception models trained in one environment may struggle to perform reliably in new and unseen environments due to differences in lighting, viewpoint, or object appearance. Additionally, ethical considerations such as privacy, bias, and fairness must be taken into account when deploying learning-based perception systems in real-world settings.

Future Trends in Learning-based Perception

Looking ahead, several trends are shaping the future of learning-based perception in robotics. One trend is the integration of multi-modal sensory information, where robots combine data from different sensors such as cameras, LIDAR, and inertial sensors to build a richer and more comprehensive understanding of their surroundings. Another trend is the development of lifelong learning techniques, where robots continuously update their perception models over time with new data and experiences, enabling them to adapt to changing environments and tasks. Additionally, there is growing interest in self-supervised learning approaches, where robots learn from unlabeled data or self-generated signals, reducing the need for human annotation and supervision.

Learning-based perception represents a transformative approach to perception in robotics, enabling robots to learn from data and adapt to changing conditions. By leveraging the power of machine learning and artificial intelligence, robots can achieve higher levels of perception accuracy, robustness, and adaptability in real-world scenarios. As we continue to advance the field of learning-based perception, it is essential to address challenges such as data availability, robustness, and ethical considerations, ensuring that perception systems are reliable, trustworthy, and beneficial for society.

Ethics of Robot Learning and Adaptation

Robot learning and adaptation have the potential to revolutionize various industries and domains, enabling robots to autonomously acquire new skills, adapt to changing environments, and interact with humans in increasingly complex ways. However, as robotic systems become more autonomous and adaptive, ethical considerations surrounding the design, deployment, and use of these systems become increasingly important. In this section, we explore the ethical challenges and considerations in robot learning and adaptation, addressing issues such as transparency, accountability, fairness, privacy, and societal impact.

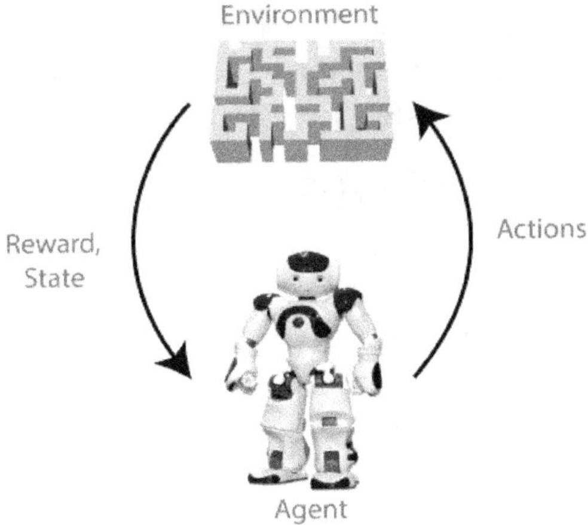

Figure 12. Robot Learning and Adaptation

Transparency and Explainability

One of the key ethical considerations in robot learning and adaptation is the need for transparency and explainability in the decision-making process of autonomous systems. As robots learn and adapt to new data and experiences, it becomes essential for humans to understand how and why these systems make decisions. Transparent and explainable AI techniques enable humans to interpret and trust the behavior of robotic systems, providing insights into the underlying reasoning and logic behind their actions. Lack of transparency and explainability can lead to distrust, uncertainty, and potential safety risks, particularly in critical applications such as healthcare, transportation, and defense.

Accountability and Responsibility

With increased autonomy and adaptation capabilities, robotic systems must be held accountable for their actions and decisions. Ethical frameworks and guidelines are essential for establishing clear lines of responsibility and accountability in the development, deployment, and use of robotic systems. Manufacturers, developers, operators, and users all bear responsibility for ensuring that robotic systems are designed, trained, and operated in a manner that prioritizes safety, fairness, and societal well-being. Establishing mechanisms for accountability and redress in cases of system failure, error, or misuse is crucial for maintaining trust and confidence in autonomous robotic systems.

Fairness and Bias Mitigation

Robot learning and adaptation algorithms are susceptible to biases and unfairness, which can perpetuate existing social inequalities and injustices. Biases may arise from the data used to train these algorithms, reflecting societal prejudices and stereotypes present in the training data. Fairness-aware learning techniques aim to mitigate biases and ensure that robotic systems treat all individuals fairly and equitably, regardless of race, gender, ethnicity, or other protected attributes.

Privacy and Data Protection

Robot learning and adaptation rely on vast amounts of data collected from sensors, interactions with humans, and other sources. Protecting the privacy and confidentiality of sensitive data is paramount to safeguarding individuals' rights and freedoms in the age of autonomous robotics. Ethical guidelines and regulations, such as the General Data Protection Regulation (GDPR), establish principles and requirements for the lawful and ethical collection, use, and storage of personal data by robotic systems.

Societal Impact and Human Well-Being

The widespread adoption of autonomous robotic systems has profound implications for society, affecting employment, the economy, education, healthcare, and quality of life. Ethical considerations in robot learning and adaptation must prioritize the promotion of human well-being, social welfare, and the common good. Ensuring that robotic systems enhance human capabilities, productivity, and autonomy while minimizing negative impacts, such as job displacement, economic inequality, and social isolation, is essential for achieving a sustainable and inclusive future. Ethical decision-making frameworks, stakeholder engagement, and public discourse play crucial roles in shaping the societal impact of autonomous robotics.

The ethics of robot learning and adaptation encompass a broad range of considerations, including transparency, accountability, fairness, privacy, and societal impact. Addressing these ethical challenges requires interdisciplinary collaboration involving experts from robotics, ethics, law, policy, sociology, and other fields. By prioritizing ethical principles and values in the design, deployment, and use of robotic systems, we can harness the transformative potential of robot learning and adaptation to benefit humanity and advance the common good. Ethical robotics is not just a technical challenge but a moral imperative, shaping the future of autonomous systems in a way that reflects our shared values and aspirations.